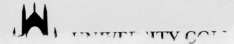

Theatre, Body and Pleasure

Drama is a medium in which one group of bodies watches another group of bodies. The theatre is a place that exhibits what a human body is, what it does, what it is capable of. It requires special things of bodies, putting pressure on its audience as well as its performers. It creates and manipulates pleasure in relation to bodies.

Part theatre history, part dramatic criticism, part theoretical *tour de force*, the central argument in *Theatre, Body and Pleasure* is that theatre is where society negotiates around bodily value and bodily meaning. It will therefore appeal to those with interests not only in theatre but also in wider questions about society, culture and pleasure.

This unique and powerful study features

- a large historical range, from medieval to postmodern
- case studies offering close readings of written texts
- examples of how to 'read for the body', exploring written text as a 'discipline' of the body
- a breadth of cultural reference, from stage plays through to dance culture
- a range of theoretical approaches, including dance analysis and phenomenology.

Simon Shepherd explores the interplay of bodily value, the art of bodies and the physical responses to that art. He explains first how the body makes meaning and carries value, and then describes the relationship between time, space and body. From here he looks at bodies that go beyond their apparent limits, becoming excessive, tangling with objects, dissolving into their surroundings.

Simon Shepherd is Direct(... of Speech and Drama, London.

Theatre, Body and Pleasure

Simon Shepherd

Routledge
Taylor & Francis Group

LONDON AND NEW YORK

First published 2006
by Routledge
2 Park Square, Milton Park, Abingdon, Oxon OX14 4RN

Simultaneously published in the USA and Canada
by Routledge
270 Madison Avenue, New York, NY 10016

Routledge is an imprint of the Taylor & Francis Group

© 2006 Simon Shepherd

Typeset in Baskerville by Bookcraft Ltd, Stroud, Gloucestershire
Printed and bound in Great Britain by TJ International Ltd,
Padstow, Cornwall

British Library Cataloguing in Publication Data
A catalogue record for this book is available from the British Library

Library of Congress Cataloging in Publication Data
Shepherd, Simon.
    Theatre, body and pleasure / Simon Shepherd
        p. cm.
    Includes bibliographical references.
    1. Theatre–Philosophy. 2. Acting–Psychological aspects.
    3. Drama–History and criticism. 4. Body, Human, in literature.
    I. Title.
    PN2039.S54 2005
    792'.01–dc22   2005013349

ISBN 0-415-25374-8 (hbk)
ISBN 0-415-25375-6 (pbk)

For my mum

Contents

Acknowledgements

I did much of the work on this book during study leave from the Drama Department at Goldsmiths College, partly funded by the Arts and Humanities Research Board. I am grateful to the Board for its support. I would also like to thank Barbara Hodgdon and Dan Rebellato, who read early drafts of this for Routledge. Their engagement with the material was very useful, lively and friendly. So too, thanks to Ross Brown and Janette Dillon, for reading and commenting on parts of this.

I realise that much of the thinking for this book was done over a period when I used to go dancing on a Sunday night at Warriors, at Turnmills. I am grateful to the organisers of that event for constructing a place of such bodily pleasure. A place that danced, militantly, in the face of death.

Parts of chapters 2, 3, 7 and 8 have previously appeared in different forms: '"The Body", Performance Studies, Horner, and a Dinner Party', *Textual Practice* 14 (Routledge, 2000): 285–303; 'Revels End, and the Gentle Body Starts', *Shakespeare Survey* 55, ed. Peter Holland (Cambridge University Press, 2002): 237–56; 'Voice, Writing, Noise ... or is Herod Balinese?', *Performance Research* 8.1 'Voices' (Routledge, 2003): 74-82; 'Lolo's Breasts, Cyborgism, and a Wooden Christ', *Cultural Bodies: Ethnography and Theory*, ed. Helen Thomas and Jamilah Ahmed (Blackwell Publishing, 2004): 170-89.

Introduction
Theatrically imagined bodies

This book proposes that theatre is, and has always been, a place which exhibits what a human body is, what it does, what it is capable of. This exhibition may amount to an affirmation of currently held views or it may be an unsettling challenge to assumptions. Theatre requires special things of bodies, and makes demands on audience as much as performer. It generates and manipulates pleasure in relation to bodies. Through this pleasure it engages those values which are held personally and culturally. Theatre is a practice in which societies negotiate around what the body is and means.

Negotiation around bodies is important, I think, because many ideas about what is good, right, natural and possible are grounded in assumptions about what the body is, what it needs, how it works. Social, moral and political values attach themselves to body shape, size, colour, movement. They also inhabit distinctions made between body and non-body, whether that be mind, spirit, object or society.

The work of the book is to substantiate this proposition and show how it operates. To set that up, the introduction offers a brisk overview of some of the main thinking about the body, specifically in relation to theatre as an art of bodies. Thereafter the book falls into three parts, each with its own contribution to the main argument. The first part deals with the relations between body and script, attending particularly to bodily value. The second explores the positioning of theatre bodies in relation to time and space, and emphasises how such positioning impacts upon the set of bodies that watches and listens. The third part interests itself in cases where the theatre seems to interfere with the supposed integrity of the body. This might be through transgression of norms of bodily behaviour or through blurring of the boundaries between body and non-body, incorporeality, flow.

Taking an interest in the body

Several stories can be told about the causes of the contemporary interest in the body.

One of the most important of these in the field of performance and theatre studies is that of the impact of feminism. In the 1960s feminist performance challenged dominant assumptions about gender roles, and it frequently did so by means of so-called 'body art'. The body of the woman was used and shown in a way that stressed its actuality as against the cultural and social meanings that had been imposed upon it. When the modern feminist movement cohered in the late 1960s it generated, among many other things, a considerable amount of work that explored the development of concepts about the woman's body and the ways in which it was represented. This work was necessary in part because assumptions about the capacity, functions and value of the woman's body underlay and justified ideas about her social role. It was also necessary because dominant (masculine) ways of thinking assumed that the body was separate from, and irrelevant to, the activities of the reason. It thus issued a challenge to men to write about their bodies. (For an overview of the body art emergence, see Shepherd and Wallis 2004; see also, for example, Jones 1998 and Schneider 1997. For a male response to feminism see, for example, Ihde 2002.)

The feminist engagement made the body into a key topic, politically and theoretically. But no coherent position or set of values followed. In her overview of this feminist work Elizabeth Grosz identifies three different positions. 'Egalitarian feminism' tends to see the woman's body as a limitation on her 'capacity for equality' while also giving her 'special insight'. 'Social constructionism' makes a distinction between biology and the way it is represented, having as its project the insistence that 'different cultural meanings and values' be given to the biology. 'Sexual difference' refuses to see the body as a biological given, but instead as something that is as it is lived. It is a place where nature and culture are interwoven. It is never neutral; the differences between bodies are both ineradicable and important. Thus, as Grosz says, 'Far from being an inert, passive, noncultural and ahistorical term, the body may be seen as the crucial term, the site of contestation, in a series of economic, political, sexual and intellectual struggles' (Grosz 1994: 19). Those struggles are ongoing.

Woven into this story of the impact of feminism are two other narratives that also make claims about the causes of a modern interest in the body. One of these features the emergence of body art itself. Within the counter-culture of the 1960s the body was given value on the basis of its naturalness, the thing humanity had in common, in a society increasingly mechanised, mediated and repressive. In the theatre this led to a valuing of the actor as against the supposedly imposed text of author or director. And it led to the prioritising of performance as a place where people could experience liberation from the everyday repressions which constrained and distorted their bodies (see, for example, Chaikin 1972 on actors; Ansorge 1975 on performances; and an overview in Vanden Heuvel 1991).

The other narrative tells of resistance to the assumed (masculinist) separation of mind from body. Thus alongside the work of feminists should be placed that of, for example, Lakoff and Johnson who claim that 'Our conceptual system is grounded in, neurally makes use of, and is crucially shaped by our perceptual and motor systems'. From here they argue towards a position that suggests that 'Because our ideas are framed in terms of our unconscious embodied conceptual systems, truth and knowledge depend on embodied understanding' (Lakoff and Johnson 1999: 555; see also Johnson 1987 and Lakoff and Johnson 2003). Lakoff and Johnson approach their 'philosophy in the flesh' as a linguist and a philospher. A century before, however, medical scientists had begun to insist on the imbrication of body and mind. In 1880 H. C. Bastian published a book called *The Brain as an Organ of Mind*. In 1915 Walter Cannon argued that emotion has a bodily basis in his book *Bodily Changes in Pain, Hunger, Fear and Rage*.

A particular inflection to this mind–body interconnection leads into another story of the causes of a modern interest. In the opening decades of the twentieth century F. Matthias Alexander embarked on a project to re-educate his body in order to recover its potential. His body, and in particular his voice, had become debilitated by learnt behaviours. What the mind learns has a physical effect, and vice versa. And as Alexander saw it, it was through this learning process that modern civilisation impacted negatively on the body, it 'contaminated man's biological and sensory equipment, with a resultant crippling in the responses of the whole organism' (Maisel 1974: xxix). While Alexander was developing his theories, much of the cultural interest in bodies of the 1920s and 1930s was taken up with a concept of the body as an appropriate complement to a world felt to be modern, machinic, efficient and fast, where the productive worker or the well-drilled army or chorus were paradigms (Schwartz 1992; Franko 1995; McNeill 1995; Segel 1998).

In the 1940s, the decade that saw modernist efficiency caught up into world conflict, Alexander's therapeutic interests were restated. In a series of lectures in 1943–4 Moshe Feldenkrais argued that human problems derived from people's adjustment to prevailing economic and marital conditions. The state of the body relates to the state of society, or, as Walter Cannon's 1940 lecture put it, the body is a 'guide to politics'. Like Alexander, Feldenkrais suggested that a person could be made to 'adjust' through a re-education of the body. So too in 1948 Rudolph Laban suggested that the alienation produced by modern industrial life could be countered through a training in movement, which would recentre the body (Feldenkrais 1949; Cannon 1942; Laban 1988). From this sort of thinking emerges the shape of the modern notion that bodily re-education is the key to a healthy and fulfilled life (the only problem, of course, being the choice of regime – Alexander technique, yoga, martial arts of various sorts, knitting).

Now if you are a sociologist reading this, you'll know that there is yet another story to be told. This one, fortunately, has also already been written, and is well documented. It begins as the story of an absence. In his overview of writings on the body, Arthur Frank notes the silence in sociology about the body. When he wrote his first overview of the field in 1990 the major initiatives seemed to be coming from 'social history, clinical practice in psychiatry and psychoanalysis, anthropology, and cognitive science and philosophy' (Frank 1996: 37). In his subsequent overview he attempts to specify the origin of the mid-1990s interest in the body, and he attributes it to modernism, postmodernism and feminism ... which is a bit like saying that it comes out of the history of western culture. Modernism, he suggests, saw the body both as 'constant in a world of flux' and 'as the epitome of that flux'. Postmodernism is presented as a division between high theory (in work by such as Barthes, Deleuze and Guattari, Foucault, and Baudrillard) and deliberately minimal, closely focused studies such as those contained in Feher's *Fragments for a History of the Human Body* (1989). Feminism's impact has already been touched on above. From here Frank then goes on to describe a general model of the relationship between body and society.

Frank's initial overview was limited to the previous decade, so that he did not attend to the work of such figures as Marcel Mauss, Norbert Elias, Erving Goffman and Mary Douglas. All of this work has an anthropological inflection, and while in 1990 its influence on sociology still seemed minimal, it had found a productive afterlife in theatre and performance studies. For my purposes here, the dissemination of anthropological work on the body into another discipline, that of performance studies, is another strand in the story of the origins of a modern interest in the body. The major figure here is Goffman. His *Presentation of the Self in Everyday Life*, published in 1956, used a vocabulary of dramatic terms to describe human behaviours in everyday life. Picking up on this, Richard Schechner opened up the category of what constituted performance. So too Mary Douglas's work made it possible to articulate the relationships between the specific performing bodies and the 'social body' of the community (in for example the work on medieval mystery plays done by James (1983)). To these should be added Victor Turner, whose anthropological method gained a heightened consciousness of performance from the work of Richard Schechner, even while Schechner thought he was being influenced by Turner (for brief accounts of all these elements within performance theory, see Shepherd and Wallis 2004; see also Schechner 2002).

Less influential within theatre and performance studies hitherto are Mauss and Elias. In 1934 the French ethnologist Marcel Mauss, describing 'techniques' of the body, observed that British soldiers used spades differently from French ones and that styles of swimming changed from one generation to another (Mauss 1992). Four years later Norbert Elias developed his thesis on the 'civilizing process' whereby societies learn, and naturalise, different manners at table, different ways of managing human waste. This work has potential relevance here in that theatre is an artform in which bodily techniques and behaviours are not only employed but also specifically exhibited, for instance in the jokes about social awkwardness in *A Midsummer Night's Dream*, *The Man of Mode*, *Caste* and *Absent Friends* (to take a random sample across the centuries). Theatre seen in this way is one of the mechanisms of 'civilisation'. And as such could become the target of, say, that feminist body art which challenged assumptions about the body, turning theatre into an explicit site of negotiation around bodily meaning and value.

And about that body art one more thing needs to be said. A considerable amount of it, whether feminist or not, deliberately put the biological body under pressure, marking it, piercing it, cutting it. This foregrounds a point that can be forgotten where the focus is entirely on learnt techniques of body, bodily behaviours, therapeutic methods: that culture and way of life, in training a body for society, have their impact on the biological thing itself. For centuries upper-class children have been trained to carry themselves in appropriate ways – decorous, upright, deliberate, indeed authoritative (see Chapter 2). Body shape has been constrained, if not permanently altered, by corsets or foot-binding. But upper-class children might also be materially different, in that their better resourced and more plentiful diet makes them taller. The biological body changes within both short- and long-term timescales: the body-builder's body and the classical ballet dancer's legs; counter-tenors singing a wider range than fifty years ago, athletes running faster than ever before.

And now there is a widespread notion that the biological thing is open to as many consumer choices as any other lifestyle accessory. Recipes for fitness and attractiveness allow for a sense of control over size: smaller through slimming and larger through body-building. Fitness and attractiveness are cultural concepts, bear social and emotional value. They also change from one society to another, whether in the recalibration of medical measures of obesity and high blood pressure or in the value placed on pumped muscles and tanned skin. As a lifestyle accessory the body changes. But these learnt cultural values in turn have material effects on bodies, effects which include killing them. As a site of representation of bodily appropriateness, therefore, the theatre may be said to contribute to a process which not only does things physically to the bodies of its performers, but also physically bears upon its audience.

Theatre as an art of bodies

As an artform theatre consciously exhibits the body. A body that is exhibited to others is almost always prepared for it, however informally. This might amount to a few moments of private mental reflection, which alerts the nerves and muscles, or to a lifetime's dedication to a technique. When a body is prepared for the theatre, this is a specific instance, and operates within the context, of the general process whereby a culture produces the body.

Many regimes of training for performance seek not only to refine and develop bodily skills but also to disseminate particular understandings, or philosophies, of performance. Stanislavsky's training system offers performers the tools for developing complex imitations of the real world even while it carries assumptions about how plays work and what stage characters are. It also defines the performer who undertakes it. For Stanislavsky the performer had an inner resource of emotional memory which could be drawn upon. For Suzuki, in contrast, the actor is taken over by the machinery of muscular exertion like a puppet becoming possessed. A body may be trained either to display its technique or to conceal it; to show that it has moved beyond the everyday or to be able to produce a recognisable copy of the everyday (Hodge 2000; also Barba and Saverese 1991; Roach 1993; Dennis 1995; Allain 2002).

Many methods of preparation for performance explicitly seek to depart from what their culture defines as everyday physicality. The precise nature and direction of that departure change according to the methods and their ideologies. I noted above that Alexander, Feldenkrais and Laban all developed techniques that were designed to compensate for, if not liberate bodies from, the physical distortion and alienation induced by modern life. In the 1970s performers might have begun their work by playing games. Play was seen as a tool for releasing body and mind from learnt inhibitions. Similarly in the 1970s, and with a similar notion of getting back to basics, various practitioners experimented with ways of ritualising the performing body, especially as a route to uncovering a primal spirituality. The quest for renewal of performance through renewal of bodily behaviour led in the 1980s to a greater concentration, not on that which is supposedly within but rather on the plurality of that which is without. Performers prepared by encountering modes from diverse cultures and traditions. This then was a form of departure from the superficially everyday, but now focused as a cultural enrichment through mingling, through the 'inter-corporeal' (the word is from Pavis 1996: 15) and through a display of skill for its own sake (Barba and Saverese 1991).

Common to all these techniques is their raw material, the human body. While that is obvious enough, different methods define, value and maintain awareness of the body in different ways. It may be the casing for an emotional inner life; it may be the substance to be purged; it may become transcendent through disorderly sensualities; it may work as mechanically as a puppet. What remains common is that it is a living entity that occupies a finite amount of space and has its own mass, energy and motor capacity. It is a material presence. As such it produces knowledge of itself and impacts upon the senses of others.

This aspect of material bodiliness was given force in the late 1980s and 1990s when what had been a somewhat discredited strand of philosophical work entered performance theory. In his introduction to *Bodied Spaces*, Stanton Garner claims that the 'phenomenological approach' can attend to both aspects of the stage – as 'scenic space ... spectacle to be processed and consumed by the perceiving eye, objectified as field of vision' and 'environmental space, "subjectified" (and intersubjectified) by the physical actors who body forth the space they inhabit'. He then quotes from the phenomenological philosopher Merleau-Ponty: 'To be a body, is to be tied to a certain world ... our body is not primarily *in* space: it is of it.' And in the same space as the performance, notes Garner, is the audience (Garner 1994: 3, 4; see also States 1985 and 1992; Merleau-Ponty 1996: 148). Theatre is an art of body and an art grounded in body.

And an art for a bodied audience

The phenomenological approach underlines the interpenetration of body and mind that was described near the start of this Introduction. For a phenomenologist, seeing is always 'bodied' seeing, mediated and affected by the physical mechanisms with which it is done. Thus one might say that 'Visual perception ... is inseparable from the muscular movements of the eye and the physical effort involved in focusing on an object or in simply holding one's eyelids open' (Crary 2001: 72). Indeed, some argue that one's whole body is affected by seeing: 'Without our knowing it, all that we see projects itself instantaneously into our musculature' (Verriest in Jousse 1990). Speaking and hearing are even more obviously 'bodied'. Speaking requires muscular activity while sound, in its pitch and rhythm, reverberates inside the body (Walser 1993). Within the theatre event there are two groups of people who might be seeing, speaking and hearing – the performers and the audience. Each group is a group of bodies.

I shall return in Part II to the bodily response of audiences, but we should note here that commentators on early film were firmly convinced that it had a bodily effect on its audience. In 1939 Walter Benjamin noted:

> technology has subjected the human sensorium to a complex kind of training. ... In a film, perception in the form of shocks was established as a formal principle. That which determines the rhythm of production on a conveyor belt is the basis of the rhythm of reception in a film.
> (Benjamin 1973: 177)

Similarly, just over a decade before, in 1927, Donald Laird concluded that loud noises have a 'profound effect on involuntary activities of the stomach' – and therefore that noise impairs productivity because its effects use up energy (quoted in Thompson 2002).

Those two observations are not only close in date, but they share conscious-ness of 'modern' living and a reference point in manual labour (Laird was observing typists). They are of their time, then, and as a consequence their concepts of bodily response are also of their time. In his history of perception, Jonathan Crary insists that different cultures have different models of the perceiving body. While in the eighteenth century a sense of touch was a component of theories of vision, in the nineteenth century sight became more autonomous, which contributed to the refashioning of an observer 'fitted for the tasks of "spectacular" consumption' (Crary 2001: 19). While vision as touch is viable in a world which has its contents in stable positions, 'in the nineteenth century such a notion became incompatible with a field organised around exchange and flux' (2001: 62). So too, while the model of the camera obscura 'defines an observer as isolated, enclosed and autono-mous' (2001: 39), cut off from the external world, a sort of disembodied mind, in the nineteenth century there developed theories of the bodiedness of looking. That position is summarised in the earlier quotation on visual perception by Crary: it is equally of its time.

Similarly Thompson argues that through the 1920s auditors were intro-duced to 'new ways of listening'. After 1927 motion picture auditoriums were wired for sound: 'the evolution of acoustical technologies in theaters and studios demonstrates how architectural acoustics and electroacoustics gradually merged'. The telephone and phonograph, by contrast, 'intro-duced people to sounds that had been severed from architectural space' and 'taught them to distinguish between desired sound signals and unwanted sounds or noises' (Thompson 2002: 234, 236). For a different historical moment, Bruce Smith attempts to describe a 'cultural poetics of listening' in the early modern period. This involves not just describing the specific mate-rial circumstances of listening – the shape and textures of theatres, the soundscape of the city – but also the 'protocols of listening', for example a decorum around sound connected to social status (Smith 1999: 8).

Listening, like speaking and seeing, happens in specific physical situa-tions, happens as part of a whole bodily experience. But this bodily experi-ence is thought about in different ways, and its physical techniques may alter, in different societies. There are cultures of listening and seeing. That said, one further point about the bodiliness of the spectators and audience needs noting.

This point, in brief, is that bodily effects emerge from two of the classic mechanisms by which theatre functions. In his discussion of empathy Ber-nard Beckerman notes the pose of a deeply engaged audience:

> leaning forward in one's seat … mirrors the forward thrust of the
> dramatic action. … Imaginatively we follow a path that runs parallel,
> not to the events themselves, but to the shifts of tension either between

characters or between ourselves and the performers. This process may be called *empathic parallelism*.

(Beckerman 1970: 149)

He then goes on to define his term: 'a kinesthetic, isomorphic response to dramatic action, by means of which the patterns and rhythms of tension find their immediate echo in the imaginative response of the audience'. The audience, however, 'need not recognise the structural patterns of an action, but they do experience the form *isomorphically* in a sympathetic pattern within their bodies' (1970: 151). The suggestion, then, is that empathy is a response of the whole physical person. Where body and brain are interconnected, this would seem a logical inference.

For commentary on the other mechanism we go much further back. In his account of the work done by theatrical performance Philip Sidney observed that tragedy 'maketh kings fear to be tyrants, and tyrants manifest their tyrannical humours' (Sidney 1975: 45). He is in effect talking about mimesis, but it is a mimesis not of actors so much as the audience. In response to the show they are led into imitation by what they watch. In 1934 Marcel Mauss seems to have observed a similar response to movies. He noted that young Parisian women were starting to walk like the girls depicted in American movies. This sort of imitation is, in turn, widely obvious in modern culture's response to its celebrities. Hair across the land has been chopped, teased and stuck in place in response to, say, Princess Diana or David Beckham. So too with clothes, so too with personal lifestyles. The star does a mimesis of celebrity, behaving as celebrities behave, and the audience does an imitation of the star. As well as the activity of actors in relation to the 'real' world, mimesis seems to describe the physical behaviour of an audience in relation to an acted world.

The interplay of bodily value, the art of bodies and physical responses to that art will occupy us in what follows. I track this through case studies of stage practices, principally within scripted drama, in the western European tradition. My method is to use 'close reading' of the sort I would do in preparing a text for rehearsal and production and situate it within a historical and theoretical context. In establishing that context, especially theoretically, I have borrowed models that sometimes put pressure on the material rather than naturally, so to speak, connect with it. But this process enables me to say things which I couldn't otherwise get to, and to invite the reader to think about whether the models and methods could be applied elsewhere.

The historical range is deliberately wide because I wanted examples that would best facilitate discussion of my various propositions. These examples are taken from canonical scripted texts from the main 'periods' of

English drama. My principles in selecting them were based on them being both generally famous and yet pleasurable for me to work on. The key thing was to model a way of dealing with staged bodies so that the reader can take the model away and apply it in other places. In each case I have tried to be specific about the material circumstances of a practice, while also trying to learn from contrasts and comparisons. This does not aim to be a history book, although there is quite a lot of history in it. Nor is it a book about actor training, directors' techniques, theatre anthropology or performance ethnography, though all of these come into it at times. It is a book, as I said at the start, about theatre as a practice in which societies negotiate around bodily value and bodily order. In that negotiation theatre is not simply an art of bodies but an art of bodily possibility, an event where the limits of body are negotiated, fetishised, imagined somehow else.

Part I

Body and script

As an art of bodies, theatrical performance both depends on and presents 'body work'. In the Introduction we saw how the body work of performance consists of two main elements. First, the body is prepared for performance, worked up to it by formal or informal regimes. Second, the preparation of the performing body is undertaken within a context of assumptions about 'body' in society and thus has a relationship – conscious or not, critical or not – with what are perceived to be dominant norms. Thus, by way of summary, the body work done by theatre consists of the construction of a particular sort of body which inevitably promotes a particular scheme of value.

In the case of preparation for performance of a written script there is a specific additional agency that contributes to shaping the body. This is the text itself. It has its effects at various levels. In the most general terms, a performer's awareness of the genre of the play will begin the process of preparing the body: it expects, for example, to hold itself differently in tragedy from farce, to have a different rhythm (see Chapter 4). In more specific terms, it organises what the body does on stage, whether it walks, jumps through hoops, giggles. In its speaking of a text the body is worked on in two ways. Most literally, that text controls breathing patterns and the way in which the body must hold itself in order to sustain vocal delivery. Less obviously it links voice into gesture. As Paul Zumthor puts it:

> Like the voice, gesture projects the body into the space of the performance, attempts to conquer this and to saturate it with its movement. The spoken word does not exist, like the written, simply in a verbal context. It necessarily belongs in the course of an existential situation ... whose totality is brought into play by the bodies of the participants.
>
> (Zumthor 1994: 224–5)

The written text of a play usually survives where evidence of physical preparation methods does not. While the written text will always have an effect on the bodies which deliver it, it has a varying relationship with the other methods that prepare those bodies. Some scripts emerge out of shared assumptions about norms of production. Other scripts seek to challenge or disrupt established norms. Some are written within company settings; others by autonomous authors.

Much of this first part of the book is concerned with the business of reading written texts specifically as an engine for producing bodies. The opening of Chapter 1 explores the issues here. It should be noted, however, that I am not proposing an entry route which will enable the staging of approximations to original performance (whatever that was). Let's remember that the script, as instruction for body work, is formulated within the context of bodies that are all culturally produced, both by physical regimes (diet, exercise, manners) and discursive ones (politeness, fashion, beauty). It is one discipline of the body among others. That context is always physically lost to later generations. While the occasion of performance has as its raw material the gathering together of bodies, the phenomenological interrelationship of these bodies is, again, not outside history. Average size and age of bodies differ according to period. So too the impact of bodily closeness will alter, not only in respect of the customary smells and dirt of surrounding bodies but also in respect of assumed norms about, say, the relationship between bodies and built environments (habitual room occupancy rates, size of buildings in proportion to bodies, accessibility and ordering of public space). Again, where the felt presence of bodies to each other is constituted from such elements, this will be irrecoverable.

My project of reading for the body here has the aim of arriving at some suggestions as to how theatre proposes, or installs, schemes of bodily value. The first case study, of Wycherley's *The Country Wife* in Chapter 1, concentrates on written script as a discipline of the body, suggesting its range of physical possibility and sketching in the value attached to bodily modes. From here follows an overview discussion of the status of 'body' and 'script' in analytical and theoretical accounts of acting and performance.

The second case study, in Chapter 2, *The Tempest*, aims to show how written text shapes a performing body in order to establish schemes of bodily value. Here production of the body is less dependent perhaps on the activity of vocalising script but emerges instead from assumptions about the performance modes and vocabularies of different genres. The play suggests, mobilises, more than one physical regime. The effect is that, while some bodies are seen to be quotations of theatrical modes, other bodies are simply natural.

The third case study, in Chapter 3, is concerned with that element of a play which is often referred to as 'business'. As such it moves to the very edges of the written script, since business seems to exist in the gaps between the lines. The chapter thus seeks to extend the ways I am engaging with the written text. In the two previous chapters bodily presentation was deliberately loaded with significance. In the business of this chapter bodies are caught up into apparently trivial routines. Consequently audience pleasure is positioned not within the embrace of orderliness but in escape from it. This invocation of pleasure in turn looks forward to the concerns of the next part of the book, which interests itself more explicitly in the audience and its physical pleasures.

1   Script as a discipline of the body

A body exists prior to the dramatic script it enacts. That script disciplines and shapes it. Within that shaping the individual body insists on its own characteristics.

The relationship between body and script is the main subject of this chapter. In an attempt to explore the detail of script's work on body there is a lengthy close analysis of one play. That analysis is prefaced and followed by commentary on the body–script relationship and its implications.

To begin with, then, let's see how the relationship of body and script has been formulated by various theorists.

The body and 'the body'

Body/script: both an opposition and a mutual dependence. The relationship has usually been tilted to one element or the other. Those working with actors' bodies have altered or ignored words; those working with the words have had only a generalised idea of the physical entity that they cue. Where textual analysis invokes bodily activity it tends to privilege that which adds to the message implicit in the words. Indeed the fashion for semiotics in the 1970s and 1980s enabled almost everything to be considered as message-bearing. The shift to a richer, and more subtle, understanding of body/script came from the newer interest in phenomenology.

Thus, as a phenomenologist, Stanton Garner takes issue with deconstructionist work on Beckett's plays which, he feels, disregards the drama. For him, the 'signifying (or representational) body is the construction of a theorizing act that brackets the living body and its phenomenal fields in an act of objectifying abstraction' (1994: 45). He demonstrates how the texts of a dramatist such as Beckett put pressure on the body and our assumptions about it. But even here, in this more subtle account of the relationship, body/script begins to tilt towards one of its elements. When Garner speaks of the living body on stage asserting a 'physiological irreducibility' (1994: 44), one of those same deconstructionists might argue that we are now at the opposite pole from theory and abstraction and are faced instead by biology as irreducible, as essence. It is necessary to recall that, as an art of living bodies, drama does not just assume biology but contributes – as indeed Garner implies elsewhere – to constructing and moulding it.

That whiff of irreducible biology, even in work which is as brilliant as Garner's, shows how tough it is to retain a firm grasp on the properly dialectical nature of the body/script relationship, the union of opposites. It is one instance of a wider philosophical discussion of the relationship between material body and the systems and discourses of culture. By way of summary of the issue Bryan Turner suggests:

> To reject Cartesianism, it is not necessary to deny the corporeal nature of human existence and consciousness. To accept the corporeality of human life, it is not necessary to deny the fact that the nature of the human body is also an effect of cultural, historical activity.
>
> (Turner 1996: 74)

But it's a very slippery dialectic. As Judith Butler notes, even the master-theorist of the interlockings of body and discursive regimes, Foucault himself, slips into an evocation of a sort of natural body which escapes the disciplines of power: 'he refers [in the *History of Sexuality*] to "bucolic" and "innocent" pleasures of intergenerational sexual exchange that exist prior to the imposition of various regulative strategies' (1990: 97; see also Grosz 1995: 217–19).[1] And then Butler herself has been criticised for confusing person and role, for giving overmuch weight to interpellation and abstract structures. As Elizabeth Grosz says, 'It is not adequate to simply dismiss the category of nature outright, to completely retranscribe it without residue into the cultural: this in itself is the monist, or logocentric, gesture par excellence.' The dialectic has to be strategically preserved: 'In the face of social constructionism, the body's tangibility, its matter, its (quasi) nature may be invoked; but in opposition to essentialism, biologism, and naturalism, it is the body as cultural product that must be stressed' (1994: 21, 23–4).

Grosz's language here emerges out of political debates about sexuality and gender in the mid–1980s. Crudely put, an essentialist position would suggest that, say, a woman is more nurturing and inclined to peace than a man because of her female nature; a social constructionist would say that she had learnt these values historically through her positioning, for example, in family and labour market. The urgency of the political debates of that period was one of the mechanisms that pushed theorisations about 'the body' into the limelight.

Those inverted commas have had to appear. They mark the fact that 'the body' became a reference point to anchor, first off, political debate and then a series of cultural and literary commentaries. Used in this way it became a sort of fetish, offering apparent connections with the real while being abstracted from its own materiality and history. Writing at the end of the 1980s Michael Feher summarised:

> the history of the human body is not so much the history of its representations as of its modes of construction. For the history of its representations always refers to a real body considered to be 'without history' … whereas the history of its modes of construction can … turn the body into a thoroughly historicized and completely problematic issue.
>
> (Feher 1989: 11)

His use of the word 'construction' refers not to Grosz's social constructionism but to the body's materiality.

In exploring the relations of body and script we regularly bump into the opposition which Feher identifies, that between representation and material construction. This is fairly deeply embedded in academic work. The editors of the 1993 collection, *Reading the Social Body*, make a virtue of it: 'These essays fall into two categories: some treat the social construction of bodies that have actually existed at some point in human history, and others discuss the representation of bodies in various artistic contexts' (Burroughs and Ehrenreich 1993: 5). On the one hand there are those who deal with the 'actually' existing – sociology which writes about ageing, diet, sport; theatre anthropology and intercultural performer training. On the other hand there are literary and cultural commentators who deal with representations in written, graphic, filmed texts – texts which use inscriptions to make reference to the body, but a body which has no actual lived history and presence.

Nature and culture, representation and construction: there are two sets of binaries. To these a third can be added: theatre and performance. Developing from the 'body art' traditions sketched in the Introduction, performance (previously known as performance art) came of intellectual age during those political debates around nature and culture. Within the polemic which was generated in order to define the emergent form, theatre was seen to belong with the business of representing, and fictionalising, the body. Performance stripped away theatricality, exposing spectators – or participants – to the actuality of the performer's body.

We return to this binary at the end of the chapter. It needs to appear in the narrative here, however, because of its possible role in shaping the circumstances which inform this chapter. At the start of this section, I noted, implicitly, that there did not seem to be a substantial body of critical work which reflected, in an appropriately subtle way, on the body/script relationship. At a time when the issues of representation and construction, nature and culture, were being picked up in academic overviews of 'the body', one might have expected that one of the leading arts of the body, theatre, might have intellectually benefited. But it is also precisely at this moment that theatre is ousted from the leading edge of the discussion by the newer form that is performance.

By contrast, in another performance mode that has risen to intellectual dominance, dance, the analysis of the relationship between body and script (here being choreography and score) has been foregrounded. For example, in her essay on 'Technologies of the Body in Baroque Music' in *The Royal to the Republican Body*, musicologist Susan McClary argues that while French music favoured moving the physical body 'at the expense of inwardness', Italian music mapped interiority: 'each divides up and shapes human bodily experience in its own way' (1998: 97). Or, again, discussing the dancer Martha Graham, Mark Franko shows how her early piece *Frontier* explored the relationship between American space and the individual body, articulating through choreography her own problematic status as woman and radical (Franko 1995: 54).

Missing from *The Royal to the Republican Body*, however, are any essays on the body scripted by dramatic text. And, apart from an essay on – significantly enough – closet (that's to say, de-bodied) drama, the same omission marks *Reading the Social Body*. And all three volumes of Feher's *Fragments for a History of the Human Body*. Where, in the minor explosion of histories of the body, is the body scripted by and for theatre? This form, written expressly for the body, seems to have no relevance in studies of 'the body'.

Body/script

The absence was filled, in part, from within drama/literature studies. In an essay published in 1999, and later included in the book *Author's Pen and Actor's Voice*, Robert Weimann approaches the issue within the framework of Shakespearean theatre. Specifically concerned with modes of acting in relation to script, he argues that there was permeability between the 'learned' and the 'common', 'between representational acting and presentational playing'. Opposing attempts to privilege either the author's text or the stage practice, he rejects the 'either/or' and suggests that we 'come to terms with the ways in which the performed play thrives on the mutual engagement of text and bodies' (1999: 420).

While some would say that it is only in literary studies that this suggestion might sound at all novel, Weimann's treatment of the relationship is subtle. Even within a very sophisticated argument, however, body/script remains a slippery entity. At a crucial juncture Weimann seems to simplify the relationship. This can be seen clearly when he emphasises the materiality of performance: 'playing in the presence of spectators is an expense of irreducible physical energy' (mmm – we have met 'irreducible' before …). Performance is never just a '*medium*', relaying the signifiers 'given in the words of the text', but an '*agency* in its own right', drawing on 'a unique and irreplaceable source of living strength that is inseparable from the transaction itself' (1999: 427). While this is a proper insistence on productive effort, I think it simplifies at each binary pole. Energy may be irreducible, but it is not undifferentiated in its application and exhibition (the singer and acrobat both spend energy, but against different resistances). This expenditure of energy is also culturally valorised – some people, for example, find it necessary to avoid sweat. And, while what has come down to us from the early modern period may be verbal texts, words comprise only one 'text' in the theatre. There are also visual and sound designs, and there is choreography. Words can perhaps be relayed, but a movement text ends up being inhabited.[2] So there are real problems with making a separation between body and verbal text. As Susan Foster says, 'verbal discourse cannot speak *for* bodily discourse, but must enter into "dialogue" *with* that bodily discourse' (1998: 186–7). There is a need for an approach which explores these modes of interrelation, the inscription of body and the bodiliness of text.

To attempt this exploration I have chosen to look at a dramatic form where there is already an apparently very close relationship between body and text. That relationship seems to be known much more widely than to a specialist group of theatre historians. Indeed, it is so firmly embedded in mainstream culture that, when the form is mentioned, the modern body knows what shapes to assume. Take this moment from the 1990s' television show *Whose Line is it Anyway?* The show was based on the wit of improvisation. In one challenge Josie Lawrence and Caroline Quentin were asked to do a dialogue in Restoration style. Instantly they were fluttering fans: chins held high, muscular tightness in the top half of the body, emphasis on the poise in shoulders and elbows while the head turned. The face was produced, through the positioning of the fan, as a place where the alternation between concealment and revelation became important. The whole activity, with its fluttering and head-turning, felt not 'significant' but busy. The corporeal stereotype of Restoration comedy appeared in an instant and was instantly recognised by its studio audience.

The Restoration and the English body

For a project such as mine, then, the Restoration is an obvious place to begin because, first, it contributes so powerfully to an assumed history, a cultural 'memory', of English body modes. And second, most crucially, the Restoration seems to be that moment when the chief mechanism for shaping body mode is dramatic text. These two elements are brought together in modern culture, not only in the fan-fluttering antics of Josie Lawrence and Caroline Quentin but in the repeated modes of advertising for Restoration comedy revivals. The copy posted outside the doors of the theatre will usually have two features – prose invocations of rollicking fun and bawdy, and pictures which consist of leery smiles and prominent breasts. Aha – sexual difference at work. Those smiles and breasts have a long pedigree. By the middle of the eighteenth century historians were looking back at the Restoration as a period when free rein was given to a decadent aristocratic culture and its sponsorship of a licentious stage. This culture was to be condemned because it reacted against, and obstructed the transmission of, the values and achievements of the 'puritan revolution' (Shepherd and Womack 1996). But while this sort of Restoration body has lived on in popular assumptions, modern historians of the period and its culture have suggested that its bodily values differed from this. They do not fully agree, however, on what they were.

Here are a couple of suggestions from a theatre historian and then a historian of acting technique. In one of the more useful books to have been written about Restoration comedy, Peter Holland (1979) suggests that in general the drama is exploring two concepts of what is 'natural' – on the one hand social ease, on the other a Hobbesian pre-social aggression. The acting style was, then, 'naturalistic' in so far as it conformed with the behaviours of social decorum. Holland's Restoration is that of the wealthy audience, with its cynicism developed in the aftermath of the Commonwealth. This contrasts with, but doesn't necessarily contradict, the story of the development of acting technique. Joseph Roach's Restoration is situated between the passion and emotion of the Elizabethan stage and the mechanised bodies of the mid-eighteenth century. The player of the seventeenth century sought to acquire inhibitions, and the end of the century established 'an elaborate network of inhibitions called theatrical decorum' (Roach 1993: 54).

These views of the acting body can be set alongside the cultural historians' narrative of the shifts from fairground and popular culture of Renaissance London to the clean-living morality of the early-eighteenth-century coffee house. The achievement of bourgeois culture of the late seventeenth century was, in the words of Stallybrass and White, the 'creation of a sublimated public body, without smells, without coarse laughter, without organs, separate from the Court and the Church on the one hand and the market square, alehouse, street and fairground on the other' (1986: 93–4). The link between the bourgeois and bodily sublimation takes us into an earlier story which tells of the close connection in early capitalism 'between discipline, asceticism, the body and capitalist production' (Turner 1996: 3). This thesis was most famously propounded in Weber's *Protestant Ethic and the Spirit of Capitalism*, but as Turner shows it was also assumed by Marxist thinkers, where it runs into problems around consumption. In Turner's opinion Weber failed to address the contradiction 'between hedonistic consumption and ascetic production' (1996: 115).

Through these different versions, one point does remain constant, namely that the Restoration is a period in English history explicitly associated with the organisation of bodily discipline (though in the wider perspective of Elias (2000) it doesn't have the same status). That association was firmly locked into Restoration culture by the theatre itself. A favoured scene, repeated in a number of plays, consists of the more or less comical training of a body in appropriate behaviour. This is an example:

> Now, if you would speak contemptibly of any man, or thing, do thus with your hand – so – and shrug up your shoulders till they hide your ears.
>
> (Wycherley 1949: 199)

Thus the instruction of a little black boy to the fool Monsieur de Paris, who is having to learn how to be Spanish in Wycherley's *The Gentleman Dancing-Master*, written in 1671/2. It is part of a whole series of instructions as to bearing, bowing, greeting, laughing that are attempted by Monsieur as he is walked about the stage by the boy. Meanwhile Prue stands to one side of the stage and complains about the lot of the chambermaid, 'who sits knocking her heels in the cold', while her mistress has sex. Against the artificiality of the body Monsieur is trying to acquire Prue seems to be natural. But as soon as she speaks about the 'carking and caring, the watching and sitting up' we see that her body too is produced, by her class and her sex. Furthermore it is difficult to keep her, in her apparent 'naturalness', separate from the artificial Monsieur, because he, as she tells us, is her only hope of getting some sex (Wycherley 1949: 199–200).

This little scene sits usefully alongside the modern commentators because it insists on placing bodies in relation to one another. When the object of enquiry is described as *the* body (singular) we perhaps lose sight of the key function of interrelationship in the work of defining bodies. Drama so often draws us into its bodily values by having us learn, and then take pleasure in, the schemes of interrelating differences. To these we now turn.

A balancing act

In Act 3 scene 2 of Wycherley's *The Country Wife*, written in 1672, the notorious womaniser Horner, now supposedly impotent, is telling his friends Harcourt and Dorilant that he is going to forgo the company of women. Just before he leaves them Harcourt asks his advice, because he is in love with Sparkish's mistress. Before Horner can give it, Sparkish enters, 'looking about' (Wycherley 1973: 3.2.53). But Horner and Harcourt continue discussing the situation for about ten lines until Sparkish joins them in conversation.

For the 50 or so lines that precede Sparkish's entry, what is the action? Three men talk. Their conversation maps them against other people (women, old leery men, rich fools) and other activities (drinking, eating, gambling). Those activities are elsewhere – nowhere – while what is *staged* is 'non-activity', talk; the men are those who refer to themselves as 'us'. Up to Sparkish's entry this is 'us' on display, working at leisure; making non-activity into spectacle, giving it – as it were – distinction. This image is reinforced by Sparkish's ten-line entry to the conversation. The performer must sustain the activity of 'looking about'. That activity, drawing on its roots perhaps in *commedia* clowning, shows the power of this persona's desire to locate and bask in the attention of others. While the pantomime goes on, the speech between Horner and Harcourt seems to become more stylish than it was before:

Horner:	Why, here comes one will help you to her.
Harcourt:	He! He, I tell you, is my rival, and will hinder my love.
Horner:	No, a foolish rival and a jealous husband assist their rival's designs ...
Harcourt:	But I cannot come near his mistress but in his company.
Horner:	Still the better for you, for fools are most easily cheated when they themselves are accessories.

(Wycherley 1973: 3.2.53–60)

The rhetorical antitheses in each line become more emphatic, recalling the shape of the formal set at wit, and behind that the stichomythia. These verbal features stress balance and organise conspicuous turn-taking. At a very basic level they trace out the rhythm of breathing necessary to deal with the lines.[3] The physical work involved combines with the perception of the rhetorical shapes to produce bodies that are themselves governed by balance. The Horner–Harcourt dialogue thus has about it the sense of stasis and containment, working within limit, as opposed to Sparkish who is driven by his desire. The corporeal balance is not, however, merely individual; it also sets up relation to another. The shape of the exchange ensures that the body *waiting* to reply is as important as the speaker. The waiting body is defined by its predeliction to participate in the balancing act, and in that way sets up a sort of repetition of another body. That repetition could be slavish, or a forced dependency; here it is a balance like mirroring, where indeed there is a form of dependency but always masked as narcissistic affirmation. This is very different from Monsieur de Paris's foregrounded tuition in solemnity. Here the bodily repetition appears to be the natural product of – while in fact it produces – the dialogue between chums. Being naturalised doesn't, however, deprive it of value, and its value, together with its shape and its degree of naturalisation (as contrasted with, say, those framed 'sets at wit'), are specific to the historical mode. So the appearance of waiting to reply here produces a feeling of harmony between the bodies that in turn makes the containment feel pleasurable. That demonstrated mutuality itself contrasts with Sparkish's solo entry.

There are, too, hierarchies at work. One differentiates Horner and Harcourt, through the contrast between Horner's habitual production of epigrams and Harcourt's more intensive use of personal pronouns. Harcourt speaks as it were from himself to himself, while Horner addresses a generality. To them both Dorilant is audience. These differences will have their effects both on the gesture and address of the body and on the real audience's perception of the body as similar or different. Such discriminations are, however, but half-realised alongside the larger differentiation between these two and Sparkish. He uses the pronoun 'I' more than anyone else. This is a verbal symptom of how much he is solipsistically governed by his desire. While he seems not to notice them, the other two take their time with a dialogue that intimately concerns him. While he does his pantomime of looking around, their bodies are observing, maintaining an alertness to the boundary between what can and cannot be overheard. Against his busy doing, they are commenting. Within the hierarchies here Sparkish's physical activity is always less important than Horner's cynical observation. Inaction is power.

Privatised lives

The second scene I am concerned with is more complex. In Act 4 scene 3, the famous 'china' scene, Horner has sex with Lady Fidget (or at least we are to *imagine* him doing so) while her husband is in the next room. Horner's pretext is that he is showing her his china collection. When other women arrive they too want to be shown his china.

The scene opens with Horner describing his sexual triumphs (under pretext of impotence) to the doctor, Quack. After 30 or so lines, Lady Fidget enters, 'looking about her'. While she does the pantomime of looking (this time the persona is driven by a desire to keep herself secret from, unattended by, the world), Horner sets up Quack behind the screen specifically to observe his prowess. Note the attitude to the stage here. Quack, on stage but not on display, has a safe and authoritative position; the fools don't know they're on display; Horner knows he is on display but is still taking a risk with regard to the outcome. The thrill is to go through with the adventure without ever appearing to be foolish. The common assumption through all this is that we are not only always observed but always vulnerable to the observer. (This might connect with Bryan Turner's narrative about the development of an increasingly 'closed' body and propriety around private space, but it contrasts with the Stallybrass and White narrative about the development of a public body and ethical coffee-house society.) The stage is not a space for play but for calculated risk. The body that will make most use of it, and thus most fun for the audience, has to produce itself as vigilant.[4]

Lady Fidget intensifies the binary between being observed and taking risk. The observers she is concerned about are the social 'world'. She doesn't know she is already observed by Quack, and us. What we see is her movement from a refusal to 'withdraw' with Horner up to an embrace of him. This movement is physically inscribed as a set of alternations between refusal and curiosity: 'let us not be smutty. But you talk of mysteries and bewitching to me' (Wycherley 1973: 4.3.48–9). On that full stop the performer's body must shift its attitude to Horner: there's a breath that breaks the two sentences; but there's a half-rhyme (smutty/But you) that re-joins them. It's a momentary glimpse of the tug between nature and culture. The effect is to make it an un-smooth transition; the muscular organisation of Lady Fidget's desire is very much on display. It becomes even more pronounced when she actually starts to speak about Horner's 'secret'. For at this point of intensified intimacy her fear about the 'world' likewise gets bigger: 'for my acquaintance are so censorious, – oh 'tis a wicked world, Mr Horner! – I say, are so censorious and detracting' (4.3.59–61). The repetition of 'censorious' is cumbersome enough, but into the syntax is placed a parenthesis – and no mere parenthesis but a form of apostrophe. The need for quite a lot of breath to manage the hurdles means that she almost pants, which makes her chest move – producing, perhaps, the bawdy breast. In conjunction with this, there is an uncertainty of control over her focus: she apparently looks outward to the censorious world and inward to Horner's 'secret', but her apostrophe about the world is directed to Horner. What we see is woman produced as that which cannot control its own performance; and what is foregrounded as the cause of this lack of control is a desiring body. The syntax may cue the actress's performance, but the image is of a character whose desire breaks through her speech. The logical climax is that it is she, not Horner, who initiates the embrace.

At which point her husband enters. The next 50 lines are a combination of asides and dialogue: she panics, and then says she is seeing if Horner is ticklish; her husband's reply gives Horner his excuse – that he is sick of squiring other men's wives about town; which makes Sir Jaspar Fidget laugh mockingly in an aside. When Lady Fidget accuses Horner of being ill-bred, her husband asks what he has done. She laughs, to give herself time, and then comes up with the idea that he has got china that he won't let her see. And she rushes into the next room. Horner, apparently trying to stop her, says:

> Lock the door, madam. – So, she has got into my chamber and locked me out. Oh, the impertinency of womankind! Well, Sir Jaspar, plain

dealing is a jewel. If ever you suffer your wife to trouble me again here, she shall carry you home a pair of horns, by my Lord Mayor she shall! Though I can't furnish you myself, you are sure, yet I'll find a way.

(Wycherley 1973: 4.3.110–15)

Sir Jaspar has an aside in which he finds this hugely amusing. Horner then has an aside: 'Nay, though you laugh now, 'twill be my turn ere long' (4.3.119). Shortly after he leaves to join Lady Fidget.

The initial interruption sets up a sequence of obstacles for the characters to overcome. They do this with different degrees of efficiency – Lady Fidget panics for longer than Horner does, the person who has increasingly less grasp on what is going on is Sir Jaspar. The differentiation between them is marked by the space assumed by the different *asides*. Hers worries about being found out, speaks incomplete sentences, addresses herself: it makes her turn inward, showing loss of control on public utterance, privatising her domain. Horner is brisk: 'That's my cue, I must take it' (4.3.84). He still has an eye on the mechanisms of performance; his subjectivity hydraulically moves into the space others create for it. There is no sense of an extensive inner personal space; if the lines are addressed to an audience they do not share very much with them. Sir Jaspar's first aside is at the other extreme from his wife: he is completely unreflexive, and he talks much more than he need do (and when he does reflect on himself later, he is wholly misguided); if he is sharing a joke with the audience, the words feel simultaneously wasted. Sir Jaspar is relaxed; that's his idiocy.

The charisma of constraint

In a mode of playing that uses the aside, it is the differentiation between asides which is crucial. They establish different body spaces and different degrees of physical control. A related display of precision, which is denied to the other characters here, is when Horner gets Lady Fidget to lock the door even while he is expressing outrage. In an instant a space that had seemed whole is broken up, secret areas are created (the instruction to Lady F); even as Horner addresses Sir Jaspar about plain dealing he plays to the audience. And – who knows – the lines about finding a way could also be for Quack. That speech, building the technique of the asides into a bravura display, depends for its delivery on the precision with which lines are directed: the angle of the head moving from generality to individual address, possibly a sharply changed intensity and focus of look. We watch the physical work that completes the isolation of Sir Jaspar, and, being addressed ourselves, are complicit with it. For the competent character, speech is management.

The asides are composed from micro-elements of technique. So too is the laughter. Lady Fidget's laugh is designed as cover. Sir Jaspar's laugh is a form of self-indulgence. As such it contrasts with the precision of Horner's managerial speech. Rather than articulate the space into sectors, the laugh fills it indiscriminately. It is redundant sound, vacuous, non-directed. Thus, left alone on the stage, Sir Jaspar is not centred in the space. He 'calls through the door to his wife; she answers within'. While he talks *off*-stage, Quack from behind his screen has a rare line directed at the audience. Quack, on-stage but concealed, has more dignity – because he has more understanding of what's happening – than Sir Jaspar who, with the whole stage to himself, is the most ineffectual character here. Authority comes from being withheld from the stage, withheld from being exposed. And, if Quack's position behind a screen gives him force, even more fascination is exerted by those behind the closed door. Between those two there is another distinction. We hear Lady Fidget: 'Let him come, and welcome, which way he will' (4.3.130). Horner is neither seen nor heard. But he has become embedded – so to speak – in our imagination. If his body has become 'sublimated', it has also become even more phallic, even dirtier.

At this point the play has invented a *mise-en-scène* where a closed door is more interesting than an open one. Part of the pleasure is that the door stands as a witty and knowing denial of what is supposed to be happening behind it, where openings are found. But within the hierarchy of characters here the more securely closed the door, the more sexy it is. It is the hidden bodies which exert the most power on our minds. We can see all of Sir Jaspar, and he is contemptible. While he shouts nervously, ignorantly, from the on-stage side of the door – where we in the audience are too – our minds are dissociating themselves from him because we know what is 'really' going on behind that door. The larger Sir Jaspar's physical performance becomes, the more fascinating become the unseen bodies behind the door. It is not just that they are supposedly having sex which makes them sexy; it is that they escape the indignity of being staged. And, because they are not staged, we don't know precisely what is going on – which way he is coming in. Which makes them yet more desirable. As we watch Sir Jaspar, then, we learn to look at the performing body with minds that desire the hidden body, looking at the staged as a sort of failure to be unstaged.

The dramaturgy suggests that a physically active comic body is an embarrassment. The more a body is foreclosed from display, the more fascinating and powerful it becomes. In both scenes we have looked at, Horner's stage power derives from emotional management and poise: very self-disciplined, very polished. The more closed off he is, the more authority he has. Being silent behind a closed door he is fascinating. In Horner we get the charisma of constraint.

Script, practice and the disappearing body

When *The Country Wife* puts its sexiest body off-stage, into a zone which is perforce unscripted, what is left exposed on stage in all its silliness is a scripted body. With that in mind, we'll return to my opening question about the impropriety of the scripted body as an object of enquiry.

That body, I've suggested, tends to slide between disciplinary boundaries: literary criticism will busy itself with text but steers clear of the acting body, which it regards as the domain of theatre studies. Theatre studies will say that, whatever the text establishes, the play can be practically performed in a multiplicity of ways. This disciplinary split between the effete relativism of 'practice' and the abstracting rigours of 'text' emerges at a theoretical level in a series of versions of the opposition of discourse and biology, representation and construction, or indeed fiction and reality.

Through one such version it slips into the very work which has the potential to demolish these binaries. Histories of acting technique are concerned with a real acting body, but in order to write their history they have to be seriously concerned with text. One of the most scholarly and unusual of such histories is Joseph Roach's *The Player's Passion* which has a breadth of reference far beyond the usual trot between Stanislavsky and Grotowski. The book's focus on the 'inner workings' of the actor's body is intended to bring to light a hitherto ignored connection between physiological concepts and modes of expressiveness in cultures ranging from early modern to modernist. In reviewing previous historians of acting Roach pauses over the achievements of B. L. Joseph, who nevertheless did not 'distinguish sharply between the physiology of character as written by the dramatist and the actor's physiology' (Roach 1993: 30). Now it might seem that the dramatist would share a concept of physiology with the actor since such beliefs, having to do with what is natural, are deeply embedded and widespread. By separating the character and actor bodies Roach is separating the fictional from the real, driving a wedge between two elements which in performance customarily interact and blur. This separation works to privilege the real, the natural body which is not only the topic of scientists and acting theorists but also the topic of Roach's book.

The tactics of Roach's argument make sense when viewed in the context of a world dominated by literary criticism. He insists on the biological presence of the acting body, where technique is brought to the text by the actor – and grounded in a scientific discourse outside that of fiction and literature. It is the combination of physiological knowledge of the body and a technique based on this which – rather than the author's text – produces the actor's body on stage. By contrast with the author's imaginings, the actor's body is that which is really natural. This step then leads to Roach's commentary on Aaron Hill's versified Diderot, 'The Art of Acting' (1746): 'the embodiment of an emotion flows effortlessly from "ideal" to physical manifestation; as Hill notes simply, "the *mov'd* actor *Moves*"' (Roach 1993: 81). The formula may be elegant but it does not tell us *how* the actor moves – within what range of gesture, with what disposition of bodyweight. Bryan Turner, summarising

Mauss, says: 'although the human body has the potential for walking, the particular form of walking which is produced within a given society or group is the outcome of training and practice' (1996: 34). In a rehearsal room, if a performer is asked to walk across the stage she might do so in a variety of ways – as a melodrama villain, as Max Wall, as a catwalk model, as a priest, as a *butoh* performer. And then again, does the performer imitate Max Wall or quote him, look to the audience or not, walk slow or fast, in curved or straight lines? When the performer moves she is confronted by choices which will lead to different sorts of effects and meanings. Caught up into a play of differences and repetitions, these choices are textual.

The body on stage may then be said to be a product not only of contemporary ideas about physiology and the technique of acting but also of a third element which – bringing back something occluded by Roach – is the script. For a script may distinguish bodies in one show from those in another, tragic bodies from pastiche tragic bodies; and it may discriminate between bodies in the same show, the easeful body from the frustrated one. A generalised notion of a culture's performing technique needs also to be alert to the particular moments at which that technique's relationship to its audience is affirmed, challenged, negotiated – the particular scripting of the body.

While the script's relationship to the body may be irrelevant to the acting historian's thesis, it needs to be foregrounded by the performance theorist, since it helps to define the terms of her analysis. Within that analysis a key role is played by another binary variant. The oppositions between technique and script, biology and discourse, reality and fiction re-assemble themselves as embodiment versus representation. Let's follow the operation of this binary in the work of another very astute and cautious analyst: in her essay on Aphra Behn, Elin Diamond argues that '[t]he gestic inference of Behn's abundant use of women-in-breeches parts is not that disguise hides a truth that will ultimately emerge ... but rather that representation is always pressured by embodiment' (1997: 73). That embodiment is, she insists, the 'experience' of a woman's body in the 1680s.

Diamond is correct to insist that the 'phenomenological experience' of embodiment may be in tension with representation. To ignore that point is to write the partial history produced by concentrating merely on semiotics or representation, to make the body '*purely* a social, cultural, and signifying effect lacking its own weighty materiality' (Grosz 1994: 21). But when we met representation before as part of a binary, it was set against (material) construction; here it is against embodiment. The occluding of construction suggests that, although there is a very proper insistence on biology, it is seen not so much as constructed but as, again, irreducible. This inflection to the binary is especially problematic within drama study, where it comes into contact with institutional pressures – and indeed another binary – particular to the discipline. We can see what happens if we move to Elin Diamond's essay on Caryl Churchill. Here she attempts to distinguish the pleasures and processes of *theatre* from those of *performance*: theatre is 'governed by the logos of the playwright's text; actors represent fictional entities of that text' while performance 'dismantles textual authority, illusionism, and the canonical actor in favor of the "polymorphous thinking body" of the performer'. Having set up that binary, she then warns against its simplicity. She wants instead to understand 'the ideological nature of representation', and she repeats: 'In theater the sexual and historical specificity of the actor's body is absorbed into a representation of the body of a character, as defined and delimited by the author's text' (1997: 84–5).

Although Diamond is sharp enough to know that it is misleading, that binary of theatre versus performance won't go away. It has all the attraction and force of what used to be called an epistemological break, as if drama studies only properly entered the (post)modern world when it learnt to dis-avow theatre and embrace performance. Its distorting effect on Diamond's argument here is that it has led her to forget the point made in her essay on Behn, where she describes how representation (presumably the domain of the author's text) is always under pressure from embodiment (specifically the performer's body) – even in the 1680s. And that point is surely right, for, as we've seen in Wycherley's text, through the control of breath patterns and balance the verbal text is *part of* the physical experience.

But more importantly, and reaching far beyond Diamond's essay, are the assumptions which that binary endlessly recycles. The actor's body is placed in opposition to the character body. The character body, being invented by an author, is textual and artificial. By implication, and following the simple mechanism of the binary, the actor's body is thus produced as 'natural'. When that happens a whole history of acculturation is occluded. Second, where the body of 'performance' is placed in opposition against theatre it can be presented as something different from theatre, a 'polymorphous thinking body', a 'semiotic bundle of drives'. But on what grounds can we explain historically why bodies that performed prior to, say, 1920 might not have been polymorphous and thinking? It may be too abstract and formalist simply to suggest the change was caused by some sort of freedom from text – we would come unstuck dealing with *commedia dell'arte*, if not with several other modes. Furthermore, the rather grand narrative which contrasts all of theatre with the 'polymorphous thinking body' tends, as a rhetorical effect, to give that polymorphous etc. a special aura. How far is it itself an illusion that works to inhibit our inspection of it as, alongside all others, a culturally learnt behaviour? The body of performance is, of course, always also accultur-ated. And in the moment at which someone takes up a position within an installation, or simply becomes lit in a bare space, in that moment they are textually positioned, not perhaps within an author's script but within planned visual parameters, within lighting design, within the institutional discourse which is 'performance'. Nevertheless it is the verbally scripted body which in the 'performance' discourse has, symptomatically perhaps, to be silenced.

The sense of that epistemological break between theatre and performance is strengthened by its reiteration in other disciplinary discourses. In his 1991 review essay on the body Arthur Frank offers as an example of the 'communicative body' – one of his four basic body types – the body of the performance artist. Performance art pieces 'seem to have a common theme of the body seeking to break out of codes in which it cannot express itself and find self-expression in a code of its own invention' (Frank 1996: 85). This observation is silent about the possibility that other dramatic text – besides that of 'performance' – might stage a body having difficulty with codes (like the boy actor playing Cleopatra complaining about being imitated by squeaking boys). It is also silent about the extent to which 'performance' is itself a genre, with learnt generic shapes. More importantly, it envisages the body as itself an author, committed to expression, as distinct from the artificial codes of others. An expressive body, speaking without mediation for itself – the moved body just moving – seems again to be an image of biology freeing itself from discourse, nature from culture. Withdrawing behind a closed door, as it were: to do the real business.

Performance theory and table manners

While Horner is off-stage, imagined to be finding self-expression, perhaps, in a code of his own invention, the audience contemplates Sir Jaspar in all his loud staginess. He is stupid because he doesn't know what is going on. Not just cuckolded, he is the one who is staged where the power lies with the unstaged. He has been set up by the others. While Sir Jaspar is caught into a fiction, Horner is imagined to be busy beyond the fictional space, behind that door. In the same way, while Sparkish does his pantomime of looking about, what's felt to be the real insight comes from the men who comment on him.

The rather tired distinction between fiction and reality here is sharpened by its relationship with other binaries which the script produces: physical restraint and directedness versus size and mess; vocal measure versus noise and exuberance. These readily generate evaluative categories: management versus clowning; planning versus theatricality. Whatever our pleasure in the clowning, the value system which runs through the binaries designates that management is sexy and charismatic and clowning is not. That value system, produced as it is by our Restoration text, has about it a strange persistence, and if we start to pick over some of the other binaries we have encountered we can detect it shimmering in the distance. For instance, if we share the belief that performance art dismantles illusionism in favour of the polymorphous 'thinking' body of the performer – and that this is useful work – we are not only looking at a familiar binary (thinking/illusion, planning/theatricality), but we are sharing the same preferences as Horner's audience.

There is another pair of terms which subsumes most of the others: the 'real body' versus the body scripted by others. For Roach and Diamond, fiction, in the form of that which is 'written by the dramatist' or 'the playwright's text', is conceived as an imposition on the actor ... much as Sir Jaspar may be said to be imposed on, set up by, scripted by Horner. Alongside and against the deliberately illusionistic world invented by dramatists the actor, we are told, brings a technique founded on science, a biologically real body, that which is sexually and historically specific. Let's take these thoughts back with us to that moment in 1672 when an audience watches three men, dressed very like themselves, standing on the forestage and sharing their light, as they comment on the activities – the large, clownish activities – of a fourth man: around those three men the aura of the biologically real, the sexually and historically specific, is not wholly absent. The audience, watching and commenting on the show, see Horner and his chums – 'us' – watching and commenting on Sparkish. And in that audience those in the least fashionable seats watch the pit commenting on the show. In this arrangement it is not simply that divisions between theatre and reality may feel a bit slippery, but that, more importantly, the presence of 'theatre' is no guarantee of the absence of sexual and historical specificity.

But that is not how *The Country Wife* has us see it. Sparkish and Sir Jaspar, those who are trapped in fictions and scripted by others, are ridiculous. And so too, in the work of modern commentators, the theatrical text – with its body scripted by others – is an imposition on, a delimiting of, the biologically real, trained – and yet polymorphous – body of the performer.

In these strange echoes between the Restoration text and the modern performance analysis we start to see that there might be a larger story unravelling around the impropriety of the scripted body. In here somewhere there seems to be an ancient distrust of fiction and theatre. Yet it is not an opposition to all forms of illusion. Some people who feel theatre is delimiting find performance fully expressive. In the same way the nineteenth-century historian who roundly condemns Restoration comedy finds Shakespearean drama noble. There is a process of discrimination going on, and we need to get hold of its mechanisms.

Restoration comedy was condemned largely because it was 'bawdy'. As we have seen, if 'bawdy' has to do with looseness, with exhibiting the body, with loss of individuality and dignity, this is not a wholly correct description. But the term was necessary as a shorthand way of bracketing off the Restoration. For within the overview of Whig history, Restoration culture was a deviant blip in the continuity between the English revolution and the eighteenth-century consolidation of the rule of men of property – that alliance of Protestantism and capital that forges English national identity. The biological form of this identity is the 'ascetic body', which supposedly lives, according to the values of moderation and restraint, a life that is well cushioned. In the process whereby puritan rigour modulates into eighteenth-century ease the Restoration stage, despite the smokescreen of Whig historiography, can be seen to produce a helpful aestheticising of that ascetic body. And, if Bourdieu is to be believed, something like that body was still with us in the 1970s: 'it is a way of denying the meaning and primary function of consumption, which are essentially common, by making the meal a social ceremony, an affirmation of ethical tone and aesthetic refinement'. He is describing the middle-class, as distinct from the working-class, meal, and goes on to note among its features 'the etiquette governing posture and gesture, ways of serving oneself and others ... the censorship of all bodily manifestations of the act or pleasure of eating' (1989: 196).

Note here Bourdieu's insistence, not so much on restraint but on the work that makes a spectacle of restraint. There is something familiar about this. It seems to echo back to 1672, to the playtext which, by my account, makes a charisma of constraint. Here the conspicuoulsy governed, measured bodies are the aesthetically pleasing – even sexy – ones.

With its suspicion of fiction, theatricality, illusion, all gathered up into the distaste for the scripted body – a body imposed upon – this trend of modern performance analysis may be said to fall into place within a long tradition of bourgeois asceticism. For those less ascetic, the job perhaps is to re-engage with slobbering theatricality at its most – um – imposing.

2 Theatre and bodily value

The history of the body is marked by changes in its value. When Monsieur de Paris in *The Gentleman Dancing-Master* wants to learn to walk and bow as a Spaniard, he is aspiring to a way of presenting his body that supposedly has authority and solemnity. But the scene is comical. The play suggests that a really valuable body would not be so rehearsed. In *The Country Wife*, the supposedly natural bodies are ones which have vigilance and self-control. In encouraging audiences to laugh at or admire particular bodies, the theatre plays its part in the mechanisms by which a society scripts and allocates bodily value.

This chapter will focus on one particular instance, Shakespeare's *The Tempest*, to show how the theatre text leads its audience to discriminate between bodily values. In doing so it defines what is proper, natural and admirable. Theatre body work is ideological.

Valuable bodies

In their discussions of the sort of body promoted by Restoration culture the histories revolved around two sets of images – the bawdy, fleshy and indulgent; the ascetic, puritan and disciplined. Each set of images also implies something about the society, so that, on one hand, there is the Restoration as backlash of sensual indulgence after the Commonwealth and, on the other, the Restoration as the initiation of the rule of men of property and capitalism. Each body type implies a type of society.

This was nothing new. For centuries the body has been seen as a metaphor for, amongst other things, the state of society. This runs at least from the early modern parables of society, exemplified in Menenius' speech in *Coriolanus*, through to a cluster of thinkers in the 1940s, including Feldenkrais, Laban and Walter Cannon's *The Body as a Guide to Politics* (1942). The anthropology of Mary Douglas (1996) mapped the relations of individual and 'social' body, which was in turn picked up by dance theory: 'By looking at dance we can see enacted on a broad scale, and in codified fashion, socially constituted and historically specific attitudes toward the body in general, toward specific social groups' usage of the body in particular' (Desmond 1998: 157; see also Polhemus 1998). But we also have to note that such body history is not simply about metaphors and attitudes.

> Every body is marked by the history and specificity of its existence. It is possible to construct a biography, a history of the body, for each individual and social body. This history would include not only all the contingencies that befall a body, impinging on it from outside ... such a history would also have to include the 'raw ingredients' out of which the body is produced – its internal conditions of possibility, the history of its particular tastes, predelictions, movements, habits, postures, gait, and comportment.
>
> (Grosz 1994: 142)

In this section I intend to track through some of the main approaches to describing bodily value, particularly with reference to the early modern period. But it is useful to have at the top Grosz's insistence on what that history ought to include, the 'internal conditions of possibility' as well as 'the contingencies that befall a body'. And, as before, the relationship is a dialectic not an opposition. The experience of physical movement, the instructions as to behaviour: each is as real, and meaningful, as the other. The tensions in this dialectic make themselves felt throughout, nowhere perhaps more clearly than in the first set of approaches.

There is a rich stream of work on the cultural text of the body in the early modern period (e.g. Stallybrass 1986; Tennenhouse 1986; Paster 1993; Sawday 1995). Much of this work derives ultimately from Bakhtin and Foucault. This has been the subject of considerable commentary, but one feature of it needs to be noted here. It seems to be more concerned with ideologies of body than with lived experience of body (which will yet always be partly a product of ideology even while exceeding it). As Gail Kern Paster says, for Bakhtin 'the body's concrete materiality – or lack of it – remains primarily symbolic. He is interested neither in actual bodily practices over time nor in the body's changing modes of self-experience' (1993: 15).[1] A similar point has been made about Foucault, in whose writings, says Bryan Turner, 'the discourse appears to be almost sociologically disembodied': 'there is a pronounced reluctance to reduce systematic thought to interests, especially the economic interests of social groups' (1982: 257). If the abstraction is re-embodied, with relation to groups with their own interests, the image of the passive lived body is once again challenged. The Foucauldian one-way street is redirected: as Arthur Frank says, 'Disciplines not only make bodies productive in terms defined by some other, whether king or factory owner. Disciplines can also be used by bodies themselves to achieve productive ends of their own' (1995: 58). Some of those disciplines are theatrical.

A more precise historical approach to bodily practice seems to be offered by those who analyse texts designed to train the materiality of the body – pre-eminently Norbert Elias (2000), with key contributions from Georges Vigarello (1989), Frank Whigham (1984), Anna Bryson (1990) and Tom Bishop (1998). Their various accounts tell of a steady increase in the restraint and 'enclosure' of the body through dissemination of techniques of politeness and civil living. But, coherent and detailed as it is, this history again has problems in relation to actual practice. First, there is a difficulty with being precise about the point of emergence of the trained courtly body. Foucault's docile body is associated with the eighteenth century; most of the historians of Renaissance courtesy find it in the Renaissance. But historians of earlier periods, including Elias, find it earlier: Jean-Claude Schmitt (1989) highlights the transmission of restrained behavioural precepts from Cicero to Ambrose; Jan Bremner (1993) discovers the ethic of uprightness in ancient Greek culture. Rather than a continuous evolution we have perhaps to think of negotiations and conflicts over bodily decorums at each period. For the prescriptions for restraint of the body are tropes regularly repeated by a set of dominant cultures. Which brings us to the second problem. Anna Bryson notes the quantity of evidence as to 'the roistering and thoroughly uncivil behaviour' of young gentlemen about town – which implies a 'less than complete' response to the courtesy manuals. Indeed, she suggests that social superiority may have manifested itself precisely as 'freedom from rules and restraints' (1990: 152). Thus, in so far as it is concerned with written rules and prescriptions for the body, the history of courtly discipline is bound within its medium – written text. Sites of bodily negotiation are elsewhere.

Some of these sites, with their different ideas of bodily potential, are examined by a discipline that has run parallel with, and borrowed from, the study of courtliness. Dance history has proved itself a potent mode of approach in recent years because it is dealing with the body as an expressive medium (Ward 1988; Franko 1993; Howard 1998; Ravelhofer 1998; see also Meagher 1966; Strong 1984). Its primary sources are less legislative, ethical ideals, formulas for courtliness, than descriptions of the body in motion and instructions for movement. It was possible to be a young gentleman without following Castiglione to the letter, but it is not possible to dance a *coranto* without observing a particular arrangement of steps. These written instructions are in turn supplemented, for the historian, by musical texts, with their specific shapes, rhythms, speeds (Ward 1988; McClary 1998). Together these materials give the impression (which might not be wholly illusory) that the operation of a historical body may be known in a way which is more direct, less mediated, than inferring it through descriptions of recommended civil behaviour (or indeed interpreting woodcuts and paintings[2]). After all, a modern body – even allowing for biological and cultural differences – can still try out the steps and rhythms, can still encounter those balancing points where culture does battle with muscula-ture; flesh can inhabit these texts.

But, even here, the intellectual constraints of received orthodoxies make themselves felt, allowing abstract models to squeeze out the evidence of specific practices, replicating the theoretical text that the academy knows it ought to speak. Thus, although the work of the dance historian Skiles Howard contributed much to our understanding of the political meanings made by courtly dances, her work was, in the opinion of Barabara Ravelhofer, fatally flawed with respect to its commentary on gender. Howard describes how male power is restated in the dominance of male dancers over female partners; Ravelhofer finds evidence that suggests to her that dance steps produced more various, if not more flexible, ideas of gender, for example the Duke of Buckingham's feminine dance. Howard's work is vitiated, she feels, by an attempt to employ – or produce – a Foucauldian scenario at the 'expense of performance practice and historical fact' (Ravelhofer 1998: 247).

I suspect that Howard found herself sucked into the symbolic domain of Foucault because she wanted to ask an entirely legitimate question: once the bodily practice has been identified, what does the body then mean?

Bodies on stage

That central dialectic reappears – body material or-and meaning, body con-struction or-and representation. And, just as one gets closer to the staged event, the problems intensify.

In dealing with early modern stage practices there have been two main traditions. One aims to describe acting practice, producing informative accounts of conventions, gestures and theories (see, for example, Brown 1953; Rosenberg 1954; Joseph 1964; Marker 1970; Frisch 1987; Roach 1993). But there is little address to meaning here. The other is a mode of semiotic reading of 'stage pictures', the organisation of scenic groups and gestural shapes, together with analysis of emblems. At its best this work is exemplified in David Bevington's *Action is Eloquence* (1984) (but see also, for example: Kernodle 1944; Beckerman 1962; Wickham 1963; Mehl 1969; Dessen 1977 and 1980; Hodgdon 1980; Slater 1982; Astington 1986; Boling 1996). The problem with this work, however, is that it tends to disprivilege bodiliness. Even in Weimann's healthy emphasis (2000) on a plurality of playing and presentational practices the actuality of bodies falters in the face of semiotics. The job then is not simply to reconcile these two traditions, but to extend their remit.

Wherever the semiotic has been in dominance in recent times, the theo-ries of phenomenology have had to take a back seat. As I suggested in the previous chapter, however, performance phenomenology may supply some tools which can extend the range of ways in which early modern drama 'means' while at the same time not losing a grasp on it as an art of space, sound, flesh. In this way, accounts of body ideologies may be grounded in the materiality of staged practices.

This should enable some of the very subtle work of literary criticism to be taken a step further. For example, in Peter Stallybrass's seminal essay, 'Patriarchal Territories', he suggests that in the second half of *Othello* Desdemona is 'reformed within the problematic of the enclosed body' (1986: 141), implicitly making her weaker. An analysis of materially bodied space can modify this suggestion. The moment she loses her handkerchief apparently changes Desdemona's attitude to the stage: she looks at it as a place where she has lost something. Within this placelessness, however, she nevertheless gives displays of bodily discipline, for example in her deliberate role of suitor to Othello, within the changed conventions of discourse, and her purposeful performance in the attitude of prayer before Iago. Each suggests a potent self-control against placelessness. Being 'enclosed' thus has ambivalent value.

The study of bodily value in the theatre moves on a step from the territory mapped out in Chapter 1, which considered script as a disciplinary regime of the body. Script establishes the activities and body type required. But so too it indicates mode of performance, performance register. In so far as the words invoke such things as genre or intertextual reference or parodic quotation, they indicate a register of movement (like a register of language), suggesting how it is done. For although the stage may share with 'real life' views on correct civility, appropriate gender behaviour, physiological mechanisms, it is also citation – a quotation of these views and behaviours (see Orgel 1985: 117), negotiating them, sometimes contesting them. The body on stage operates through, on one hand, a range of generic possibilities, and on the other a series of degrees of explicit quotedness. It may be made to 'speak' by the script, but when the body is speaking you can sometimes hear the characters' lines differently – as parody or quotation. In enacting a gait within a particular register, or in generically juxtaposing that gait with another, the stage may have the effect of making strange that which in another context seems natural, normal, proper. In this way the scripting of bodies may put pressure on culturally circulated ideas about, and especially valuations of, particular bodies.

Performance phenomenology not only has its uses in dealing with the staged bodies. It also invites reflection on the audience. A performance is thought of as social event, a gathering of bodies as much as minds. The audience 'is situated in the phenomenological continuum of space through physical proximity, linguistic inclusions, and the uniquely theatrical mirroring that links audience with performer in a kind of corporeal mimetic identification' (Garner 1994: 4; see also Wilshire 1982; States 1985 and 1992). Effects are produced in the spectator simply as a result of materially sharing the space with the performance. Many of these effects, bypassing the intellect, are felt in the body and work powerfully to shape a spectator's sense of the performance. And in many cases they are actually scripted by the performance-makers – in *Shakespeare's Art of Orchestration*, Jean Howard argues that the audience is taken up powerfully by such non-verbal phenomena as the rhythms of filling and emptying the stage (1984: 128, 103).

In that the scripting of bodies leads to effects which are kinaesthetic (see p. 74), the mobilisation of bodily value is ideologically more successful because it produces responses that are felt rather than discussed. In making that point, it also has to be noted that there might not be conscious intention on the part of the makers of the work. They may be unconsciously operating within their own ideological constraints as to what is practical or proper. To illustrate how the produced text will indicate this residual ideological shape I shall borrow from Richard Dyer's analysis of the film *In the Heat of the Night*. Sidney Poitier and Rod Steiger have different acting styles; the difference is compounded by ideologically shaped conventions of film lighting which disprivilege black skin, so that Steiger 'can display a range of modulations of expression that indicate the character's complex turmoil of feelings and reminiscences. Poitier, by contrast, remains the emblematic, unindividualised, albeit admirable, black man' (Dyer 1999: 99). Alongside the film's liberal project, the materiality of the bodies tells a different story.

All that said, it is to the story told by the materiality of the bodies in *The Tempest* that I now turn.

A queen enters

You can recognise the queen of the gods not by her face, nor by her clothing, but by her bearing. 'Great Juno comes,' says Ceres in *The Tempest*. 'I know her by her gait' (Shakespeare 1987: 4.1.102).

In a production of the play that wanted to ensure, rather than estrange, the wonder of the masque, Juno's bearing would not work to establish personal idiosyncrasy – a characteristic slouch, for instance – but would produce instead a sense of typical majesty and divinity. And an audience would probably have little problem in sharing Ceres' ability to recognise a person from the way she holds herself. They have not seen Juno before, but she must be the one with the divinely queenly pose.

This seems commonsensical stuff. But it begins to unravel when we ask how a divine being actually holds itself. What makes it distinct from a mortal stance? And do queens move differently from ladies, from serving-women, from kings? These questions are not just relevant to actors, whose work is to make the representation. They are also relevant to those who watch and interpret the representation, in that modes of bodily organisation don't only suggest social status, category or occupation, but at the same time imply qualities – seriousness, wastefulness, triviality, majesty, etc. An audience can be made to feel that a queen is dignified or that she is affected, that she has natural authority or unnatural pomp. In so far as it suggests that which is natural, right, proper, good, the actual movement of the body plays a key part in the ideological work done by a play.

I am going to try and substantiate that assertion by looking at how the text of *The Tempest*, in scripting its bodies, speaks its class attitudes without, it seems, breathing a word.

Courtly geometries

Juno and her divine gait appear in the masque organised by Prospero to celebrate the betrothal of his daughter Miranda to Ferdinand. The entertainment consists of entrances and speeches by three goddesses, a song, and then a dance by nymphs and reapers. It is, of course, famously dispersed before it can reach the customary climax in the mingled dancing of masquers and spectators. Rather than blurring the distinction between masquing fantasy and daily life, the ending of this entertainment throws into high relief the contrast between the masque's way of inhabiting the stage and that of its on-stage spectators.

By contrast with the newly fashionable and lavish masques of the royal court, Prospero's is a rather simple affair, a quotation of the mode (see McNamara 1987; Orgel 1987; Bevington 1998; also Brissenden 1981). But it does enough to suggest the atmosphere and, most importantly for our purposes here, the physical regimes of the masque. These regimes were mostly focused on courtly dancing, which has been very well documented in some enthralling work by dance historians (e.g. Ward 1988; Franko 1993; Howard 1998; Ravelhofer 1998). The masquing body would seem, to put it summarily, to exemplify control and balance. As Skiles Howard says, quoting Caroso (1600), 'The courtly body danced according to "the laws of symmetry and perfect theory", with geometry realized on the body by costume and choreographic design' (1998: 103). That geometry may also be said to inhabit the musculature, in so far as gestures of arms and hands tended to be inhibited: with the emphasis being on the feet, the body's verticality is promoted. Thus with regard to the popular early Renaissance form of *basse dance* (or 'measures' in English), Arbeau (1588) recommended 'the steps should not be so big as to deform the erect posture of the upper body' (quoted in Franko 1985). Another restraint on the masquing body comes from the geometric choreography mentioned by Howard. This traced on the floor geometric shapes, with their significant hidden truths, or spelled out the names of watching princes. As Mark Franko (1993) points out, the body that takes its place within the delineation of a whole form has limits placed on its capacity for individual expressivity. Within this physical context, it is not only the dancing body that shows its discipline. Prospero's goddesses have to enter and stand, rather than dance. But their exhibited gait will also presumably be governed by the rules Franko summarises: 'The correct carriage of the head mirrors that of the eyes and of the body in general … The precepts of physical rectitude, while calling for an immobile stance, preclude rigidity' (1985: 57, 58). They presumably don't wave their arms around in ways which are fast, unexpected or mimetic.

This discipline of the body does ideological work: courtly dance

> could demonstrate measured proportion not only by presenting bodies exemplarily, but also through the ballet's very organization and its choreography. The structured joining of both the different arts and the choreography within and between them produced metaphors of harmony in the aural and sociopolitical senses.
>
> (Franko 1993: 32)

This ideological production from a combination of elements can be exemplified from a masque that was produced close in time to *The Tempest*. Ben Jonson's *Masque of Queens* (1609) has already received a great deal of critical attention (Gossett 1988; Maurer 1989; Orgel 1990; Lewalski 1993; Holbrook 1998; Howard 1998), so I shall do little more than sketch in the points which exemplify the main argument here. The masque is celebrated for introducing an antemasque: witches do a magical dance 'full of praeposterous change, and gesticulation' (Jonson 1941: lines 35–6). The 'confused noise' at their entrance is accompanied by visual confusion. They make strange gestures – using those forbidden arms – and carry a clutter of spindles, timbrels and rattles; attention is called to the strange movements by their noise. The queens replace the witches with dances at the end that are 'euen, and apt' (line 754), 'as if Mathematicians had lost proportion, they might there haue found it' (lines 754–6) – inscribing order on the ungoverned physicality. Jones's drawings of the queens depict heads with elaborate crowns and helmets, their breasts and torsos enclosed in stage armour. Thus, apart from the learnt decorums of courtly dance, the upper body was also costumed into stillness, its muscles tensed to bear the loads upon them. With its high centre of gravity, the body is enacting control, balance, highness.

And, in turn, the attentive spectator was supposed to absorb this high virtue. Sir Thomas Elyot describes a form of dancing which displays 'prudence', and remarks that this will be 'well perceyved, as well by the daunsers as by them which standinge by, wyll be diligent beholders and markers' (1907: 97). The geometric and allegorical shapes were meant to be read by spectators. This act of close concentration, this diligence, has the effect, in John Meagher's words, of 'imparting moral improvement to the beholder' (1962: 265–6). Or, indeed, political 'improvement': the political job of the aesthetics, says Franko, was 'the cultivation of a malleable, hyperreceptive subject-as-spectator' (1993: 35). This, it should be said, was the model rather than the actuality. The high virtue of the dancing may well have appeared more rarefied and special because of its contrast with the behaviours of the courtly audience when, immediately after the masque, they flung themselves at the food, the drink and each other.

In the masques for James the idealised spectator made a close reading of the choreography situated within, and reinforced by, the visual rhetoric of Jones's stage design. The measured bodies spoke and danced in front of scenery which gradually intensified its focus on a magical vanishing point. In the antemasque to *Queens*, Jones's designs for the House of Fame which replaces the witches' scene have a strong emphasis on the vertical columns. This emphasis is replicated by the upright, column-like bodies of the queens, in their hard casings (Franko 1985: 57–8; Vigarello 1989; Cunnar 1993; Howard 1998: 60, 101). As the masque proceeds, the vanishing point is in turn lined up with the precise position of the watching monarch (Orgel 1975). He was not only the single best-placed recipient of this spectacle; he was also, in the terms of its ideological rhetoric, the only begetter of all that noble symmetry. The vanishing point is opposite what has to be taken as the point of origin.

Although Prospero the magician is more truly the point of origin than James I ever was, the staged circumstances of *The Tempest* masque relax the rigorous system of visual focus. Prospero invents the masque as a gift for Miranda and Ferdinand – their responses to it are as interesting as his, and perhaps gesturally more foregrounded since they will be enacting wonder while he presumably watches it and them. Now in itself the prince's look at the masque audience is wholly in keeping with this sort of event – as Franko says, 'his subjects inhabit – actually constitute – the geometry of the ballet's landscape as his ideal field of vision' (1993: 39). But if Prospero is watching Ferdinand and Miranda, so too is the theatre audience, particularly if, as I suggest, those two are gesturally foregrounded. So in what we might call the *theatricalised* masque of *The Tempest* the princely perspective elides with that of the paying spectator. We shall return to this elision of class positions later. The second, brutally obvious, point is that this is all a fiction. Masques for James could be upstaged any moment by eruptions within the delicately maintained network of diplomatic allegiances, by mere nuances of disquiet from those who possessed the power to dispossess. The spectacle of the masque, however splendid, always existed in relation to the spectacle of the audience, where there were very few neutral observers. At the same time that staged splendour had a one-night-only transience combined with an elevated indifference to the potential problems of its circumstances. As such it offered its spectator a tense but deep engagement. By contrast Prospero's masque is a much less complicated source of pleasure. Its spectacle, filling the stage physically and aurally, offers plenitude – plenitude organised by choreography and harmony so that the fullness does not bewilder the senses, and is repeatable day after day. In a sense, of course, it is a gesture towards, even a laconic simulacrum of, plenitude.

Most famously something happens to this masque which seems never to have happened at this point to James's. The climax of mythic splendour is forestalled; its originator closes it down. In the innovatory *Masque of Queens* the rough people, the witches, were part of the antemasque, which gives way to the masque proper. Here the reverse happens. Far from resolving disorderly elements, this masque is broken apart by them. The artifice, always slightly too relaxed fully to entrain our focus, must yield place to that which seems much more 'real' – the world of the masque's audience, its creator and the plot against him.

At the moment at which the masque is aborted the theatre audience might have a sense of two sorts of action on stage: that of the artifice of the courtly entertainment, and that of the 'real'. We probably knew, anyway, that the masque's apparent fullness was only a quotation of plenitude. By contrast the really authentic matter is the operation on a human being of thought and emotion (of which more later). The 'real' is felt to be superior because this is the narrative which affects people we have come to care about, or at least be interested in; and indeed it is superior because it can abolish masques.

Low centres of gravity

Once we concentrate on the plot against Prospero, we discover other ways of feeling about the stage action. Most audiences guess that the plot won't work because it relies on the assistance of clowns. These clowns are seen to be people who easily succumb to their own most base desires. They are clumsy in what they do and without purpose in achieving the objectives set. It is in relation to them and their appearance that an audience might well have – consciously or not – another sense of two sorts of action on stage. This time the division is not between artifice and 'real' but between clowning and the seriousness of Prospero.

What precisely does the clowning here involve? A certain amount of physical comedy is required by two separate routines in relation to a concealed Caliban. First there is Trinculo's discovery of a creature beneath a gaberdine, and his attempts to identify what it is; next there is Stephano's encounter with what has now become a 'monster', a thing with four legs and two voices (Trinculo concealed with Caliban) (2.2.18–102). The physical comedy in each case is predicated upon simple but unremitting emotional drives. Trinculo needs to escape from a darkly threatening storm. Lines are given to the actor early in his entrance to enable him to establish the precise location of the storm over his head (2.2.20–1): he can look toward it, his body can adopt an attitude toward it, he can cower away from it and we shall still know it's there. Since there's a storm, of which he is terrified, he needs shelter. The logic is simple, almost hydraulic. But the *only* shelter that is available already has some horribly smelly creature underneath it (2.2.25–7). Strong smell is a richly productive ruse for comic performance, much more so perhaps than straightforward curiosity or even fear. The source of the smell provokes curiosity of course, but it also defines a threshold at which the smell becomes repellent: there's a nicely precise line at which the nose sniffing inquisitively becomes the nostrils filled with stinking air, and then the business of struggling through stench to get closer to the source. The extra push towards the repellent smell is provided in this instance by the threat of the storm. The Trinculo actor is thus supplied with a drive to seek shelter, and an obstacle to that drive which is almost intolerable. The business of the interplay between fear and disgust can continue for as long as the actor can sustain it. Lines are, of course, not necessary.

Stephano is also in the grip of a monolithic drive. He drinks alcohol as a solution to the problems which confront him. Once again there is an available physical structure: each problem makes him drink; the drunker he gets, the more problematic and imponderable the problems become; as the problems get apparently bigger, his response gets more urgent and simultaneously more incapacitated. He has the additional advantage of a stage prop – the bottle – which commences on its own journey around the stage space (2.2.72ff). The habit whereby Stephano pours drink into his own mouth leads him to pour drink into other available mouths – the monster's when he finds it (2.2.80), and then the second 'mouth' (2.2.90). This has little to do with greed, then, but with a logic that requires all orifices to be filled.

The presence of a single dominant drive is a defining element of the mode of characterisation here. It's a shape that remains in place even though the drive changes. Trinculo moves from being fearful in the first half of this scene when he discovers the monster through to a mocking contempt for it (2.2.138ff); in the next of his scenes (Act 3 scene 2) he has become jealous of the monster's relationship with Stephano. The emotion may change in relation to the object, but what remains constant is the obsessive force with which it governs the person – the jealousy has the same singlemindedness as the fear.

The mode of acting required of the Trinculo actor (as too with Stephano) is that he be completely taken over, as it were possessed, by a dominant drive. A model for this sort of acting is the *commedia dell'arte*, an improvised form based on various stock personas. Although there is little evidence, one way or another, to suggest that Trinculo was actually acted as a *commedia* persona, current opinion does now lean towards the belief that, in general, Shakespeare and his actors were influenced by *commedia dell'arte* (Lea 1934; Steele 1977; Clubb 1980; Mellamphy 1980; Grewar 1993 and 1996; but

Richards 1989 and 1994 disagrees). *Commedia* types have been identified by a number of scholars in Shakespeare's work (in addition to the preceding references see Campbell 1925 and 1932; Yates 1936; Moore 1949; Melzi 1966), and it has been suggested that, since Italian troupes had been visiting England since 1573, performers had become familiar with the form:

> most of the actors who were to work with Shakespeare – and perhaps Shakespeare himself – were not only acquainted with the stock characters of *commedia dell'arte*, but may actually have been using its comic conventions and the technique of improvisation in the plays they were performing.
>
> (Grewar 1993: 18)

The residual presence of improvisatory method is detected by Richard Andrews in the 'elastic' gag, 'capable of being protracted or curtailed at will, according to the audience response' (1991: 26). On the other hand, Shakespeare has Hamlet express hostility to the disruptive activities of clowns, and, if David Wiles is right, the person playing opposite the Trinculo actor in the role of Caliban was Robert Armin, a performer whose hallmark was a quality of intellectualism (Wiles 1987: 155). With this caution in place, it might still be productive to explore *commedia* – not to argue the case for a hidden performance history but to try and formulate some general points about the clowning body.

The *commedia* personas all had their own specific physical characteristics and routines (Rudlin 1994). In the early days they may not have actually worn face masks – Richards and Richards say that references to masked actors and the mask itself were rare (1990: 114). But, if a persona has physical characteristics, when performers take on their persona they put on, as it were, a particular muscular organisation, a bodily attitude. The shapes of these bodily attitudes seem to be visually memorialised in the conventions for graphically depicting *commedia* routines. This muscular organisation is something very different from the learnt, and naturalised, behaviour that is called 'habitus' (Mauss 1992; Bourdieu 1977 and 1989) in that it is *put on* and then *relinquished*; it thus may be said to operate as a mask. What is this operation? In modern mask-work when the performer puts on the mask she or he becomes taken over by it, so that there is a sense of being 'led' by the mask; not looking through its eye-holes but looking *with* it, having one's belly or nose conduct negotiations with the world, seeing as the mask sees. In part this psychic effect is produced from a respect meticulously given to the mask, a willing submission of 'everyday' subjectivity to something indistinctly 'other', projected onto the mask. This may be strengthened by contemplation of a face mask in the mirror, and is almost always sustained in place by the responses of other masks.

[A *zanni* or Pulcinella] should be ridiculous in his movements: in the way he puts on a hat, walks, runs, affects gravity or haste in his deportment. He should be ridiculous in the tone of his voice, which ought to be excessively shrill, or out of tune, or raucous. He should be ridiculous [rather like Stephano perhaps] in the dignified roles in which a blockhead incompetently pretends to be a prince, a captain, and so on.

(Perrucci quoted in Richards and Richards 1990: 137)

Once a performer is in the mask the characteristic actions which derive from the mask continually reproduce and re-emphasise the shapes and muscular tensions which construct the force of the identity. As Laughlin, McManus and d'Aquili say, 'sustained and intense concentration on a physical activity' leads both to psychic energy and an experience of greater energy flow in the body; later on they observe that 'an excited somatic system produces an excited consciousness, and vice versa' (1990: 299, 319). In the range of physical disciplines which comprise what we have very loosely to call 'masked clowning' a new sense of the body emerges from zones foregrounded by muscular focus, perhaps a changed centre of gravity, new points of tension and energy. In turn this changed muscular arrangement produces a different relationship to the space around the body and to other individuals. One's sense of one's body in space has bearing on the formation of subjectivity (see Chapter 5). It is thus in a very developed sense that we speak of the person being taken over or possessed by the mask – a seemingly new subjectivity is not merely licensed but produced while the mask is worn.

This subjectivity of the mask has bearing on both agent and effect of performance. In their work on ritual, Webber, Stephens and Laughlin endeavour to explain how symbols 'operate both to organise and to transform consciousness and cognition'. There are some symbols which 'direct the flow of experience, focus attention, and integrate information' on a scale that exceeds our conscious awareness. When symbols of this sort penetrate the brain they use their information 'to activate neural structures not ordinarily accessible to normal consciousness'. A key concept in their 'biogenetic structuralist' argument is the tri-une brain in which there remain older brain forms from an earlier stage of evolutionary development, together with traces of archaic experiences. A potent symbol can evoke neural models of a 'genetically older date', hence its power. The reason that the authors spend time on the discussion of symbols is because the ritual mask is an outward transformation of the sort of potent symbol which crosses cultures and evokes archetypes (Webber, Stephens and Laughlin 1983: 204, 211).

Webber, Stephens and Laughlin are writing about masked ritual, indeed ritual in the Americas. So it's a far cry from the rather European clowning of *The Tempest*, and the student of Shakespeare may feel well justified in putting to one side both ritual ceremony and the tri-une brain. But the biogenetic structuralist work gives emphasis to two key points: first, it reaffirms the depth of the possible relationship between mask and brain, where the brain must not be seen as functioning in the same way in different sorts of performing – where masked clowning may activate a different aspect of the brain. And second, it insists, irrespective of one's views on the tri-une brain, on the power of that which is archetypal, not just in ritual but also in clowning. Alongside, and partly hidden by, the picture of Armin's intellectualism we have to retrieve a sense of the gag being bigger than the clown – where the clown actor is triggered, in a way not necessarily conscious, into what feels like the physical and somatic logic of a routine. In short there's a mode of comic playing where the rational, and indeed the conscious, are disprivileged.

One of the classic markers of the force of unconscious desire in *commedia dell'arte* is that it ruptures proprieties: masks usually find themselves in territory which is bawdy, obscene, scatological. As Thomas Nashe put it at the time, 'squirting bawdy comedians' (Nashe 1972: 115). The impropriety is usually so studiedly in your face because it grows logically out of given circumstances. Thus in *The Tempest* when Stephano discovers a monster with, apparently, four legs and two voices he carefully distinguishes between the 'forward voice' and the 'backward voice' which 'is to utter foul speeches and to detract' (2.2.87). Where there are two voices in a body, the backward voice uttering foul speeches can only be the arse. Into this 'mouth' Stephano also pours alcohol. The temporary blurring together of the functions of arse and mouth feels a lot more improper than Stephano's likening of Trinculo, once he has pulled him free, to the 'siege' or shit of the monster (2.2.101). It works a nice variation on the stories of being (re)born from the sea – not here from foam or a fish's mouth but from a monster's arse. But it brings to an end the arse jokes, it produces no new action. In the next scene the obscenity (if obscene it be) is mainly around pissing. In a short, and highly obscure, group of four lines, Trinculo expresses his jealousy of Stephano through puns alluding to urination and defecation:

> *Stephano*: thou shalt be my lieutenant, monster, or my standard.
> *Trinculo*: Your lieutenant, if you list; he's no standard.
> *Stephano*: We'll not run, Monsieur Monster.
> *Trinculo*: Nor go neither; but you'll lie like dogs, and yet say nothing neither.
>
> (3.2.16–19)

If you blink you miss them – it's a mere token gesture towards the traditional obscenity of clowns, but it helps to make more appropriate the later drenching of these three in horse piss.

At this juncture a schematic summary of clowning and masque bodies might be useful. In the received conventions of depicting *commedia* performance – with its possible links to the Shakespearean stage – the clown is angled at the hips, bent forward or back, arse or genitals out, knees bent, twists to the shoulders. The angles tend to be off the vertical, spines curved, shoulders rarely horizontal; the centre of gravity has to be low enough to allow bent knee postures. These might be said to be not only low in physical terms, but morally 'low': 'the prominent choreographer Fabritio Caroso', says Barbara Ravelhofer, 'harbours deep suspicions of knees spread too far apart as if "to urinate"' (1998: 250). The chin is thrust forward, the nose exaggerated. In the drawings Inigo Jones did for masques, by contrast, the forehead and cheekbones are important – and the bodies are vertical. The limbs of the masque dancers conform to geometric patterns, imaging cosmic order; what they do is not a picture of geometry but geometry itself, abstract. Vitruvius, whom Jones followed, says, in John Peacock's words, that 'units of measurement which the architect uses are derived from parts of the body ... these various measures go together to make the perfect number' (1990: 160; also Vigarello 1989). The dancer is taken over by a network of relations and patterns, a geometric figure; the clown is unable to be taken over by the 'proper' sense of relations because s/he misunderstands, the body does not enact poise or balance.

There is a kinaesthetic empathy between spectators' musculature and performers. In addition, the courtly masque body produces in the spectator a sense of that which is 'high'. It is an art that deals in the capacity of the body to seem 'abstract'. Watching it involves the work of precise looking, a valuation of accuracy and wit and poise. In turn, the watcher becomes poised. We are engaged with an art that is abstracted, disciplined, otherworldly. Far from being abstract, the clown body is indecorous. Its appetite leads it into repeated attempts to achieve satisfaction. This then leads to a sense of superfluous – because repeated – activity. In *The Tempest*, furthermore, the clownish drives don't take us into exciting and risky areas. Stephano and Trinculo are actually pretty dull. Experience of their activity can lead to a feeling that the physical is both superfluous and tiresome – or, in the classic petty bourgeois formulation, unnecessary.

An anti-theatrical coup

With this clowning around we are hardly in the presence of carnival. If you're reading the play you may note that the scripting of the comedy is pretty straitlaced, but in performance we are also aware always of the presence of Prospero and his agent Ariel. Alongside them the clowning feels trivial, almost pointless – especially in its more obscure moments. While the clowns are later distracted by some clothes – 'glistering apparel' – hung on a line, which Prospero describes as 'trumpery', he himself is pursuing his mission for justice and true order. While the clowns waste time trying on the robes they've found, Prospero is alert to the 'minute' of their plot (4.1.141). In our reflection on this division between the parties we should pause and note that Caliban too is dismissive of that glistering apparel, which he calls 'trash' (4.1.223), and that he worries that the activities with the robes will 'lose our time' (4.1.248). He, as much as Prospero, has a sense of mission. If Wiles is right about Armin playing this role, then the casting gives force to the distinction being posited here. Armin the intellectual is not one for trumpery.

That trumpery enables Stephano and Trinculo to play at the roles of king and subject – with Stephano in a robe giving jerkins as rewards to Trinculo. The wardrobe that they find is very like a theatrical wardrobe in that it is associated with the performance of fictional roles.[3] This glistering apparel is the stuff of the stage: as Peter Stallybrass says, 'the theater insisted upon staging the magic of clothes', much to the disapproval of anti-theatricalists (1996: 307). Prospero, a man who knows when to end revels, traps his enemies with the apparatus of playing. The bait is very precisely in line with the activities of one who can cause actors to melt into thin air, who can cause an insubstantial pageant to fade … or indeed with someone who can give an instruction that some trumpery be fetched, and, when it appears, it turns out to be glistering apparel.

But how far does that sort of moment really position Prospero as antitheatre? When that apparel appears it may well exceed what an audience expected – it has a similar sort of visual splendour, unexpectedness, even fullness, as other apparitions in the play, albeit on a smaller scale. And its appearance works to enhance the status of Prospero, for not only can he cause such stuff to be produced but at the same time he also regards it as trumpery. The more an audience is delighted with its appearance the stronger seem Prospero's magic and cynicism. The glistering apparel may be a minor *coup de théâtre* but it is superseded by Prospero's attitude to it, thus achieving a sort of coup of anti-theatre.

Anti-theatrical as the attitude might be, that coup works to enhance the status and indeed charisma of Prospero. As an audience temporarily delights in that glistering texture and surface, Prospero is a step behind that surface, somewhere less accessible, putting on a show, inviting others to delight in the surface which does not impress him. His charisma consists not in surface but in depth. Prospero is a fictional creation who seems unimpressed by the apparatus of fiction. To the extent that he has both charisma and authority, in which an audience believes, he must himself – despite his pronouncements (or perhaps because of them) – be a very substantial piece of theatre.

Saying that leads us to a remarkably obvious point. When Prospero ends the masque, the entertainment, pleasurable in itself, is replaced by something much more pleasurable – the emotional seriousness, the apparent psychic depth, that speaks great poetry. It is the speech about the ending of revels that we know and love, not the revels themselves.

The various bodies

In one sequence, in Act 4, we see masque performance, a man in the grip of a passion that 'works him strongly' (4.1.144) and clowns playing with robes. Each of these elements in the sequence requires a *specific and distinct bodily discipline*. That of the masque and the clowning I have described at length, with the assumption that the interaction between Prospero and his 'family' is in a more familiar, more documented mode. These are not, then, just different social groups: they are different ways of being on stage, different registers, differently used bodies. The moments of transition between one mode and another are marked both by the acting out of aggression – Prospero's passion, his intention to plague the clowns – and by theatrical devices which deliberately uglify – the 'confused noise' which replaces graceful music, the clowns 'all wet'. So there is a feeling of contest, rather than symbiosis, between these modes. And that contest sees one of the three victorious.

The relationship between these modes of playing may, with hindsight, be seen to be working itself out in a domain more extensive than that merely of *The Tempest*. The company performing the play, the King's Men, had, since the opening of their Globe theatre, apparently made a pitch for artistic and social pre-eminence. Richard Wilson has argued that the opening scene of the opening play at the Globe, *Julius Caesar*, enacts a distaste for poorer elements of the audience: 'The first words on the stage of the Globe can be interpreted, then, as a manoeuvre in the campaign to legitimise the Shakespearean stage and dissociate it from the subversiveness of London's artisanal culture' (Wilson 1993: 47). Against Wilson's point, some historians are sceptical as to whether different theatres deliberately played to different sorts of audience. But, whatever the reality of its composition, the Globe audience, along with that of other amphitheatres, was nevertheless characterised by satirists at certain junctures as being of less sophisticated taste than those who watched the more expensive fare on offer at the hall playhouses, with their literary, satiric plays. In this context, when Hamlet hears news of the fashionable boy players, *Hamlet* shows that it is up with the fashions. Its literary protagonist also has views on modes of performance, warning against old-fashioned gesticulation and the dangers of letting clowns upstage you. Spoken at the Globe this advice shows circumspection about the supposed traditional fare of amphitheatres, with their ranting and clowns. Put simply, it is as if the theatrical world of both Hamlet and *Hamlet* positions itself between the clowns of vulgar taste and the coterie plays of the rich. Ten or so years later, the King's Men owned one of those elite hall theatres (and did *The Tempest* in it), though they still also played the Globe. But by then a different mode and venue had come to typify the performances of the most seriously elite. Under James, the court masque had rapidly acquired a pre-eminence.

None of the foregoing is meant to imply that the King's Men were excluded from court performance: they were not (and they were, after all, the King's Men). The argument is not solely about social status; it is also about artistic forms and artistic identity (which eventually leads us back into the social). The King's Men seem to have been making a bid for pre-eminence in a competitive world by claiming to play a form of 'purposeful', and generically self-knowing, drama; their star, Richard Burbage, was praised for becoming his parts (rather than assimilating them to his star identity, as did Edward Alleyn). As Andrew Gurr puts it, they chose, somewhat riskily, to perform 'a new kind of repertoire', rejecting the appeal of theatres such as the Fortune or Red Bull to supposedly old-fashioned citizen taste (1987: 151). At about the time of that choice, the viewpoint spoken by Hamlet was not too far removed from the dramaturgy of his tragedy – drama should be purposeful rather than extravagant, functional rather than distracting. At a much later date, after Shakespeare's death, two established members of the company, in role in Massinger's *Roman Actor* (1626), have a conversation in which they emphasise how their performances

> endeuour
> To build their mindes vp faire, and on the Stage
> Decipher to the life what honours waite
> On good, and glorious actions.
> (Massinger 1976: 1.1.21–4)

And, another adds – for this is fiction – 'For the profit *Paris*,/ And mercinarie gaine they are things beneath vs'. Later in the play Paris recalls playing a tragedy of theirs in which an enacted murder produces a display of troubled conscience in a guilty watcher: Hamlet's functionality still celebrated, by the company, in 1626 (1.1.26–7).

In *The Tempest* we can perhaps glimpse one moment in the process whereby Shakespeare's company define themselves and their mode of playing against other modes – the clowning of vulgar amphitheatres, the masquing revels of a tightly circumscribed royal court. The fictional gesture by which revels are ended is made by a star actor working with a company that had high artistic ambitions in a world of entrepreneurial contest between companies. The King's Men wished to dissociate themselves from the vulgar while also exercising a freedom to experiment artistically, without being bound by absolutist authority and its circumscribed world of compliant expensive masques.

A gentle start

In my schematic account the three modes – masque, clowning and serious 'real' – all coexist as possible options, possible body stagings. This is not, however, the experience of *The Tempest* audience. The narrative and dramaturgy of the play work to produce a sense of Prospero's natural superiority. The way he and his 'family' behave on stage seems to be something we should take as authentic, real, as against the artifice or insubstantiality of masque and clowns. With Prospero we come to acknowledge, with poised resignation, that there comes a time when revels need to be ended.

When Prospero interrupts the masque he 'starts suddenly'. He is in a 'passion'. Ferdinand invites Miranda, and the audience, to observe how the passion works Prospero 'strongly'. For a brief interval, unusually, we look *at* Prospero, rather than with him. What we see is as much a performance as the masquing was, but it's a performance which sets up, assumes, produces, a very different relationship between movement and motivation of that movement. The masquing figures adopted formal movements and dance measures because those were the conventions of the masque – they move according to appropriate ceremony. This ceremonial movement seeks to be an image of something outside the human being – measure, 'highness'; it is movement made abstract. When we see the passion working strongly on Prospero we see the outer behaviour as the direct result of inner emotion – this is movement that expresses something from inside the person. The contrast here between ceremonial, abstracted movement and what we might call 'motivated movement' gains significance from contemporary attacks on ceremony and custom – modes of behaviour that are not natural (where this term, like several others, is to be recognised as ideological).

The work of the French philosopher Montaigne offers us, in hindsight, a useful gloss on the relationship between passion and ceremony. Montaigne dislikes the artificiality of ceremony in general and elaborate dancing in particular:

> some Ladies make a better shew of their countenances in those dances, wherein are divers changes, cuttings, turnings, and agitations of the body, than in some dances of state and gravity, where they need but simply to tread a naturall measure, represent an unaffected cariage, and their ordinary grace; And as I have also seen some excellent Lordains, or Clownes attired in their worky-day clothes, and with a common homely countenance, affourd us all the pleasure that may be had from their art:
> (Montaigne 1908: 116)

Against ceremonial behaviour, which is acquired, learnt, Montaigne places spontaneous feeling. He recommends that the body express such feeling, however ungraceful or indecorous the movement might be: 'If the body be any whit eased by complaining, let him doe it: If stirring or agitation please him, let him turne, rowle and tosse himselfe as long as he list' (1908: 619). (Similarly one should not fear to raise one's voice if to do so will allay grief.) The very clumsiness of a movement resulting from pain, its conspicuously unplanned agitation, is a sign of the authenticity and *naturalness* of the emotion which motivates the movement. Within the religious and political debates at the turn of the century in England, this authenticity – or as we might call it this purity of feeling – was a combination of nature and godhead speaking through the individual. To puritan polemicists ceremony was associated with both idolatrous state religion and established courtly wealth.

Set against the masque Prospero's passion displays his naturalness, his distance from empty – or duplicitous – ceremony. But there is another possible contrast at work. When the Prospero actor gives a display of passion working on the character he is doing something similar, albeit fleetingly, to the clown who enters in the grip of a dominant emotion. The difference, however, is that when Trinculo and Stephano are emotionally possessed and driven they are in the grip of physical needs, appetite, which they need to satisfy; their needs do not relate to a mind. Prospero's passion, by contrast, arises because he has forgotten a deadline – 'The minute of their plot / Is almost come' (4.1.141–2). For the short period that passion works on him we see the rage for order. As Prospero does his passion, the spirits depart and Ferdinand and Miranda look on. The stage is being cleared of its artifice, returned to truth, but we don't yet know what action Prospero will take. We are not looking at action so much as reaction. The outcome of this passion will be a course of action that prevents something happening, a plan to forestall someone else's plan.

But we are not immediately told what that preventive plan will be. Instead Prospero gives a display of how to control passion. It is turned into, or replaced by, poetry. The speech about ending revels seems to be intended to cheer up Ferdinand, who is looking dismayed. His dismay is presumably a response to the sight of Prospero's passion. So by cheering up Ferdinand, the passion is also cleared away. Of course, it is a strange recipe for cheerfulness: a confirmation that the playing is over and a vision of the littleness of life. But once he has spoken this vision, Prospero can acknowledge that he is old and vexed. Speaking that speech seems not just to be emotionally motivated – coming from an old man's vexation – but it is also part of the process of moving from passion to repose. The demolition of pageants, indeed the very poetry itself, has a higher function – serving to establish individual repose, individual resignation in the face of life's decay.

At the end of the speech he sends Miranda and Ferdinand away so that he can walk alone, to 'still' his beating mind. That desire to be alone contrasts with the behaviour of the clowns. Trinculo would rather be under Caliban's gaberdine than face the storm: the dramaturgy of their first scene impels each into the company of another. And that scene tends to disturb rather than promote stillness. We have already noted the range and sorts of move-ment – responses to rain, stench, drunkenness. If their movements highlight appetite and gut instinct, if their centres of gravity are low, if they joke about shit and piss, then they might be seen as corresponding to lower body parts. In relation to them Prospero's movement can be seen as purposeful and functional, rather than driven and wasteful. It is a response to his higher body parts, specifically his mind: after a passion has gripped him he then says he will walk to still his beating mind. Contributing to a whole tradition of acting as the display of bodily inhibition (Roach 1993: 52), Prospero will move in order to make himself more still.

What Prospero dislikes about Caliban is that his mind is governed by his body – as his body grows more aged the mind becomes more cankered, he says. The episode of Prospero's passion shows how the mind can control strong emotion and how body movement is beneficial when controlled; to walk to still the mind is to move with plan and purpose. The contrast between Prospero's mode of being on stage and that of the clowns schemati-cally arranges itself as a contrast between high and low, where the action against the clowns expresses not merely a distaste for lower body parts but revenge against them. It also expresses a contempt for waste. Prospero and Ariel watch, invisible, as the clowns' appetite for trumpery wastes their time – and in doing so keeps Prospero's plan right on schedule.

The contrast between the body stagings is, unsurprisingly, a contrast between sets of values. The contrast enables a definition of what in its 'naturalness' and 'realism' would otherwise be pretty slippery to pin down. Prospero's way of being, his place and values are defined as what the others are not. On the one hand there is the courtly masque, on the other clowns; each is felt to be artificial, digressive from the main busi-ness. More precisely, in terms of values, there is fragile ceremony on one hand and on the other ill-disciplined appetite and waste. Prospero, fictionally a duke, is located elsewhere by the scheme of body stagings. His mode of being is between courtliness and lower orders. He moves in a way which is 'natural', since it is not meretriciously ornamental; disci-plined and orderly, since it is not wastefully overcome by appetite; more passionate than geometric, more rational than possessed; not caught into patterns or *lazzi*, but vertically still. Neither courtly nor clown, Prospero presides over a sort of household with servants; but it is a household which does not manufacture or produce – he does not labour or trade. His posi-tion is that of the gentleman.

Clearly that assertion is nonsense in terms of what Shakespeare scripts. Prospero, as I said above, is an aristocrat – with, we could add, kingly powers. But what the storyline offers us is, I suggest, contradicted, albeit silently, by the – how shall we put it? – body language. In the mode of acting done by Prospero and his family – or, to be more precise, in what that acting is not – it is the *gentle* body which is felt to be authentic, natural, real. The position which is, nominally, princely is concretely embodied as something different. The mode of that embodiment, and its behaviour, imply – without the need for verbalisation – the triviality of the courtly on one hand and, on the other, the contemptibility of the clownish. Separated as much from what is higher as from the low, its attachment to discipline, measure, individuality, purpose and time-keeping shows how amenable it is to a vision that we have later come to characterise as bourgeois.

This scheme of contrasts produces a sense of the authenticity of Prospero's position. The clowns, on the other hand, are ridiculous because they aspire above their social rank. And there is a parallel, if less ridiculous, piece of social blurring in the masque. This occurs in the dance, which now at last we need to look at. Nymphs and reapers dance 'country footing'. But they do so within a courtly masque. The stage direction requires not only that the reapers be 'properly' habited, but also that the dance is 'graceful'. Alan Brissenden notes how unusual it is for a Shakespearean stage direction to describe a dance in this way, and conjectures that it 'possibly indicates an insistence that this dance should be particularly attractive and orderly' (1981: 100). Contemporary notions of gracefulness in dance would inhibit the dancers from showing the irregularity and 'freedom' that Skiles Howard associates with real country dancing (1998: 2; see Franko 1985 on grace). We are, in short, watching courtly dancing playing at being 'country' – sliding down in degree just as the clowns aspire upwards.

The inauthenticity with regard to social position may for some in the audience have been adumbrated by more general prejudices not only about clownish wastefulness but about mereticious dancing. To a puritan such as Prynne dancing was both wasteful and scandalous, and the dancing he had in mind was also imported from France (Ravelhofer 1998; see Ward 1988 on French dancing masters; Holman 1993). While Prynne's voice was particu-larly strident, the attitudes about courtly decadence and foreignness were not uncommon among the London mercantile and manufacturing communities (Heinemann 1980). This might give significance to the tendency for city masques to abstain from dance. Where an antipathy against dancing comes into alignment with a valuing of productive work in relation to degree, it might find everything it opposed condensed in the sight of graceful dancers dressed as reapers.

Prospero enacts for us the destruction of this masquing fantasy. So too he terminates the folly of clowns. But although these things are demolished within the fictional narrative, Shakespeare's text has a deep need of them. For those clown scenes supply one of the parameters which places, defines, that otherwise slippery thing which I have called Prospero's realism. By successfully defining that realism the clown scenes give authority to the values which come with the realism – discipline, measure, etc. (And quickly, having said that, we have to recall that, in the dialectical scheme here, Prospero's measure is felt to be functional – unlike the ceremonial discipline of masque movement.) Once established, these 'realist' values confirm the waste and triviality of the clown mode. There's something going on which is back-to-front.

Which brings us back to the revels speech. What the speech doesn't tell us is what Prospero has got planned for the next ten minutes. He is certainly not resigned to the Caliban plot and will take action against it. The dramaturgy suggests that the plan is already formed in his mind for, when he sends Miranda and Ferdinand away, even before thanking them for their farewell wishes he has summoned Ariel:

> *F* and *M*:   We wish you peace. *Exeunt.*
> *P*:   Come with a thought! – I thank thee. – Ariel, come!
> (4.1.164–5)

While we may dwell, with Ferdinand, on the beautiful necessity of the revels' ending, and then pity an old man who confronts his own infirmity, we have missed something. The old man has a plan in his head and is yet moving towards the full achievement of his revenge. Far from stilling his mind, he has launched into a new action; far from being resigned, he is going to plague the plotters 'Even to roaring'. And while the 'insubstantial pageant' might have faded, he has sent for a set of glistering apparel to be spread out attractively for a new audience.

Theatrical activity will carry on. But it has been obscured by a rhetorical gesture that invites us to contemplate the ending of revels. It is this gesture which has caught the imaginations of so many commentators on the play. What is happening here is that Prospero's contempt is being elided with that of Shakespeare, so that the play appears to be acting out the abandonment not merely of revels but of clowning too. That leaves us with the serious part of the play, which is the 'realist' part – the part that denies its own theatricality, or at least has contempt for trumpery. That part is most closely associated with Prospero, the man who ends revels. At the heart of *The Tempest*, then, is a mode of theatrical playing which identifies itself as anti-theatre. That anti-theatre is attractive and familiar because it gives defining form to the gentle, and later bourgeois, body. While it modestly demurs at the theatrical the gentle body finds in the vigilant maintenance of its tidy uprightness a spectacle that is, as it were, highly satisfactory.

3 The wrong dog (an account of significant inaction)

In one of the episodes of the Seattle-based sitcom *Frasier* there has been a sword-fight between Niles and his wife's lover, a fencing master. Niles loses, and only then they discover that they have been fighting at cross-purposes. For the fencing-master only speaks German; the other person who speaks German is the Latino housekeeper, and her only other language is Hispanic. Frasier has to translate from Niles to the housekeeper to the fencing-master. After the fight the German admits he loves Niles's wife, but that she would not have him. Each line, or monosyllable, of the conversation is passed up and down the line of four people, together with the appropriate gestures. It ends with Niles, overjoyed, embracing Frasier, then the housekeeper, then – almost – the fencer, and leaving (Channel 4: 1999).

If you were describing this bit of the show to someone, what would you call it? Comic routine? Business? *Lazzo*, even? And then, what do you say about the relationship between this routine and the rest of the show? And what pleasure do you get out of it? By the time you're onto the next bottle of wine you might be asking what cultural work the routine does. And – slurring slightly – how it might be culturally evaluated.

After looking at script as a discipline of the body and practices which establish bodily value I shall now try and think about what one does with script which consciously lets the bodies go free. How does it work and what does it do? To get there this chapter looks at the doings not just of Niles but also at Mischief and Mrs Holroyd, Deleuze and Guattari, Launce and, most importantly, Launce's dog.

Business class

The *Frasier* sequence has precursors going a long way back. It also has a generic name, indeed several.

Someone reading the text of Latimer's *Maria Marten* would come across this stage direction 'Business continued ad lib' (Latimer 1928: 39). The author's script invites the performers to take control. The business relies for its development on their invention and it becomes their property. They may well bring to it gestures and gags that they've worked up elsewhere. The author is not concerned with specifying the precise detail of the activity; and the printed text is not concerned to record what they did. The 'business' is a gap in the text.

Another instance of performer interpolation appears in *commedia dell'arte*. The improvised playing of a scenario will include *lazzi*. These, said Riccoboni in 1728, are the actions of masked characters 'when they interrupt a scene by their expressions of terror or by their fooleries' (in Gordon 1983: 4). Such fooleries were taken from the 'stock of materials' which a performer had collected together from printed texts and commonplace books, to 'insert into their dialogue as occasion permitted' (Richards and Richards 1990: 149; see also Rudlin 1994). Although they improvised, it was the job of at least one of the performers, according to Perrucci, to keep the scenario in his head. Into this *lazzi* would be inserted, as a new or expected source of fun or to sustain the playing when the improvisation flagged. Like business, *lazzi* generate performance material as they go along. Thus in the *lazzo* of Pulcinella's goodness 'on hearing from the Capitano or others that they intend to kill him, and not being recognised, Pulcinella praises himself saying, "Pulcinella is a lively chap, simple and good"' (Richards and Richards 1990: 136, 176). Once a performer starts on this, the self-descriptions may become steadily more extravagant as Pulcinella inadvertently edges closer to being recognised. Part of the audience's pleasure comes from the sheer extent of what can be produced out of the original familiar starting point; the delight is in watching production happen.

The generation of material from a *lazzo* ends in the return to the scenario. So, like business, it has a place in the overall scheme of things, even though that place may be less circumscribed. Like business and *lazzi* the Niles routine is funny because it develops a logic of its own, which can be recognised – both as a logic in itself and as a logic seen elsewhere. Of course it's not invented at the moment of performance but – like some *lazzi* – carefully rehearsed in advance. All three sorts of playing seem to belong loosely to a class of interpolated rather than scripted material. Their different relationships with the scripted is one of the things we shall explore.

Launce and his dog

The problem with discussing *lazzi* is that their detail, being unscripted, is not precisely known. There is, however, a comedy contemporary with the earliest *commedia* which offers us written text, not only for the clowning episodes but also for their relationship with the rest of the play. The Launce monologues in *The Two Gentlemen of Verona* feel disconnected from the main action, according to David Wiles, because Shakespeare has scripted a show which will allow the clown, Will Kemp, to show off his skills. The writing clearly derives from comic playing, but it also operates to join that playing with the other scripted material (Wiles 1987: 73).

Each of Launce's two lengthy monologues (at Act 2 scene 3 and Act 4 scene 4) is marked as disengaged from the main action. In Act 2 scene 3 Panthino enters with the words 'Launce, away, away! Aboard! Thy master is shipped, and thou art to post after with oars. What's the matter? Why weepest thou, man? Away, ass, you'll lose the tide, if you tarry any longer' (Shakespeare 1968: 2.3.31–3). Launce's weeping is, initially, a response to the departure from his family, and then becomes an extended demonstration of the hard-hearted nature of his dog, who is the only one who does not cry. The demonstration of the leave-taking has been enacted by Launce, using his shoes, his staff and his hat to represent his family. The dog remains the dog. The audience is caught up into the elaborate business of representing the departure – the precision with which the shoe must correspond with what it must represent, and the resistance to representation of the dog. During this speech Launce's drive to ensure that all positions are appropriately represented leads to uncertainty about who he is: 'This hat is Nan our maid. I am the dog. No, the dog is himself, and I am the dog. O, the dog is me, and I am myself' (2.3.20–2). Panthino's entrance not only brings the constraints of a world of masters, with their timetables, projects and instructions, but it also relocates Launce back into a system of representation where his identity is defined by reference simply to his master – no longer being, multiply in one person, himself the story teller, the family members and the dog. And the tears cease to have meaning. Launce commits a fault in the act – or, rather, the non-act – of 'tarrying'.

In the same way his master, in Act 4 scene 4, blames him for 'loitering'. In each case Launce's monologue is designated as a waste of time in relation to the storyline. Furthermore, in the second of these two episodes, Launce's activity is also outside the proper system of exchange and circulation between people, on which the storyline is founded. Proteus had sent Launce with a gift of a little dog to Silvia. He wants to know how she reacted to it. Launce tells him she said it was a cur, and has sent it back. But what Launce has in fact brought back is his own dog – which is the dog he actually offered to Silvia, since the original dog was stolen from him.

Before Proteus' entrance we have already heard how Launce's dog behaved in Silvia's company: stealing a capon's leg from her plate, pissing under the Duke's table and finally cocking his leg against Silvia's farthingale. The supposed activities of the dog allow us to imagine a sullying of that which should be respected and idealised. But much of the laughter derives from the presence of the actual dog on stage. Launce's speech doesn't require that it perform any particular routines or tricks – it can remain wholly indifferent to Launce (or piss on the stage). It becomes funnier the more indifferent it is, since Launce always takes the blame for it anyway. The dog, as an actual dog, is allowed to stand outside the scripted and choreo-graphed relations between humans (and is thus very different from a trained melodrama dog, which carries the human narrative, often in its mouth, turn-ing up with, for instance, the crucial piece of evidence that saves the hero from death). Launce's dog – and Launce's monologue about it – are comi-cally engaging but at the same time apparently extraneous. Launce is dis-missed from the stage to find the right dog. His presence with the wrong dog merely vexes his master.

Doing what comes naturally

The scripting of Launce's activities establishes discrete orders of activity and representation. Where elsewhere fictional persons are consciously embodied by human actors, Launce addresses a shoe as his mother and emotionally connects with a dog which is simultaneously produced as indifferent. Launce's activity is thus superfluous to the economy of representation. And although his extended solo turns may be no longer than a soliloquy by Proteus they are made to feel less tightly focused. Proteus speaks of his feelings, and in speaking of them tries to make sense of his relation with other characters in the story. Launce not only describes but also enacts scenes that happened elsewhere, outside the story. In doing his enacting he interests the audience both in the depicted scene and in his work of enactment. The activity is referred to as non-activity – tarrying or loitering.

The verbal markers that specify non-activity have parallels in other sorts of play. 'Oh, your servant, sir; are you at your raillery, sir?' (Wycherley 1973: 3.2.82). Sparkish the fop responds to being teased by Horner about his mistress. From here they proceed to talk about going to the theatre, the merits of poets and Sparkish's fear of being satirised on the stage: 'they make a wise and witty man in the world a fool upon the stage, you know not how. – And 'tis therefore I hate 'em too, for I know not but it may be my own case' (3.2.109–12). Horner and his two friends provoke the fop to display his atti-tudes. His greatest folly is that he does not understand the mechanisms of the stage, or that any and every space may be performance space. But, as with Launce's loitering, this episode of 'raillery' is outside the action in the sense that it does not change the situation. It is an elaboration on – a development of and response to – the comic persona who is the target of the raillery.

Just as with Launce's leave-taking and Niles's jealousy, we quickly get the point about Sparkish. We are looking at something which doesn't take its rationale from communication of information. These characters are locked into satisfying their needs. It's a mechanism that works by repetition and accretion. And, far from being answerable to any other system, it generates its own logic. So it seems to be trying to repeat itself for as long as it can; and at the same time it is elaborating itself. As this elaboration, this accretion, proliferates it threatens to obscure the original shape, the logic, that tries to replicate itself. What might begin from the dominant desire of the persona – to explain, to show off, to be jealous – is then taken over by something bigger – a mechanism that seems to have a *compulsion* to repeat, indeed a desire of its own. It might be called loitering, or raillery, or business: all of them are sequences structured by the mechanism of repetition and accretion.

What adds to the sense of performers being caught up into a routine is the idea that they cannot actually perform. They are people merely doing what comes naturally in their situation. Endlessly explaining, endlessly obsessive, they appear to have yielded up any capacity to create or govern their own performance. This idea is established when the performers of a French burlesque ballet (c. 1622) recite:

> Not one of us knows how to dance;
> Our steps are performed without reflection,
> We walk in any which way,
> As people who have never learned;
>> (the *Ballet de l'heure du temps*
>> cited in Franko 1993: 97)

They dance as if they can't dance. So too Launce's clowning is offered up as a waste of time. The performance in each case is highly skilled, but it sets itself against proper staged performance.

In putting it that way I have stepped away from defining raillery or business simply as a turn or set-piece. Part of the focus has always to be on the relationship between what appears to be autonomously extemporised and what is marked as significant for the purposes of plot. The shape and function of this relationship change in different modes of drama. They achieve a particularly subtle form in naturalism. Have a look at one of Lawrence's heroines working in her kitchen: 'She carries a basket heaped full of washing, which she has just taken from the clotheslines outside. Setting down the basket heavily, she feels among the clothes. She lifts out a white heap of sheets and other linen, setting it on the table' (Lawrence 1974b: 149). The performer does what is expected with washed laundry. Her activities are shaped by the function and nature of the objects she handles – the heavier damp garments are separated for drying, the linen is folded; it's not used to make an elaborate hat. A performer who stands folding laundry makes the movements, and takes the time, necessary to getting the fabric flat and the creases straight. This is certainly not theatrical 'incompetence' but it can feel as if it is extraneous to plot. Such activity is presented as a task which is 'routine', in theatrical terms marking time, as it were, before the next thing happens. It is an illustration of the stuff of the everyday, the given circumstances within which the story will happen. As such its function is to guarantee the authentic ordinariness of what is shown.

In the tightly scripted stage directions of the naturalist text, the detail of the daily routine is left to the performer to work out: 'She continues placing the flannel garments before the fire, on the fender and on chair-backs, till the stove is hedged in with a steaming fence; then she takes a sheet in a bundle from the table, and goes up to Blackmore, who stands watching her.' A change to that ordinary daily activity, where it becomes proper action, is then carefully marked. Blackmore says he needs to wash his hands before taking the sheet; she insists on getting him a clean towel, even though he says it is unnecessary. She takes it to him in the scullery:

> *Blackmore*   [*softly, now she is near him*]: Why did you trouble now? Pride, you know, pride, nothing else.
> *Mrs Holroyd*   [*also playful*]: It's nothing but decency.
> *Blackmore*   [*softly*]: Pride, pride, pride!
> [*A child of eight suddenly appears in the doorway.*]
>
> (Lawrence 1974b: 150)

The clean towel suddenly acquires special status as fabric, being invested with interpersonal significance. The ordinary routine has been made to turn into an image of a potential, and difficult, change in the situation of her daily life. Action happens.

Inaction, of a significant kind

Business and its like can produce a sense of disengagement from the rest of the play. It may be possible to specify this relationship theoretically.

Hitherto I have described the opposite to business, the thing it's disengaged from, as 'action'. In dramatic theory this is a precise term, with its roots in Aristotle's theory. There it is considered more important than character: 'while men do have certain qualities by virtue of their character it is in their action that they achieve, or fail to achieve, happiness' (Halliwell 1987: 37). Through action, plays model how the significant human events typically happen. It is not to be confused with mere plot (see Shepherd and Wallis 2004; also States 1994). A much later reworking of the concept of action also suggests a word for its opposite. Manfred Pfister's definition of an action may be summarised as 'something which changes the situation'. For activity which does not change a situation – as, famously, in *Waiting for Godot* – he uses the word 'event'. Now the change in a situation is something difficult to define precisely, and hence the division between action and event is also slippery: 'An event is anything that happens; actions are events which change the situation' (overview of Pfister in Wallis and Shepherd 1998: 69, 70).

The problem with adopting Pfister's blanket-term 'event' is that in a variety of different cultures and their dramatic practices there seem to be names for activity which is not action. The list includes sport, game, gear, gestes, raillery, turn, ranting, *lazzi*, business, extemporisation, even 'riff' perhaps. These words don't all mean the same thing or point to the same staged activity. They do, however, fall into place in conceptual binaries, where each pole of the binary holds the other in place. Thus we might have work–game, doctrine–japing, civility–raillery, earnest–careless, decorum–rant. Such binaries can be produced as much by choreography as by verbal script. Mark Franko gives an illustration in his discussion of burlesque ballet:

> Because the *entrée* was itself separate from dramatic action, it, like the interlude, was fundamentally digressive. Rather than becoming dramatic, the *entrée* maintained its resemblance to the interlude: that is, its digressive quality, while losing its structural justification for digression.
>
> (1993: 85)

Where the qualities and ideological import of action change, so its other pole must also change. But what shall we call this pole? Pfister's 'event' obscures the varied histories of the terms, and it is too neutral. Event is a sort of action without consequences. Some of the activities under discussion here are, by contrast, both interruptions and interpolations into action. Sometimes they clearly come from elsewhere, belonging with games and routines that are transmitted, in basically unchanging shapes, across texts and histories. 'Event' gives a sense of unproductive action, but we also need an idea of something which lives on elsewhere, beyond any particular action. We are dealing not so much with what is lesser than action, then, but with action's other, which I prefer to call inaction.

There is another possible word: 'play'. Certainly in the eyes of its theorists play has some of the features of what I have been trying to describe. It appears to be voluntary activity (Huizinga 1949), just as inaction appears to be outside the obligations to carry out the requirements of storyline and author's text. Although it has its internal rules, play, like inaction, can be seen as time out (Caillois 1961) – like Launce's loitering it is something separate from a highly organised society. So too, in its superfluity, its time-wasting, inaction runs counter to organised and structured narrative, as if the performer is released from the author's control (but only 'as if'). Play has a neurophysiological function within learning processes: 'Models of the world are complexified through action in the world either by increasing the complexity of sensory information about domains already modeled, or by increasing the spatiotemporal range of the world modeled' (Laughlin, McManus and d'Aquili 1990: 178–9). Similarly inaction can make more complex the sense of dramatic shape (having to deal with something that looks 'disconnected', for instance) and of the possibilities of the stage (Launce playing games with the rules of representation). Yet for all these parallels there's a crucial difference. Play is something people do rather than watch. And the doing of it, in adults, produces a state of being that Mihaly Csikszentmihalyi describes as 'flow': a state of concentration, merging action and awareness, with a noncontradictory goal, often a compressed sense of time, and a loss of ego (1975; summarised in 1979: 257–74). The audience at a performance – especially where someone is getting caught up into an obsessive routine – is, by contrast, presumably well aware of its own separation from the staged activities. Furthermore, rather than being pushed to choose between play and organised society, the audience is invited by the contrast between inaction and action to look at a *relationship* between two things. For all these reasons inaction, again, seems the preferable term.

That relationship between action and inaction does of course change in different cultures, as too does the status of playing itself. Before I look further at this relationship, I should clarify how this inaction is also 'significant'. In the various examples so far described, there are particular sorts of signifi-cance: naturalism's kitchen activities and the texture of authentic ordinari-ness; Launce's games with representation and his failures at the system of romantic exchange; the capacity of *lazzi* to bring into the light the shapes of obsessive fixations; the effect of raillery in relation to display and self-objectification. But, above all, the inaction acquires significance through being marked as inaction, the thing which the action is not. The binary rela-tion itself produces inaction as significant.

Two left gloves, and Deleuze's battle

This inaction is not just significant. It is also deeply pleasurable. As a first step towards describing the pleasure let's specify what the inaction *does*.

When Molière's miser Harpagon discovers he has been robbed, he searches for the thief: 'Where is he hiding? How can I find him? Which way shall I go? Which way shan't I go? Is he here? Is he there? Who's that? Stop! (*catching his own arm*) Give me my money back, you scoundrel! Ah, it's me!' (Molière 1982: 159). The emotion, working free of rational controls, elabo-rates itself into a routine – the *lazzo* of searching. The more it searches the less important it is that anything is found. Empty space is filled by movement that goes nowhere; the body seems to break into parts. At its climax there is an image of a man arresting himself, devoured by his own energy.

Harpagon, like Launce, is not making the best use of his solo time. Nei-ther meditates on the purpose of life or the mechanisms of revenge. They are people governed by obsessions in such a way that they lose grip on the system of exchanges and interchanges going on around them. Like the dancers in that burlesque ballet, their 'steps' are performed without reflection. So why might this be pleasurable?

Have a look at the opening act of Pinero's *Trelawny of the 'Wells'*. There is extended business with a glove: 'Ablett is now going about pouring out the ale. Occasionally he drops his glove, misses it, and recovers it.' Working as a butler at Trelawny's farewell dinner, Ablett has arrived with two left gloves. He tries initially to force one of them onto his right hand; and thereafter is vexed by reappearances of the recalcitrant glove: 'By an unfortunate chance, Ablett's glove has found its way to the plate and is handed to Gadd by Ablett' (Pinero 1995: 230, 231). For the audience the 'private' business between the butler and his glove becomes more interesting than his public role serving at the table. We watch a drama between a human being and an object, between will and circumstance, where the object appears to follow a narrative of its own as it moves around the stage.

The business here produces pleasure for the audience by several means. First, the pleasure in watching Ablett partly comes from the sight of him being taken over by his desire to wear both gloves, to be complete. This desire is more powerful than his social duty. A second source of pleasure has to do with the perception of space which is generated by the business. For now, rather than concentrating wholly on the farewell dinner, the audience is also watching for the movement around the room of the unhanded glove. Why should a new perception of space be pleasurable? Theorists of space suggest that a sense of where and how we are in space plays a part in shaping our identity (Colomina 1992: 83; Grosz 1995: 85–93). As space is reshaped, the relationship to it changes – there are new points of focus, different hierarchies between spatial axes and domains, a newly positioned centre. In stage space these shifts, which could normally be risky, are set within a safe framework, like a maze or hall of mirrors.

A third source of pleasure in the glove business comes from the relationship between the human body and objects, where those objects change their function or cease to be functional. The butler's 'work' alters in status when the glove narrative begins to put pressure on it. Once again the sense of the subject is altered. Objects are no longer merely 'object' – inanimate, without agency, only ever moved or used by a subject (compare Sofer 2003 on fans). The glove that won't fit denies its usability, and, with the human desire for completeness projected upon it, it appears to gain a will of its own. Of course this is all fiction, illusion: but at the same time a new placing of subjectivity, in the interplay between body and objects, is being fantasised by the stage.

These pleasures are not inevitable. A dramatist can restrain them: 'Minnie Gascoigne is busy about the fire … She lifts lids of saucepans, etc., hovers impatiently, looks at clock, begins to trim lamp' (Lawrence 1974a: 99–100). This woman could be playing the *lazzo* of waiting, where the familiar social situation could develop into an elaborate routine with lids, where those lids themselves somehow become responsible for the frustration (the lid that doesn't fit, the one that gets stuck). But in D. H. Lawrence's script here, the normal rules of kitchen space are observed, as too are the correct treatment and status of objects. Rather than express all the feeling through and against lids, Minnie must also do hovering. That hovering is constructed from elements which together suggest a fairly precise frame for Minnie's behaviour: she is waiting for an arrival that is late. The frame locates Minnie in relation to a significant narrative. It is not like Mrs Holroyd putting clothes to dry simply because the job needs doing. So in each case, although the domestic work is characterised as the particular sphere of the woman, there are different effects of constraint.

Lawrence was specifically scripting Minnie not to get locked into the routines of cooking and trimming. In other episodes of inaction Pulcinella, Launce, Ablett and Sparkish all get taken over by the routines they are in. This effect of lost initiative is well illustrated in a dance described by Mark Franko from the burlesque ballet *Les Fées des forêts de Saint Germain* (1625). A group of Will-o'-the-Wisp Spirits leap about, playing a violent ball game. As Franko notes, the existing contemporary drawing of this dance doesn't show a ball:

> Thus, in addition to simulating the combat implied by the game of 'balle forcee', the dancers also represent the movement of the ball itself. The pun signals a transition in the ballet from mimetic to 'metaphoric' movement: the dancers are both the players and the played.
>
> (Franko 1993: 91)

So too in *The Two Gentlemen of Verona* when Launce uses representation to distinguish between the members of his family, he ends up blurring his sense of self. To show different relations he makes use of his shoes, staff and hat. As he reaches the dog he runs out of signifiers. So he decides he must represent the dog. But the dog is there with him: 'No, the dog is himself, and I am the dog' (2.3.21). Launce, losing grip of his identity, exchanging himself with the dog, is not, however, a split subject, mad. Like the dancers of *Les Fées* he is taken over by the internal rhythm of his activity. The firm grasp on singular identity is relaxed within a safe framework. Those dancers are caught up into, yet contained by, the typical movements of the ball game.

Although the thing is engineered by a performer, the effect is of that performer being caught into a rhythm, a 'routine', that is larger than s/he is (see Chapter 4). The routine acquires an incorporeal status that coexists with, and even apparently overtakes, the bodies that actually make it happen. Thus the significant inaction may be said to produce for itself something akin to a virtual presence. And it may, thus, also be called an 'event' – but in a different sense from Pfister, that of Gilles Deleuze. To illustrate his 'event' Deleuze gives as an example the military battle. Ronald Bogue summarises:

> A battle may be viewed exclusively in terms of bodies – those of the combatants, of their weapons, their cries, their wounds – but there is also a

sense in which 'the battle' itself is an incorporeal surface effect produced by the bodies, a kind of floating entity which is everywhere apparent and nowhere localizable.

(1989: 69)

Deleuze's example is relevant to the episode of significant inaction in another way. For the battle, as Bogue says, 'is a vital entity with a life of its own, an aggregate of metastable states, a structure of *loci* of potential energy, of possibilities of development' (1989: 69). The appearance of improvised activity is engaging because it always contains possibilities for development – the dancer who announces that he doesn't know how to dance is placing himself outside the known terms, the predictable shapes, of the dancing rules – and thus opens up a space for all manner of uncertain outcomes. So too, if you act with a dog, you set up a situation where the dog, without a human sense of protocols, may behave in unpredictable ways. Many of the routines of game, raillery, sport, revelry have, for their duration, a sense that they can always go in a new direction. Thus the main experience of significant inaction is of a potency, a capacity for a range of outcomes. Not something finished but a state of becoming – 'not a thing, but a verbal infinitive capable of various actualizations, not "the battle", but "to battle"' (Bogue 1989: 70). Or: not the game, but to game; not the play, but to play.

Inaction, interaction, flow

It is crucial that the analogy is with a verbal infinitive. A present-tense transitive verb links two agents or names together: 'I embrace you', 'stone breaks glass'. The verbal infinitive doesn't have a subject or an object, it is not in the service of names. The linguistic operation here can provide a model for the nature of 'business'.

Let's take as an example the task which Launce messes up. He is supposed to deliver to Silvia a small dog given by Proteus. The dog is stolen so he substitutes his own. This set-up can be modelled by analogy with the syntax of verbs. Proteus the gift-giver and Silvia the receiver are the most important entities in the process. Less important is the person who carries out the instruction to deliver. Least important of all is the dog, that which is given, not even human. Yet the dog, part of the act of giving, is fundamental. If the dog is stolen, and replaced by another dog, the act of giving changes its significance. That in turn changes the relationship of the two most important people. When Proteus puts a clown in charge of the verb – to give – that verb ceases to be of proper service to the named lover (Proteus) and the loved (Silvia). Launce, faced with the instruction to give something to Silvia, substitutes his own dog. In doing so he demonstrates the fluid, and anarchic, possibilities of the verbal infinitive. 'To give', on its own, doesn't distinguish between what is given or how. Launce's dog, capable of all sorts of transgression, and showing no remorse, is a signal that the verb has escaped the service of the nouns.

Furthermore, in Shakespeare's text Proteus' dog – the gift dog – is unseen, only ever a word, immaterial, whereas Launce's dog stands there, flesh and blood. Proteus' dog, like a properly trained noun, will take its part in the syntax of his relationship with Silvia. Launce's dog meanwhile is just *there*. It is thoroughly present in that it can freely take its liberty of the stage, and showing, by being there, that it is incapable of fitting into any meaningful exchange between the characters, unable to be substituted for a nonexistent dog. At the same time of course it is not intentionally showing any of this, it is simply a trained theatre dog. It is, as Deleuze might have it, 'not fully individuated and it does not exist in any separate, transcendent realm. It is at once mere surface-effect and vital potential energy of individuation' (Bogue 1989: 70).

Or – alternatively – it's just the wrong dog.

That dog standing there on stage for real, with its capacity for eating and pissing, is felt, by Proteus, to be not what he had in mind in terms of gift-giving. Launce's dog exceeds the demands of storyline interactions, messes the neat circulation and exchange between characters. Similarly the adventures of Ablett's glove cut across his efforts to comply with the social conventions of appropriately delivering food to its recipients. 'Business' places itself outside the proper logic of exchanges between people. It resists established protocols of difference. Within the routine of inaction an audience enters a domain where positions blur. The major blurring is between agent and routine, but also person and object, game and player. The emphasis falls much more onto *interactivity*. Polarised positions being occluded, the inaction insists on a state of flux.

This state of flux is something more than a blurring of signifiers, of the game playing the player. There is about the flux a feeling that the business or *lazzo* is unstoppable. At the heart of it is a productive energy. The performer, who is apparently not carrying out the delivery of a script, produces the material, the jokes and elaborations, which will in turn enable her to carry on carrying on. And the longer it goes on, the more powerful seems its grip on the performer. It is as if the performers are caught up in what might be called an onward *flow of energy*.

In a moment I shall develop this idea of a *flow* of energy. Before doing so, however, I want to comment on another effect of inaction. It is to do with its impact on what is around it. For in order for a storyline to function as a story, and for one situation to produce another, certain basic concepts have to be accepted – about the identity and shape of the space, the relationship between humans and objects, the logistics of exchange between humans, and the discrete individuality of each person. For these concepts to be accepted they have to be understood and trusted, they have to work according to established rules. They have, in short, to follow that which has been codified for dramatic performance. The inaction works in such a way as to question the meaningfulness and function of these concepts – it questions their codification. When it has us look afresh at the space, at the behaviour of objects, at melting individuation, it may thus be said to be *decoding*.

So, alongside that sense of a flow of energy, inaction also has an effect of unpicking the dramatic rules, or codes, that have been established. Each of these aspects has bearing on the audience's sense of what is going on in front of them, and its pleasures. That said, I want to pause. For, described that way the action–inaction binary appears to be a transhistorical machine, working the same way at all times. Yet it actually appears in different modes in different cultures. So it now becomes necessary to ask how far the characteristic aspects of inaction can be accounted for in relation to the dynamic of a particular historical society.

In order to attempt this move into a more historically focused account, I have chosen to draw on a model developed by Deleuze and Guattari in *AntiOedipus* (1984). That choice has been motivated in part by an interest in testing the usefulness of the model within the context of dramatic analysis.

In *AntiOedipus* Deleuze and Guattari write a history of civilisation, critiquing and building on traditional Marxism, and polemically grounding their account in the desire and limits of the human body. As Alphonso Lingis notes, they are opposed to an exchange concept of society and resist the analogue of that society, the integrated body (1994: 289–303). They extend the idea of human production, conceiving of the parts and activities of the human body as being connected together, in binary relations, as 'desiring machines' which both produce and cut off various flows – of milk from the breast, of urine, of semen. These flows are experienced as endless flux, originating always elsewhere. By extension, when they start mapping forms of social organisation – or 'social machines' – these flows are seen to consist of money, labour power, debt, or just energy itself. In the story they tell, the prime function of the social machine 'has always been to codify the flows of desire, to inscribe them, to record them, to see to it that no flow exists that is not properly dammed up, channeled, regulated' (Deleuze and Guattari 1984: 33; see also p. 141). A simple form of coding, practised by primitive society, amounts to 'reciprocal adaptation, the respective embrace of a signifying chain and flows of production' (1984: 148).

This model offers a way of thinking about inaction in relation to the main storyline. The episode of inaction is filled by a flow of energy – the elaboration could proliferate, producing more production, carrying on carrying on – but it is to be broken by the cue-line which returns us to the 'signifying chain' of the story. Launce's inventive weeping is ended by Panthino's entry to remind him of his function as a servant of Proteus.

Now the fate of flows is not always to be coded. They can also be decoded, and re-coded again. In elaborating on this process I shall endeavour to situate inaction within a large historical scheme.

Decoding Mischief

In the morality play of *Mankind* (c. 1470) as Mercy tries to get rid of Mischief, Mischief justifies himself: 'I say, sir! I am come hither to make you game.' Shortly afterwards the Vices New Guise, Nought and Now-a-Days enter. There is music and they do a dance. Mercy protests at the 'revel'; and they try to get him to dance (Wickham 1985: 9). Then there is a change in the middle section. The Vices are formally identified. Their voices are intercut with, balanced against, Mercy's. The sequence ends when Mercy identifies himself. After mocking his Latinate speech, the Vices burst into more obscene and nonsensical chatter. In a passage of 45 lines or so Mercy has two. The speakers are caught into a pronouncedly rhythmic verbal wildness, 12 lines of which are taken up with leave-taking and departing, where the verbal language becomes almost a function of the physical activity. The change to Mercy's solo speech after they have gone is a change to stillness and verbal dominance, commenting on the preceding events and warning.

At his original entry Mischief apparently 'decodes' the action: his entry lines parody Mercy's speech. Then Mercy asks 'Why come ye hither, brother? ye are not desired' (Wickham 1985: 8). Mischief is set up as an intruder, inappropriate. A more thorough – and genuine – decoding of the space happens when the Vices dance. It must, as Nought says, be violent – the performers may do what they please. After they have finished they attempt to get Mercy's clothes off in order to involve him in the dance. The energy of the dance seems to be flowing over Mercy's assumed *gravitas*. But here the text produces a delicately precise control mechanism. As New Guise and Now-a-Days are pulling Mercy into the dance, Nought advises him not to dance. A tug-of-war routine seems to be taking place. Nought is pitched against his companions. And so it's he who is given the line that can move them on to the next section: 'But, sir! I trow, of us three I heard you speak' (Wickham 1985: 10).

By placing the identification section *after* the dance, the playtext effectively re-codes what we are seeing. Attention is drawn back to the things of which Mercy speaks. Furthermore, the flow of energy introduced by the dance is ended by one of those who nominally represent the decoding, Nought. Rather than being taken over by the routine, Nought assists with the re-coding. Once the identification has happened, the Vices become obscene and nonsensical: the words are made to flow according to principles that are not linguistic and not depending on the signifier (compare this with

Deleuze and Guattari's account of dream images (1984: 244)). By now, however, the audience is placed to see and hear the obscenity as 'idle' words, an illustration of the sinfulness of the speakers. But this re-coding is fragile, for the obscenity is quite funny (well, I think so). Re-coding becomes firmer with the departure of the Vices. They go; Mercy stays. In hindsight the dancing amounted to the same thing as the obscenity, and the earlier energy is brought into equivalence with the redundant capers of the departure. The game is evacuated: Mercy can rightly call it idleness.

In this illustration of the decoding/re-coding process, the significant inaction is – apart perhaps from the dance – always allocated a place within the main action. And it has no real capacity to decode. Its energy is turned into an illustration of energy. The play thus demonstrates its capacity to manage the inaction–action binary. This point gains especial force if you consider it to have mumming and folk-play roots (Denny 1974). Far from passively offering the banal insight that game is idleness *Mankind* proffers itself as active agent in the always necessary work of re-coding.

Seen in this way the morality text assumes – and demonstrates – a despotic vigilance over its maintenance of codes. As a step towards a large historical schematisation of coding, let's now contrast this pre-industrial morality play with a melodrama of early nineteenth-century industrial society. The 1840s' script of *Maria Marten* invites 'business ad lib'. Maria is dressed as a man; the clown Tim becomes jealous of the affection shown by 'his' Anne towards this strange man. He threatens reprisal if they kiss; they do so; he threatens again; they do so; etc. It goes on as long as the performers can sustain, or be sustained by, its elaboration. Although Maria wholeheartedly enters this routine, she is also, we know, disguised by instruction from the villain, whom she is on her way to meet at the Red Barn, where he will kill her. While the kissing business goes on, this murder narrative is forgotten. Furthermore, Maria's status also changes, from that of victim whose vulnerability is marked by her alien clothing to comic agent who is empowered by disguise. The melodrama business, the inaction, transmits a flow of energy which is almost irreconcilably different from that of the action, and it decodes its space.[1]

Melodramatists often made provision for business in order to capitalise on the talents of the company's comic performers, whose pulling power might often be greater than that of the writer. This insertion of business has often been taken as a symptom of how far melodrama was driven not by the principles of art but by the principles of the marketplace. Instead of the coherent vision of the writer, there is the apparent anarchy produced by the need both to give space to a range of star turns and to cater for a variety of audience demands. In melodrama, the dramatic form most clearly associated with entrepreneurial capital, the carefully coherent codes of proper art apparently give way to the irruption of decoded flows of energy.

The larger historical scheme motivating this diagrammatic move from medieval to capitalist is suggested by Deleuze and Guattari: 'the Urstaat was defined by overcoding, and its derivatives, from the ancient City-State to the monarchic State, already found themselves in the presence of flows that were decoded or in the process of being decoded' (1984: 252). The history of social machines told in *AntiOedipus* begins with primitive territorial society, moves through the despotic barbarism of the Urstaat, through to capitalism. The codes established by primitive society, against exchange and commerce for instance, could not sustain themselves against being broken down by private property, wealth, etc. Hence these decoded flows needed to be overcoded or re-coded by the Urstaat. Capitalism by contrast works by decoding flows (1984: 225). But it needs to resist the headlong rush into the schizophrenic condition of complete decoding, so it puts brakes on the process by re-coding (1984: 250). None of this story concerns economics alone, for such a separation in human productivity is not possible. The history of the despotic Urstaat partly concerns the invention of writing (1984: 202). Each social machine produces its own type of representation.

Abstract and global as all this might sound, Deleuze and Guattari also insist that something such as the structure of a musical chord can have a deliberately tense relation with 'social production': Ravel 'chose to end his compositions with abrupt breaks, hesitations, tremolos, discordant notes, and unresolved chords, rather than allowing them to slowly wind down to a close' (1984: 31–2). And if a musical chord, methinks, why not a clown's routine?

Significant inaction: culture, Shakespeare and *Frasier*

My use of Deleuze and Guattari's history of 'social machines' is intended to suggest a way of culturally reading, and perhaps evaluating, a dramatic event through an analysis of the relations between what it marks as inaction and action. It's a version of Eugene Holland's argument that 'The concept of decoding ... enables us to explain the semiotics and psychodynamics of texts historically in relation to ... the rhythms of capitalist development' (1996: 242).

The game of the morality play is not as radically separate from the action as is the business of the melodrama; one text re-codes, the other decodes. Between these poles, by way of another example, we might locate Shakespearean comedy (always on the middle ground). Launce and his dog have occupied much of this chapter. But they belong to a very early comedy. Move later, to *As You Like It* and *Twelfth Night*, or to the fool of *King Lear*, and you find a very different clowning. Gone are the solo turns; the clown has songs and meaningful retorts. David Wiles (1987) suggests that this development arises out of the different performing persona and talents of Robert Armin, who fancied himself as something of an intellectual. But an explanation of the cause doesn't remove the textual effects. The clown, in Armin's hands, becomes a clear-sighted observer, cynical and self-interested in Touch-stone's case, melancholic in Feste's and downright inscrutable in the Fool of *Lear*. Thus the clown is still given a characteristic voice and indeed 'licence', and still inserts moments of apparent inaction, in the form of extended banter or a riddle. But the banter and riddles are seen to contain significant meanings which have bearing on the main action. Indeed, this apparent 'inaction' is part of the cognitive apparatus of the action proper.

In short – and to return to the terms I used above – Shakespeare's clowns are progressively re-coded, their potential for independent flows of energy curtailed. Now the economic organisation of early modern theatre shows all the signs of early capitalist enterprise, with ticket sales forming an income stream that was more substantial than the nominal patronage framework. So according to the Deleuze and Guattari model we might expect the movement to be towards a decoding, and greater 'anarchy'. But Shakespeare's company in particular was apparently making a bid for cultural (and economic) pre-eminence, aiming for 'authority' (Gurr 1987; Wilson 1993). Thus the re-coding of clownish enthusiasms might be seen as playing a part within the negotiation of a cultural place by the company. Hamlet is somewhat scathing about performances in which clowns are allowed to upstage the serious action, even though *Hamlet* lets the gravediggers do a turn.

Capitalism, in Deleuze and Guattari's story, is in a contradictory situation. It has continually to be vigilant about its drive to decode:

> Concerning capitalism, we maintain that it both does and does not have an exterior limit: it has an exterior limit that is schizophrenia, that is, the absolute decoding of flows, but it functions only by pushing back and ex-orcising this limit.

> (1984: 250)

Capitalist theatre culture has promoted, 'licensed', a diversity of forms and practices, where the venue or the star might be as potent as the dramatist. Everything thus made free, all alike purchasable, is then re-ordered in terms of social value, cultural authority and art.

So what to make of that bit in *Frasier*? We could call it the *lazzo* of transla-tion; it comes after the mock heroic swordfight and ends with Niles's exit line: 'Give me five seconds, then tell him he's fired.' The mock-heroism, the cow-ardice and the upper-class lifestyle are the norm for the snobbish, self-serious Frasier and Niles. Their world, and comedy, are textured by regularly epi-grammatic dialogue. The *lazzo*, by contrast, dwindles to a set of noises, and then the sequence of hugs – which nearly has Niles embracing a male stranger. It's also dependent on the work of all four players. The time out for the *lazzo* takes the players away from their customary mode (which they share with other sitcoms) and also produces them as team players. This latter effect fits with the show's publicity image. The former effect contributes to the sense of *Frasier*, at its best, as having less adherence to a formulaic structure woven around verbal punchlines than other sitcoms. The physical rhythm of the *lazzo* is allowed to be more forceful than the camerawork, which is often a controlling presence in this genre. So the relationship of inaction and action, while being carefully editorially monitored, constructs a sense of actual performing, a sort of delightful human agency.

The stars are given space, it seems, to display their real clowning ability. The series has strong enough performers, it says, not to need scripting and camera. It can embrace decoding. But the whole thing, within the structure and texture of the series, is also very arch. It is, as it were, a quotation of decoding. Hence it displays self-knowingness. This then underscores the image of intelligence and cultural competence of the series. Which in their turn authorise its occupation of its cultural niche.

In dealing with significant inaction we are coping with that which is, by definition, outside theme and thesis. Its routines problematise the relations of body, script and value. They also have an unclear relationship with social order. But they are the stuff of drama, and there needs to be a way of speaking of them. Which is why Deleuze and Guattari find themselves somewhat improbably looking after the wrong dog.

Part II

In time and space

Theatre is an art of bodies witnessed by bodies. Witnesses are something more than passive viewers. In the act of witnessing a person attests to the truth of something that is or was present for them. In its religious usage the act of witnessing is done by a person attesting to the truth of the godhead, possessed physically by that truth and seeking to make that truth known to others.

The audience members as witnesses are physically engaged by that which is present to them, to the extent that they might be physically possessed by it. One of the outcomes of possession is that audience members attempt, during a performance, to assert out loud, to announce publicly, the truths that they believe exist – 'Don't believe him', 'Look out behind you', 'Oh yes it is!'

This book's Introduction suggested that the processes of perception, hearing, speaking may all be said to be bodily. While an audience is not prepared in the way that performers are – although it is prepared – it is nevertheless bodily engaged by the performance as soon as it begins to listen and look. That engagement, coming on top of the expectancy that entered the auditorium, is part of the way the audience's body is worked on. The show physically organises the audience's feeling of pleasure. Verriest summarises this idea:

> As our eyes follow the mimic actions of an actor on the stage, all the movements made by the latter project themselves into our body with an intensity which varies according to our individual excitability and our present level of stimulation.
>
> (in Jousse 1990: 23)

In the 1580s this effect confirmed Stephen Gosson in his hostility to theatre. Unconvinced that theatre had a moral impact, he noted how an audience responded to stage action: 'when Bacchus rose up, tenderly lifting Ariadne from the seate, no small store of curtesie passing betweene them, the beholders rose up, every man stoode on tippe toe, and seemed to houer ouer the praye' (?1590: sig. G5). It is a model of muscular empathy that can still be observed, especially in sporting performances. A common instance is the excitement of the football match which energises the bodies of the spectators. There's no rational need for the upper body to rise as your team gets close to the opposing goal. As Roger Caillois puts it in his wider discussion of games, 'A physical contagion leads them to assume the position of the men or animals in order to help them' (1961: 22).[1] This physical contagion is possible in all performance–audience relationships, but it is most obvious where cultures of spectating assume – and construct – emotional expressivity.

In the 1970s that physical contagion was given a name by drama theorists. In *The Dynamics of Drama* (1970) Bernard Beckerman suggests:

> Although theater response seems to derive principally from visual and aural perception, in reality it relies upon a totality of perception that could be better termed kinesthetic. We are aware of a performance through varying degrees of concentration and relaxation within our bodies. From actual experience performers can sense whether or not a 'house' is with them, principally because the degree of muscular tension in the audience telegraphs, before any overt sign, its level of attention. We might very well say that an audience does not see with its eyes but with its lungs, does not hear with its ears but with its skin.
>
> (Beckerman 1970: 150)

Beckerman had developed this idea from a reading of contemporary philosophers of perception, in particular Rudolph Arnheim and Michael Polanyi. In *Art and Visual Perception* (1956) Arnheim insisted that visual perception was separate from kinaesthetic activity, which at that time denoted 'the physical forces that move muscles, joints, and tendons' (1956: 339). It was not these forces, only messages about their effects, which were transmitted to the brain. But then a qualification had to be made:

> If these messages are accompanied by experiences of tension, this surely is not due to a direct grasp of muscular energies, but to perceptual forces aroused within the cortical brain centers by the stimulation. If it is admitted that such experiences of tension are inherent in kinaesthetic perception, there is no reason why they should not accompany visual perception in the same way.
>
> (Arnheim 1956: 339)

If visual perception is accompanied, or indeed reinforced, by kinaesthetic sensations these will result from the initial experience of 'visual tension'. The kinaesthetic for Arnheim is still primarily to do with muscle awareness and body image. But the door is opened for Beckerman's meaning by the concession that kinaesthetic stimulations are 'a kind of sympathetic resonance, which arises sometimes, but not necessarily always, in the neighbouring medium of muscle sense' (Arnheim 1956: 339).

Michael Polanyi's *The Tacit Dimension* (1967) was based on a series of lectures given in 1962. In his first chapter he argues that 'by elucidating the way our bodily processes participate in our perceptions we will throw light on the bodily roots of all thought' (1967: 15). The process is to do with two different ways of responding to the world – by consciously attending to it and by being unconsciously, 'tacitly', aware. We use our body to attend to things outside us, but we also think about our body in terms of those things outside. In doing so, however tacitly, 'we incorporate it in our body – or extend our body to include it – so that we come to dwell in it' (1967: 16). Once he has introduced this idea of knowing something by 'dwelling' in it, Polanyi is able to add a new dimension to the concept of kinaesthetics. He refers us to German philosophy at the end of the nineteenth century (specifying Dilthey and Lipps) which 'postulated that indwelling, or empathy, is the proper means of knowing man and the humanities' (1967: 16). Thus kinaesthetic perception is identified as the foundational principle of empathy.

Picking up from Polanyi, Beckerman firmly insisted on the bodily basis of theatrical reception:

> Nor do we have to discriminate the dramatic signals mentally in order to react. Perception includes subception, bodily response to stimuli before we are focally aware of the stimuli. In theater, this means that our bodies are already reacting to the texture and structure of action before we recognize that they are doing so.
>
> (1970: 150–1)

As Polanyi might put it, we are unable to discriminate or know the constituent signals because we are attending to the performance as a whole; nevertheless we are still incorporating those signals into our bodies. For Beckerman kinaesthetic perception functions even where there is an absence of understanding. It is stimulated partly by space, the presence of other people and time-span.

This model of bodily response has been of particular use to dance theorists. Alexandra Carter suggests that the kinaesthetic impact of ballet derives from 'a bodily response to the richness of colour and texture on stage, the complexity of patternings of large casts and the aesthetic values of classicism – clarity of line, formality of shape, virtuosity, harmony' (1999; see also Manning 1997). Ann Daly connects the kinaesthetic impact to Kristeva's 'semiotic', which is characterised as 'pulsing, kinetic, heterogeneous space whose meanings are much more fluid and imprecise' than those of the 'symbolic' which has a logic and is 'translatable' (1992: 244).

Time-span, pulsing, shape and space: these seem to be some of the crucial factors in the way a performance apparently works on its audience. They are part of the mechanism of kinaesthetic engagement. That mechanism is analysed in the two chapters which follow. These assume that, while audiences will of course vary in their states of excitability and cultural competence, the written text can indicate what is being produced for them, what is deployed in order to organise pleasure.

My analysis thus looks in some detail at the rhythmic organisation and spatial arrangements assumed and generated by performances. Within this I argue that senses of rhythm and space have bodily impact on audiences, and, from here, that such impact is part of the mechanism whereby theatre, through the theatricalised body, engages with its cultural context. Chapter 4 begins with Ayckbourn but then ranges across various periods; Chapter 5 is much more tightly focused on mid-nineteenth-century 'sensation' drama.

4 Just at that very moment

The organisation of body rhythm

Through the second act of Alan Ayckbourn's *Absurd Person Singular* Eva is trying to kill herself. One of her attempts involves a can of paint-stripper, with a very tight top. Her efforts to undo it lead to the following sequence:

> She struggles vainly, then goes to the room door, intending to use it as a vice.
> At this moment Marion enters.
> Eva is pushed behind the door, and, as it swings shut, she clings to the handle and falls across the floor. While the door is open the dog barks and raised voices are heard.
>
> (Ayckbourn 1979: 64)

A door opens and closes

What is funny about the door sequence? Partly it is the surprise of Marion's entry. Eva's suicide activity has been unnoticed by the other characters, but shared by the audience. Their attention is focused by the struggle with the top of the can, which has its own dynamic – desperate woman, recalcitrant object. It continues long enough to get an audience engaged. The performers and director will have explored how long to wait before opening the door. That opening is a surprise; but not unexpected. Eva's previous attempts had also failed. This failure is part of what is becoming a predictable pattern, a set of variations on a theme. It is both surprising and regular.

The door, having opened, must close again. Comedy comes from the realisation that objects have their own logic, and that human activity is vulnerable to this logic. The vulnerability derives less from human passivity than human desire and determination. Eva falls with the door because she won't let go of the handle. The more ferociously she grips that handle, the more comically pleasurable will be her fall.

The door's operation is itself emphasised by the change of sound, which helps to hold that moment when the door is open. For that brief time what hangs in abeyance is the mechanical logic that will surely follow from the closing of the door. While it is open, with all the noise of the room beyond, behind it, in silence, is Eva. An audience knows she will re-emerge, but neither when nor how.

The re-emergence shows the human body humiliated by objects, and falling flat. But the humiliation is also militantly insignificant, ignored on stage. Eva's project is upstaged by Marion's drunken curiosity as to what the others in the room are doing. Eva will pick herself up and set off for the next door with her tight top which, throughout the sequence, has remained, of course, unmoved.

In the production of this sort of comedy, both in writing and performing, much of the technical skill lies in the establishment of sequences or routines that have their own sense of inner logic: cause and effect, necessary unfolding, accident and repetition. The relationship of cause and effect does not depend on human intention. Eva intends to kill herself, but she is caught up into a world of objects with purposes of their own: the door will close once opened, the can will hold tight to its top. That Eva is tangled into something larger than herself is something of which modern farce audiences are usually all too well aware. They expect the door suddenly to open; they know, in general, the sort of thing which will happen next. Indeed, so insistent is this sense of a larger logic that it appears to be autonomous. The actual relationship between human effort and comic sequence is apparently inverted, in that human activity, rather than producing it, has the task of fitting appropriately into the sequence. When the entrance of the Marion actress feels comically just right, she is said to have excellent 'comic timing'. As a performer she is sensitive to the inner logic of the sequence that in part she constructs.

One of the pleasures in watching farce is the enjoyment of displays of 'timing'. A well-timed comic accident is a fantasy of fulfilment. While the character may be tripped up, the performer offers an image of human physical ability completely adjusted to the sequence in which it operates, completely filling the space allocated to it, delivering everything required, and enabling the sequence to be complete. Timing is part of a dramatic rhythm, which in turn relates to the experience of culture. Let's unpack this by beginning with dramatic rhythm.

Dramatic rhythm

All drama has to organise its own temporal flow. This organisation is its rhythm. It is felt in 'the functioning of structure, beats and accents, tension and release' and through these has an effect on its audience (George 1980: 12; see also Hadomi 1988). Most contemporary theatre workers would recognise, and probably use, the words on George's list. In a good rehearsal, says Bogart, 'You place your hands on the pulse and listen' (2001: 52; see also Laban 1960;

Barker 1977; Bogart 1995, Rabkin 1999; Hodge 2000). My interest here is in the relationship between dramatic rhythm and a sense of bodiliness.

A way into that can begin with Francis Fergusson's (1953) book, *The Idea of a Theater*, first published in 1949. In *Oedipus Rex*, says Fergusson, the clear 'tragic rhythm of action' is produced by a sequence of purpose, passion, perception (1953: 31): purpose moving forward encounters crisis, which leads to a new perception which redefines purpose and initiates a new movement. Taking this model from Kenneth Burke's work on rhetoric, Fergusson then mapped it onto an account of ancient ritual form as it appears in Greek tragedy, which he got from the Cambridge School of Classical Anthropology. Through its rhythm drama is linked back to its supposed primitive roots. The firmness of that link accounts for its power over audiences.

Fergusson's focus was limited to a supposed ritual origin. A broader general connection between dramatic rhythm and human life was proposed by Suzanne Langer (1953), who argued that particular dramatic rhythms related to different aspects of biological process. Comedy, for example, presents the 'rhythm' of a continually renewing life process. Against that may be set the movement towards death of almost all living forms, which has 'a series of states that are not repeated: growth, maturity, decline. That is the tragic rhythm' (1953: 323).

For Langer, 'The total action is a cumulative form; and because it is constructed by a rhythmic treatment of its elements, it appears to grow from its beginnings. That is the playwright's creation of "organic" form' (1953: 356). Or as Jacques Lecoq was to put it (in French in 1997), 'To enter into the rhythm is ... to enter into the great driving force of life itself' (2000: 32). This rhythm makes drama something deeper than an ordinary imitation, for rhythm connects through not to the intellect but to the basic bodily processes of human life: in 'the realm of physiology ... the basic vital functions are generally rhythmic' (Langer 1953: 355). A similar point was made by Henri Lefebvre when he argued that rhythm has to do with bodily need (1992: 205). By contrast 'conscious acts' tend to be 'not repetitive' (Langer 1953: 355). The point, says Langer, is not to turn the play into an illustration of the world outside it but to attend to the 'created form' itself: 'Tragic action has the rhythm of natural life and death, but it does not refer to or illustrate them; it abstracts their dynamic form' (1953: 360).

Langer's emphasis on a bodily, rather than intellectual, engagement with drama was restated by Beckerman's attempt to explain in detail how drama works on an audience. It is done, he suggests, by manipulating the processes whereby audiences attend to a performance, setting up a 'rhythm of involvement and disengagement' (1970: 41). This rhythm is generated from the sequence, and intensities, of the 'segments' out of which the performance is made. To engage an audience, a 'theatrical segment must have a rhythmic character. Its pulsation must be organic, involving not so much a beginning, middle, and an end, but intensification and decrescence' (1970: 51). This pulsation is present even in non-verbal performance – in an acrobat's show, the somersault is the 'crux', the lead-in is 'intensification', and the relaxation into bowing is 'decrescence'. The rhythm derives from physical rather than representational processes, and interacts with the bodily, rather than conscious, process of watching.

The model of intensification, crux and decrescence is intended as a move beyond Aristotelian drama, something applicable to all performance, not just that which is dramatic. Thus, while a written play may seem more constructed, more sophisticated, than an acrobatics display, it still has

> A rhythm of intensification and decrescence ... and it is awareness of this rhythm that makes play reading enjoyable. By becoming sensitive to the open spaces in the dialogue, we begin to feel the gestures, the reactions, the pauses that they imply, and thus begin to sense the pattern of the action.
>
> (Beckerman 1970: 62)

Note what the concept of rhythm opens up here: an awareness of it can turn reading into feeling, it can produce bodily engagement with the dramatic text. It is a method of corporeal reading.

Beckerman's attempt to explain the precise bodily engagement of the reader as much as the audience can be supplemented with a model from literary theory. Beginning from poetry rather than drama, Hans Ulrich Gumbrecht (1994) says that rhythm in speech is experienced both through perception (through identifying sound qualities produced by a voice) and kinaesthetically (defined as an awareness of one's own body as organ of sound production or reception). Speaker and listener become as one through their shared bodily awareness of rhythm.

In this respect rhythm, says Gumbrecht, has three main functions, of which two will concern me here. It is 'affective' and it is 'coordinating'. The 'affective' function derives from the inability to separate the form of the rhythmic utterance from perception by one's own body. This works to undo the normal behaviour of a 'civilized' body, which has learnt to defer or repress involuntary body movements triggered by perceptions of, say, danger. In 'prehistory', says Gumbrecht, drawing on G. H. Mead, bodily stimulation inevitably, and simultaneously, accompanied such perceptions. In 'civilization', through conceptual refinement, dangers can be anticipated as future events, and the bodily response to them thus becomes a matter of choice. Rhythm's effect amounts then to 'a reshaping of "lucid consciousness" into conditions that border on the "trancelike"' (Gumbrecht 1994: 178).

From here Gumbrecht goes on to demonstrate how rhythm coordinates behaviours. To do this he uses Maturana's notion of 'consensual zones', which occur when two systems are coupled. In a simple coupling one system reacts to a change in the other. In consensual zones of the second order, behaviours arising from the primary interactions between systems are in turn shaped by the process of interaction. Language belongs here, being capable of 'constantly new reactions to the newly produced parts' of the consensual zone. As such it is productive. But rhythm is non-productive, simply offering 'a recurrence of behavioral sequences'. It is thus in consensual zone one. Here there is no mechanism for differentiation between orders of interaction. Thus: 'The *behavior-coordinating function*' of rhythm 'is characterized by the absence of a difference between the self-reference of one coupled organism and the self-reference of another' (Gumbrecht 1994: 180).

Gumbrecht's language-based work offers a more detailed way of underpinning Beckerman's points about the effects of dramatic rhythm. His model does not assume that the mere bodiliness of rhythm will automatically guarantee its effect on an audience. There is a need to specify the particular operation of rhythm on perception. But the model is useful in another way too.

It stresses that rhythm in part *produces* the body, stimulates bodily movement, un-civilises. In the work on dramatic rhythm up to Beckerman there was a tendency towards an idea that rhythm is in touch with the processes of natural life. That idea famously had expression in the late 1940s in the work of Rudolph Laban, who argued that the child was born with a natural desire to move; it 'repeats rhythmic actions for the sake of moving' (1988: 17; see also Laban 1960: 17). A play that has dramatic rhythm itself is seen as 'living', developing the characteristics of a body, with its pulsations and so on. Thus, in short, at the heart of 'dramatic rhythm' there is the human body. It gives its life to the play, for the play is an art of live bodies. Bodiliness not rhythm appears to be the crucial factor.

At the same time, however, Beckerman suggests that the body is a function of the dramatic text. The 'open spaces in the dialogue' imply 'gestures' and 'reactions'. This assertion leads into an apparent contradiction. In the written play, however 'living' it seems, these bodies are in actuality constructed by the written text: gestures implied by spaces in dialogue. For a person who reads the play prior to performing it, s/he is discovering its implied gestures in order later to make these gestures 'live'. As Gumbrecht's model would have it, it is the rhythm which works on the perception, and stimulates the body.

Thus, as I describe in Chapter 1, the written text produces its particular body, suggesting to it the gestures and breath patterns it should make, just as the training regimes of an acrobat produce a body that can automatically adjust effort and balance as it somersaults securely. The acting bodies thus formed are specific to particular sorts of text and theatre, and hence they are both shaped by, and contribute to, the 'dramatic rhythm' of the text. As an agent of body rhythm the acting body works on the bodies of the watching audience. Let's track this, then, by looking first at the production of what I am calling body rhythm

Producing body rhythm

The most obvious cases of body rhythm in performance may be those where body is structured by music or collective, non-musical, rhythm – dance and drill. Another case where the body is clearly governed by rhythm is in the delivery of emphatically metrical verse. Take the example that follows.

New York, 1930: a workers' theatre group is performing a sketch that depicts how capitalist industry oppresses its workforce. The fictional boss shouts instructions at his employees:

> Faster, faster, shake it up.
> No one idles in this shop.
> Time is money, money's power.
> Profits come in every hour.
> Can't stop profits for your sake.
> Tempo, tempo, keep awake.
> (Bradby et al. 1980)

The whole sketch – called *Tempo, Tempo* – is written in this metre, and it is internalised in the body through the work that is necessary in order to deliver and sustain the verse rhythm. This entails an organisation of enunciation and breathing, deploying effort through a range of muscular units. The thorax expands and contracts.

In his efforts to revitalise theatrical practice, Artaud suggested that the way to discover the all too often neglected musical tempo of drama was through the mechanism of breathing, and in particular the distribution of breath (1970: 90). While the body can be trained to control its breathing, the tendency is to breathe where the text marks it – by metre or syntax. This is very obvious in the verse of *Tempo*, but in the apparently more natural blank verse there is still the basic structure of a iambic rhythm – together with a rhythm derived from syntactic units. And it's those that also structure prose. Thus the characteristic carriage of the body in Wildean comedy, with the chin high and the chest raised, may well derive not only from the postures of late nineteenth-century fashionable display (Kaplan and Stowell 1994) but also from the breath production required for the epigrammatic syntax. So too, as I observed of Restoration 'wit', the timing of interpersonal exchanges will induce rhythmicity. Van Leeuwen says that: 'Like all human action, speech has rhythm, a regular pulse. In conversation speakers even attune to one another's rhythm, so that the same pulse underlies the speech (and gestures) of both' (1999: 42). But there are other factors at work besides speech.

Ayckbourn's *Absurd Person Singular* opens with Jane in her kitchen. This is described as a 'model kitchen' for its day (1972), albeit on a 'modest scale'. Jane is 'bustling round wiping the floor, cupboard doors, working surfaces – in fact, anything in sight – with a cloth. She sings happily as she works' (1979: 13). The text's instruction sets up a number of frames which between them produce the particular body here – setting, costume, required activity, required and 'accidental' sound (her singing, the bustling and wiping). The stage set controls the shape and dimensions of the space within which the body can move. It also affects range, character and quantity of movements: a fitted kitchen has lower cupboards, upper cupboards, drawers, surfaces. Where the set is practicable the body can stoop and reach, can interact with the setting at many various levels and places; but each gesture has a physical limit set to it, not simply by the dimensions of the space but because drawers and cupboards will only open in particular ways. It is busy activity but contained activity. The body does what the set allows it to do: a director such as Richard Foreman very consciously sets this up: 'The objects I build and incorporate into the set are meant to suggest, through their design, different ways that the performer can manipulate his body' (1992: 64). Different possibilities are offered by a blasted heath and a fitted kitchen. So too, different possibilities could be offered by the costume the performer wears, not only in its physical characteristics, its weight and shape, but also in what it suggests about its appropriate use. Jane is dressed for a party: the dress will in part control how she walks and bends, but so too the effort to keep it clean and smart will affect the quality of her movement.

The opening direction requires a basic repetitive activity from the performer's body, wiping surfaces. Any such simple work exemplifies what Laban calls 'occupational rhythms', with their pattern of exertion and recovery (1988: 32). If the activity were polishing handles, putting away crockery, picking up flecks of dust, there would be more variety. But the required activity is uniform, and because the kitchen is of the sort to which suburbia of 1972 aspired there are many surfaces to wipe. Jane's vocal text is simply singing. It signals happiness in her work. It also signals self-absorption, and a degree of vulnerability. This is deliberately not sound projected out to the audience, nor is it the ambient sound of the stage. It is isolated amongst the rest of the noise that accompanies the opening of a show, as an audience settles. Its internal song rhythm is subjected to a larger, more haphazard scheme of noise. Lastly here, the settling of the audience recalls a further frame to the performer's body, one unmentioned in the text's directions. The performer knows that the genre is farce; many of the audience may know this too. In this genre order, and its attendant properties of tidiness and cleanliness, will usually become disordered. So too self-absorption is usually broken in on by others. The wiping, then, is a sort of quotation, not so much of actual suburban behaviour as of typical farce behaviour.

The Jane body has a rhythm of its own – it is indeed a performance of being self-absorbed. It is also, however, an image of a body caught up by a rhythm. Jane's activity is perhaps less a controlling force on the kitchen than a function of it. At the end of the act, after the disastrous drinks party, Ayckbourn reprises his own image. Jane is again alone in the kitchen: 'She picks up the damp cloth and wipes first where the glasses were standing and then slowly, in wider and wider circles, till she has turned it, once more, into a full-scale cleaning operation. As she cleans she seems to relax. Softly at first, then louder, she is heard to sing happily to herself' (1979: 46). Jane's 'real' characteristics, her basic bodily rhythm, reassert themselves after the hilarious panics. It is a picture of both calm and entrapment, where the work is not so much human decisiveness as a function of setting; effort is not expended to transform anything, simply to be. The 'real' rhythm of Jane is the rhythm of her kitchen. The re-emergence of the singing seals the irony on this utopia – a perfectly content abandonment of self in the circumstances of the 1972 dream-home fitted kitchen.

The precision of that particular farce-body rhythm, and its constituent elements, can be highlighted by contrast with a moment taken from John Latimer's popular barn-storming 1840s' version of that domestic horror tale, *Maria Marten*. Following a dream premonition by her mother, Maria's father arrives in the barn where Maria's body is buried. He begins to dig. The action of digging produces a very different bodily rhythm from that of wiping. There is more exertion, and, since the spade goes in and out of earth, more pronounced rhythm. Here too, as with the wiping, music will probably have accompanied the activity. *Maria Marten* is, however, melodrama, so the music comes from the pit band. Mr Marten's digging body would not so much be isolated by music as at one with it. He is the agent that will enable a revelation of the truth. There is a lantern regularly refocused on the digging, and snatches of conversation as bits are revealed. All emphasise the passage towards the necessary discovery of the horrific sight. While Jane in her kitchen gives herself to smooth surfaces, closed doors, preserved appearances, Mr Marten in the barn penetrates, disrupts, opens. In each case the body rhythm is established by a specific muscular activity and a sound text that supports the movement.

The muscular activity will be modified by the dimensions of its range and reach (size and shape of kitchen or barn) and by its material accoutrements (costumes, props): the weight of the spade requires a disposition of balance in a way that a wiping cloth does not; a costume can constrain muscle groups by tightness or weight – ruffs, corsets, cloaks. And the overall rhythm of the body will in part be conceptually determined. This is fixed at the most local level by the actor's understanding of the character's positioning in the narrative and in the immediate fictional setting (Jane as a function of the suburban house, Mr Marten as an agent of discovery and change).

At a more general level it is fixed by assumptions about what farce or melo-drama are. This is part of the process of preparation for the performance. In rehearsals for the Ayckbourn play, the Jane actress will very likely have had her body inducted into the typical shape of farce (even though Ayckbourn himself would recommend that she plays it for real). Actress, director and company will also, presumably, have experience and expectations, derived from their cultural knowledge, of the playing style and genre. The body rhythm produced by rehearsal partly comes from physical training and partly from conceptual assumptions. Each might be supposed to govern the production, for instance, of a generically appropriate relationship between body and setting. So in rehearsal a farce actress may well attend to gesture, timing, balance around the opening of doors, in a way which is of less concern to the naturalist actress. What emerges, however consciously, is a displayed attitude to doors which coincides with the expectations, however conscious, of the farce audience. So farce plotting and set don't simply produce a specific range and dimension of movement, they also call for a certain quality of movement – the performance of an appropriate farce assumption, for instance, about the liabilities of doors. Body rhythm, then, is partly muscular deployment and partly ideological deployment.

Pause

Now that I have sketched in the concept of body rhythm here, I want to pause and summarise the overall argument.

The contention in this chapter is that a play's rhythm works on an audi-ence. It does so through the agency of the performer body rhythm which stimulates response in audience bodies. The audience bodies are not, how-ever, without their own rhythm, which is derived from their everyday lives. In watching, the rhythm of their bodies may be confirmed or drawn into a new rhythm by the play. For dramatic rhythm has a relationship to, but doesn't always replicate, the dominant rhythms of its culture. At a concep-tual level what might appear to be contested or confirmed is a proper atti-tude to time. Physiologically, however, the work is done through body rhythm. Thus body rhythm is the agency whereby a play may negotiate with its audience an affirmation of or deviation from the rhythmic experience of their everyday lives.

Dancing through life

This argument has already been foreshadowed in a different disciplinary area, dance. Very obviously music, or an equivalent, supplies the rhythm that is taken up by the body. But in certain dance practices this rhythm explicitly relates to a recognisable real world, both in deriving itself from that world and in reflecting it. Thus for Rudolph Laban in 1950, although the performer 'uses the same movements as any ordinary working person, he arranges them into rhythms and sequences which symbolise the ideas that inspire him' (Laban 1960: 93; see also Burt 1998). Laban's position here follows on from earlier German musicology. In 1896 Karl Buecher argued in *Arbeit und Rhythmus* (1896) that work led to music, for in all societies each time of year has its own 'work sounds', and each type of work its own music; rhythms have an influence on work and techniques of work shape worksongs (quoted in Blacking 1987: 57). A very similar position, closer in date to Laban, argued that poetry developed from songs anciently established to keep a unified work rhythm (see for example Caudwell 1937). But even modern industrial work, Laban said, despite its negative effects, can form the basis for the development of a new form of dance which will assist in coping with the modernity of 1948:

> the great variety of operations in the more than eighteen thousand occupations of modern man demands the study and mastery of the common denominator of the technical exertions involved in all his working actions. The common denominator is the flow of movement.
>
> (Laban 1988: 11)

Without necessarily being consciously derived from working activity, dance could still be associated with a felt sense of modern labour. The celebrated example of this, contemporary with both Buecher and Laban, is that of the Tiller Girls, founded in England around 1890, who did highly drilled routines in rigorously geometric lines. The mode spread to Europe and the USA, with Tillers performing at the Ziegfeld Follies in 1922 (Nield 2004). In a 1927 essay Siegfried Kracauer likened the repetitive steps in long lines to the operation of a factory machine (Burt 1998; Franko 2002). But the parallel was also apparent to the women themselves, who spoke, somewhat playfully, of being 'Tillerised' by the training – a pun on the system of organising factory labour famously devised by F. W. Taylor (Bailey 1996; see pp. 88, 147).

Body rhythm in dance, then, has been said to relate to both the lived experience of 'social rhythmicity', through work rhythms impacting on the body (though it could also be the rhythms of city life), and a more conscious sense of the speed and mechanisation – the temporal flow – of the age. Social rhythmicity and temporal flow will, inevitably, also be experienced by the audience. This is a point argued by analysts of social dance. Tagg, as a musicologist, asks how 'individuals socialise their time sense through music in different cultural contexts' (1984: 24). Of the dance craze of the 1970s, disco, he argues that the music's metronomic beat invites dancers to accept regular clock time, as contrasted with the effects of rock. In the case of urban blues, a music that had begun in a rural environment was adapted to the new gridwork streets, rectangular blocks and machinic work of the city. The development of the new musical form, Tagg argues, was a vehicle which assisted people's bodily adaptation: 'the performer or listener could be preparing himself affectively for the rhythm and sounds of the life he has to lead in an attempt to master it on an emotional level' (1984: 29). Or as Blacking puts it more generally: 'Dance and song can be understood as primary adaptations to environment; with them, mankind can feel towards a new order of things and feel across boundaries' (1987: 60). Building on Tagg's work Frith (1998) insists that rhythm is always a cultural, not a natural, phenomenon. Its appreciation is socially learnt. Nevertheless, the experience of music can appear to absorb the dancer into 'implacable sonic flow' (Frith 1998: 155), an ideal time outside the everyday. Music, and dancing, are ways of experimenting with time.

Drawing the above points together, we can suggest that at a dance performance two or three different rhythms are present – the rhythm of the show and its bodies and the rhythm already internalised in the audience bodies, from their everyday lives. This second rhythm may have an extra element, which is the audience's own experience of dancing. The dance performance becomes a negotiation, through body rhythm, of the experience and sense of temporal flow in a particular culture.

Muscular loyalties

If that is the model from dance, can it be applied to drama?

I have noted how the Jane actress may have prepared for delivering farce. The reference point for her is not the world of work but the conventions of a genre. There are, however, other methods of preparation of the performing body which much more consciously engage with the 'lived' as that which is explicitly located outside dominant theatrical practice. By way of example, Alison Hodge describes the 'night running' which features in Gardzienice's training. Stamping their feet on the ground a bunched group run in darkness over uneven ground (Hodge 2000: 236). Or, describing his own practice, Richard Foreman attempts to use 'the raw materials of everyday life to externalize on stage a rhythm and sensibility that exist deep inside me' (1992: 30). Whether the focus is outward, to a body under actual duress, or inward, to a sensibility that can find no existing equivalents in the world, these preparations seek to bring to the audience, through the rhythms of body and performance, an authentic inwardness. For the Gardzienice running enables a sense that the 'inward self' is growing (Hodge 2000: 236).

These two examples, out of many possible ones, are of their period in that they are more interested in the limits of subjectivity than the world of work. The parallel with the dance examples I noted above could be made more precise, however, if we looked at material from a similar period. I want to do that now, though not mainly to elaborate on connections between performance and work. My example is intended, instead, to introduce a further stage of the argument.

In 1922 the Soviet theatre maker Meyerhold made some notes on physical preparation for actors:

> If we observe a skilled worker in action, we notice the following in his movements: (1) an absence of superfluous, unproductive movements; (2) rhythm; (3) the correct positioning of the body's centre of gravity; (4) stability. Movements based on these principles are distinguished by their dance-like quality.
>
> (Meyerhold in Braun 1969: 198)

In his productions he organised all elements of the stage picture into a rhythmic unit, bringing individual bodies into harmonic relation not only with each other but with the scenography and furnishings of the stage. An individual's gestures are inserted into a larger pattern. More than this, an individual character may be played by several performers, as a rhythmically repeating image.

Three points should be noted here. First is the requirement, 20 or so years before Laban, that the performer learn from the efficiency of the worker. Second, a rhythmically coherent image ensures that the audience is always aware of the person as a member of a grouping, so that a basic tenet of Marxism is turned into a source of theatrical pleasure. Third, the concept of work is very much of its time. 'Modernism' at this period tended to romanticise the efficiency of the productive body – seen, for example, in Dziga Vertov's film *Enthusiasm* (1931) where miners' movements are abstracted and practised in unison, or in the admiration for the 'efficient' factory practices of Taylorism which Lenin shared with Meyerhold. Thus, in summary, the body rhythm here worked both to connect its audience to a world of work and to take on an attitude to that world, identified as Marxist and modernist.

What is less clear is the issue of how the rhythm works on the body of its audience. In dance it happens principally through sound. As musicologists say, sound can enter the body directly, bypassing the intellect, as vibrations (Walser 1993; also Storr 1992). In spoken or mimed performance the mechanism would be more reliant simply on kinaesthetic response, which again is supposed to be a direct impact, through the eyes, onto the nervous system. There is, however, another possible channel of rhythmic infection of the audience, and that is through the effect of 'group body rhythm'.

A very obvious example is that of *Tempo Tempo*. The advice to the worker-performers who did agitational pieces was that they be closely attentive to speaking and moving in unison with others. Charlie Mann's notes on his own sketch, *Meerut* (1933), insist that it must be thoroughly rehearsed and done with intensity, with the mass speaking 'as perfect as possible', 'staccato and clear' (Mann 1985: 106–7). The end result, as in military drilling, is production of *esprit de corps*. It works, argues de Landa, according to the mathematics of apparently chaotic phenomena, which show that when almost any group of individual members 'oscillate or pulsate' they reach a synchronised state, a 'body' greater than the individual bodies (de Landa 1998: 64; see also Foucault 1979: 151–2; McNeill 1995).

The creation of a 'group body' has an effect on those in the group. McNeill (1995), for example, tracks the development of gymnastics clubs, from their formation in 1811 as part of the revival of Prussian identity after defeat by the French through to mass gymnastic displays in the 1920s and 1930s and their function in defining national and political consciousness. Alongside what happens to those within it, the display of the rhythmic 'group body' facilitates expansion of the group. Watchers want to participate in that group body, to share its rhythm. McNeill suggests that the pleasure for individuals in the drilled group is that 'surrendering personal will to the command of another, while simultaneously merging mindlessly into a group of fellow subordinates, liberates the individual concerned from the burden of making choices' (1995: 131). This potentially also describes the effect of witnessing or participating in a rhythmic performance, where indeed the effect of the body-group rhythm operates to blur the separation between witnessing and participating. That is how it worked for Hitler's rallies, with their 'muscular expressions of loyalty' (McNeill 1995: 147).

Hitler's was a consciously brutalist version of it. In his seventeenth-century bid to establish absolutist culture Louis XIV introduced elaborate courtly dancing alongside military parades. This version perhaps more conspicuously activates the pleasures in self-display as the route into participation in social rhythmicity. The pleasure of joining in with a 'group body', or imagining that you could, is perhaps one of the pleasures of performance in general.

Getting there in time

In the case of Meyerhold and *Tempo Tempo* the body rhythm, both individual and group, was explicitly connected to a sense of temporal flow in society. *Tempo Tempo* addressed itself to industrial workers with experience of monotonously regulated time. In so far as rhythm is the organisation of temporal flow, the passing of time here is constituted by the rhythm of the factory machine. The connection between rhythmic delivery and the supposed experience of industrial production is made explicit. And the precision of the link between the performance and its audience's culture in turn demonstrates the sketch's authority to speak to them – and for them. Meyerhold's

purposes were less locally agitational but his attitude to work and its efficien-
cies was, as I have noted, very much of its time.

These observations take me to the next stage of the argument. I've said
that a show has body rhythm which works on the bodies of its audience. That
audience, we must now note, arrives with a sense of temporal flow, knowing
and feeling how time is conceived and properly observed in their culture.

That both Meyerhold and the performers of *Tempo* should be so concerned
with rhythm and time is itself symptomatic of the culture of modernism. Historians of the period have shown how, throughout it, contemporaries were
observing that society was becoming mechanised, moving faster, producing
'intensification of nervous stimulation' as Simmel put it in 1903 (Simmel 1997:
175). Cultural commentators noted that the emerging artform of film seemed
peculiarly appropriate, in its capacity for instant transitions and discontinu-
ities, to this new faster society (Donald 1995). That proposition constitutes
what has been called the 'modernity thesis'. In his review of that thesis Ben
Singer suggests that its most controversial element is an assumption that 'the
intensity of modern experience generated in individuals a psychological
predisposition toward strong sensations' (2001: 103). Such an assumption
seems to be predicated on the idea that human biology is flexible enough to
change in relation to environmental shifts, which is unlikely. But, says Singer,
recent neurobiological work has identified 'neural plasticity': 'neuron properties and connectivities that change as a function of visual experience'
(2001: 106–7), producing flexibility of response to the environment. Furthermore, without making an argument about the sensory apparatus, it is
possible to suggest a qualitative as opposed to structural change in perception: 'a key qualitative modification of perception caused by metropolitan
experience would involve patterns of eye movement as the individual faces
diverse stimuli' (2001: 108–9). Human strategies for attending to and making
sense of phenomena around them can be learnt and altered.

Perhaps the most important part of Singer's argument for our purposes
here is that he takes seriously what contemporaries said about the bodily
experience of urban modernity. Walter Benjamin talked about nervous
impulses flowing through the body. After summarising the processes of
'psychophysiological excitation', stress production, Singer asks in relation to
the urban sensory overload: 'what does the experience involve on a physical
level?' (2001: 116). From here he can return to where he started, to suggest
that the process of adaptation to the tempo of urban life would enhance a
readiness to enjoy 'cinematic dynamism' (Singer 2001: 118). For my purposes
the process of adaptation to a social tempo might also produce assumptions
about a body rhythm appropriate to contemporary living (whatever it is).
That body rhythm can be modelled, explored, contested by the stage in relation to an audience which has its own rhythms adjusted to perceived contemporary tempo. 'I hoped', says Richard Foreman, 'that the rhythm of my

plays of the late seventies, early eighties, would induce a fast scanning mechanism in the spectator's brain' (1992: 22).

The late melodrama studied by Singer coincided with the period of supposed 'speed-up'. If one moves to middle-period melodrama one can observe as much concern for time, but felt in a different way. One of the famous big effects of Boucicault's *The Corsican Brothers* (1852) comes in two parts. At the end of Act 1 the hero's brother, who is in another country, appears gliding up through the hero's floor, then walks through the wall, while the back of the scene disappears to reveal a glade in the Forest of Fontainebleau where the brother lies dead. Then Act 2 scene 4 opens as an 'exact reproduction' of this tableau (Boucicault 1987: 126). The thrill comes not only from seeing across impossible distance but also from the experience of simultaneity. When the stage transforms itself instantaneously from one setting to another, and especially when it precisely replicates an event, then the time taken to travel the distance between one place and another becomes radically condensed (and the exactness of the replica in fictional time undercuts the experience of real staging time).

This apparent vanishing of time was an effect created in the mid-nineteenth century by the invention of telegraph, first demonstrated in 1837, then publicly exhibited in 1841. The speed taken by information was no longer bound within assumed relationships between time and distance. But telegraph only made actual what the stage had already imagined. Earlier on melodrama had developed the sudden transformation scene. It asked for modes of acting that specialised in moments of silent individual apprehension and mutual realisation. In these moments the body acts as if it is in two places at once, both here now and reliving trauma of the past (Shepherd 1994). In the suspense narrative, when it is necessary to make a discovery or escape before the inevitable happens, time duration has to be wished away. The audience is made to want the truth or the rescuer to arrive almost immediately.

This sort of narration was played in a society experiencing new forms of time, produced through the organisation of factory labour and the structure of the working day, which Marx so eloquently evokes in *Capital*. That new temporal flow was also produced by the imposition of standard time across the country, coinciding with the development of railways. 'Railway time' and its effects were, somewhat ambivalently, imagined by Marx's contemporary Dickens in 1848 in *Dombey and Son* (1982) (see also Kern 2003). The suspense narrative in which a hero races against the clock – perhaps to rescue a person tied to the railway track – requires for its effect that the audience assume a temporal apparatus that is separate from, and impervious to, human effort.

The general proposition is, then, that drama, not only in its explicit concerns but also in its rhythmic process, is tied to the conceptualisation of time which it shares with its audience. The various conceptualisations have been roughly mapped by historians of time. Zerubavel (1981) locates the division of medieval and modern as a change from a world governed by liturgical seasons to a society governed by the clock, precise measurement, linearity and production. Maier (1987) models concepts of time from the nineteenth century through to the present. These run from a linear time assumed by nineteenth-century bourgeois/liberal society, through fascist challenges to 'liberal' time in the 1920s and 1930s, to a post-liberal society that relaxes linear time (in concepts such as 'quality' time, 'flexi-time', video playback – and marked perhaps in the aleatoric work of Happenings). These concepts are circulated within what Maier calls a 'politics of time', where 'those who govern or want to govern advance characteristic ideas of how society should reproduce itself through time' (1987: 152).

An example of the theatrical equivalent of Maier's relaxation of linear time might be the work of the late 1950s and 1960s, which favoured that which was aleatoric, or the pause, or the cyclic structure. The Happening of the mid- to late 1950s opened up human activity to chance and arbitrariness (Suvin 1984; Kirby 1985). The atmosphere of Pinter's so-called 'Theatre of Menace' is partly constructed by pauses, those moments when dialogue parts to reveal impenetrable depths below, where the real stillness of time is asserted against the efforts to maintain daily norms. Similarly, the sense of cyclic structure favoured in the 1950s and 1960s, in a work such as *Waiting for Godot* (or indeed the first version of *Rosencrantz and Guildenstern are Dead* (1967)), produces a sense that human activity goes nowhere, that it amounts to an attempt to pass the time, avoiding any direct address to the assumed pointlessness of human life. All these games with staged time may emerge perhaps out of a shared sense of the redundancy of human agency in the new mediatised post-war culture.

We also have to deal with drama which doesn't foreground the issue of time. Before looking at an example, I want to return to Maier. Having identified his time concepts, he suggests: 'The new awareness of time was reinforced ... by the rationalization of space that distinguished the seventeenth and eighteenth centuries' (1987: 155). This had an effect on the way that builders used architectural space, so that an attitude to time is shown in the design of the late seventeenth-century grand palace. Or indeed in railways, connecting up space within standardised time. Or Hitler's imagined eternal architecture. For our purposes, if the built scene adopts an attitude to time, then perhaps scenes built for theatres do likewise, in the sense that 'scene' would mean not just the scenic setting but the structuring of the action of both scene and whole play.

To the example then: Middleton's tragedy *Women Beware Women* comes from the early 1620s. At one point it does indeed foreground time as an issue between people. But the whole play, even when not apparently discussing time, is taken up by a rhythmicity which modern audiences tend to find unsettling. As Richardson (1987) says, plays both talk about time (within the fiction) and they take time (in their staging). Many accounts of the temporal worlds of plays from different periods seek to show how what the plays say about time is culture-specific (see, for example, Bennett 1983; Spingler 1991/2; Maquerlot 1995; Venet 1995). There has been less discussion of the time that plays take.

Alvin Toffler (1970) argues that individuals carry in their heads a 'temporal map' which gives them a sense of order and duration for temporal events. For example, the schedule is a deliberately imposed temporal control. For certain socio-historical groups, such as western European puritans of the late sixteenth century, the value placed on schedule derived from a larger ethic of production and use. Scheduling stages, as it were, the proper balance between activities, and marks the ability of the individual mind to place itself in control through the instrument of the schedule. Middleton images this when the 'factor' Leantio has stolen his new wife away from her parents: rather than linger as a pair of newly-weds he parks her with his mother because he has to return to his business. The value he places on a schedule derived from a production imperative enables him to withstand the temptation simply to indulge, and 'waste' time over, his and his wife's desires. As Glennie and Thrift put it, power relations 'constitute (and are constituted by) practices about time' (1996: 292). A clash between time practices can be dramatised in a way which negotiates, confirms or contradicts, the audience's assumptions about time.

The unsettling rhythmicity in *Women Beware Women* may derive from its dissolution of expected proprieties about tragic body rhythm. In phrasing it that way I am skirting around what an original audience may have felt, because we don't know. The play's critical, and theatre, history in the twentieth century, however, tends to suggest that tragic expectation is thwarted. The most notorious example is the killing of several characters in a court masque at the end. It is often felt as too fast, and too mechanical. Indeed, the bodies are explicitly caught up into the machine of the masque (one dying in mid-air). The dramaturgy might be anticipated by moments such as the dialogue in Act 4 between Leantio and Bianca, both now prostituted and both now lavishly dressed. The mode of the exchange, in verbal terms, apes the sets at wit common in earlier comedies. They each inspect the other's clothing and furnishings, both condemning and enjoying the wealth. So the body postures are of display and critical observation, neither having ethical authority, both caught into an engine of repetition. Again in Act 4 the Cardinal arrives morally to reprove his lecherous brother. He has two lengthy speeches, his entry is accompanied by lights – which remain burning for the whole scene of moral enlightenment. His brother does indeed fall to penitent weeping. But after the Cardinal's exit, he notes that his lover's husband is due to be killed tonight so he can enjoy her legally tomorrow. The big effect, with its rhetorical words and lights, is trashed. In this respect, as in the others, the spatiality and rhythm that might be assumed proper to early seventeenth-century tragedy seem to be distorted, disallowing appropriate cathexis of the tragic body. Within a larger scheme Middleton's dramaturgy may be seen as a staging post in the gradual move towards replacing tragic cathexis with tragi-comedy and the development of the self-knowing quotedness of 1630s drama.

The 24-hour clock

An audience arrives with the attitude to time of its culture. But it also arrives with a body structured, physically engaged, by its culture. It is in its engagement with this that the play does its deepest work.

I need first to explain the point about the audience arriving with a body rhythm of its own. A society's mode of temporal organisation helps to produce body rhythms. As Zerubavel (1981) says, the 'temporal spacings of recurrent activity' inform the rhythmicity of social life. A body that clocks on and off will learn particular expectations about temporal organisation and live them as the rhythm of daily life. Early in the twentieth century F. Matthias Alexander observed that the body can be put under stress, and physiologically distorted, by the routines of work. He developed regimes of physical education to counter this effect and restore the body to balance and health. The deep emotional and psychic effect of muscular stimulation or constraint began to be tracked at a similar date. In 1915 Walter Cannon noted, in his book *Bodily Changes in Pain, Hunger, Fear and Rage*, the 'close relation between emotion and muscular action' (1953: 225). And from here developed a tradition of exploring the emotional/psychic response to rhythmic stimulus (see, for example, Neher 1962; also the overview in McNeill 1995). This has tended to foreground explorations of drumming, trance and shamanism, but Alexander, and later, in the 1940s, Moshe Feldenkrais and Laban, had a broader sense that the body responded to, and was stimulated in particular ways by, the rhythms of work and everyday life.

If the body in general internalises social rhythmicity, then bodily effects in theatre presumably flow from the placing of performance attendance in relation to the rest of daily life – such as, for example, the Elizabethan afternoon performance which the legislators of the city saw as a distraction from the working day and potentially a threat to evening prayer; the evening performance in an industrial neighbourhood which comprises a series of shows over a four-hour period; the one-off play seen before or after dinner at a restaurant; a weekly visit as part of a fairly closed self-referential group known as the Town; the yearly civic event of the English medieval town or fifth-century Athens. Each of these impresses on the audience body differing regimes of dress, behaviour, and 'occasion'; each requires or leads to differing amounts of activity surrounding the theatre visit. When the body arrives it is already in a more or less heightened state of openness to rhythmic possibility.

And in this state of openness it is confronted by the play's own rhythms. These rhythms will encompass the physical activity of the performers (body rhythm, individual and group), the shape of the work as temporal flow (dramatic rhythm), and the work's own declared attitude to time. It will also be encouraged to take pleasure in the bodily event or rhythm offered for attention. Acrobats, gymnasts or dancers are celebrated because of what their bodies can do, rather than what messages they carry. But spoken drama also offers opportunities for fixing pleasurable focus, creating cathexis, on a sort of acrobatic body, being dextrous for its own sake. Examples might be the speed and precision of repartee, the gravitas of soliloquy, the precisely timed farce entry. Alternatively there are those moments of calculated displeasure, the negative cathexes, such as the early modern mad body that cannot sustain the stillness of soliloquy, the Restoration fop whose repartee is too esoteric or overdone. A pleasure choice between two body rhythms is one way in which the stage locks the spectating body into its negotiations over rhythm.

Another way is a choice between perceptions of temporal flow and attitudes to time. There is, argues Eviator Zerubavel, an ongoing tension in people's lives between an 'organic' and a 'mechanical' periodicity (1981: 11): the one seeming to flow from natural requirements; the other seeming to be imposed in the form of scheduling. In Lynch's argument this tension is characterised as an opposition between body and mechanical time. This positioning of organic as good against the mechanical as bad can be seen as symptomatic of the moment when it emerged, within a culture that tended to stress the value of 'play' and achievement of freedom through the liberated body.

And it is within that culture that Ayckbourn invented Jane. So let's end by seeing what a 'rhythm analysis' (in Lefebvre's phrase) would make of her.

The hostess is in crisis. She needs to buy more tonic without anyone noticing. And then she pauses, temporarily frozen into immobility because her kitchen only has a 24-hour clock. In 1972 this would have felt very modern, and specifically 'European'. Its effect is that she has to calculate what the 'real' time is, her body caught into stasis by a new mode of measuring time: '*She runs to the centre of the room and looks at the clock*. Nineteen-twenty-one. [*Hurried calculation*] Thirteen – fourteen – fifteen – sixteen – seventeen – eighteen – nineteen … seven-twenty-two' (Ayckbourn 1979: 30). She goes to the back door, opens it, steps out, feels the rain, closes it. Finds in a cupboard some different footwear (choosing between plimsolls and men's wellington boots); finds a large man's raincoat. Looks at clock. Goes to door, steps out, feels rain, finds from cupboard a man's hat. Debates about wearing it. Goes out.

Jane moves between clock, door and cupboard. The clock remorselessly ticks on, so she needs to get out of the door; outside the door it is raining, so she needs to protect her party clothes; the cupboard keeps yielding up the wrong objects. Each time she is in a dilemma about putting on the garment she has found, but pressure of clock and rain force her. It is a classic comedy machine.

Lynch would presumably note the opposition between body and mechanical time, with Jane's dilemmas highlighted in relation to the force of circumstances. That may be an attitude to time, but rhythm involves more than this. Jane is watched, at her first performance, by an audience in Scarborough. The play's genre, and possibly its venue, put it at some cultural distance from the more 'experimental' dramas and performances of the late 1960s, with their aleatoric or cyclic structures. Its apparent assumptions about male and female roles put it, seemingly, at some difference from 'Women's Lib'. The bodies move within 'smart'/'party' costumes, are not messy, naked, 'liberated'. It's a joke that she has to put on man's clothes. The fuss caused by the clock is an indication of how unnatural Europe is. Several elements of the play establish it as the expected culture of a regulated middle-class Englishness.

But the emphasis has to be on that which is 'expected', rather than necessarily delivered. Ayckbourn was playing games with the form. Farce was by now deep in the tradition of middle-class Englishness, popularised by the Whitehall farces, starring Brian Rix, on television. In 1972 it moved to a rhythm which was culturally secure and familiar at a time when the artistically experimental and socially revolutionary were becoming more intrusive. Fetishising timing and routine rather than pauses and gravitas, it is orderly without being solemn; entertaining but not arty. Within a couple of years or so the audience would be dancing to clock-time disco. But that audience was not at first uniformly sure about what Ayckbourn had given it.

Even as the Jane character runs through a series of hopeless dilemmas, the Jane actress has the opportunity for precisely ordering the attitudes to and relationships between clock, door and cupboard. Done well, it is highly dextrous performing. And one of the things it performs is the ability to organise, the thrill in handling several challenges at once. Within the frame of the kitchen, and dealing with a clock associated with the husband, this is a particular display of woman's capability. It is not the politics of women's liberation; it is precision within domesticity. The Jane character ends Act 1 as a sort of automaton, a function of her glossy modern kitchen. But the Jane actress plays her dilemmas within an overall skilful routine. Pleasurable cathexis attaches to her timing. This then enables the audience to share, and enjoy, a body rhythm which works to establish, at some distance from 'experiment' and 'politics', the glamour of precise timing.

5   'Look out behind you'

Lady Audley's Secret, written by Colin Hazlewood in 1863, was a sensational success. It had the right features. A young woman, apparently deserted by her husband, changes her identity and marries again – to an old man well above her station. The first husband reappears, so she kills him. But over time her crime is uncovered and she herself is revealed as being of unsound mind. In the original novel she is tucked away into a madhouse in Belgium but in Colin Hazlewood's play she goes completely mad in front of us and then dies. Dramatised for different theatres, the story found its place within the 1860s' fad for 'sensationalism' (see Hughes 1980; Kalikoff 1986; Pykett 1994).

This chapter uses Hazlewood's *Lady Audley* and its sensationalism to explore the relationship between space and bodies in performance. It begins from the assumption that the play handled its story, which was neither more nor less shocking than many other melodrama stories, in a way which felt 'sensational'. It argues that the deployment of space is a key instrument in this effect.

The opening hypothesis is that there is something about the way that the play moves that in turn moves the audience. '*Enter Lady Audley at back*' (Hazlewood 1972: 249).

A model

This is not a particularly novel hypothesis. In developing his phenom-enological approach to modern drama, Stanton Garner suggests that a partic-ular sort of visual arrangement can have its effect on spectators. Thus, in the work of Samuel Beckett, the required off-centre positioning of characters visu-ally indicates their decentredness – 'marginalized in time and space, disjointed from the gestures they make ... consigned to an unending linguistic evasion' (Garner 1994: 76). Informed by the operation of kinaesthesia, reactions to Beckett's work are 'grounded in direct perceptual response, embodied in the tensions of visual arrangement'. And these tensions are felt because they frustrate what audiences bring with them, 'the perceptual inclinations and tendencies of the spectator as visual processor of theatrical imagery' (Garner 1994: 79).

The audience arrives with 'perceptual inclinations' which, like its sense of daily rhythms, are derived from its culture. This is the material on which Beckett works, breaking those shared visual conventions. Describing this activity, Garner refers to depth and, above all, symmetry and centredness, where the audience is produced as unsettlingly always off-centre. The disturbance here derives from the upsetting of deeply held concepts and expectations, often derived from perspective and a sense that centrality in the auditorium mimics that on stage.

Bearing in mind, then, the general effect of kinaesthesia, and learning from Garner's account of Beckett, let's return to *Lady Audley* and my opening hypothesis that its effect has something to do with the way it moves. In developing and testing that hypothesis I hope to be able to add something to Garner's assertions about proximity of bodies. '*Lady Audley* (*coming down*): What do you mean?' (Hazlewood 1972: 251).

The subject of theatrical space

In 1850 Charles Dickens published an essay about one of his favourite theatres, the Britannia Saloon in Hoxton. He tells how he had difficulty finding a place in what was a hugely crowded theatre. The reason for its popularity, suggests Dickens, was in

> its being directly addressed to the common people, in the provision made for their seeing and hearing. Instead of being put away in a dark gap in the roof of an immense building … they were here in possession of eligible points of view.
>
> (Dickens n.d.: 178)

Dickens may seem to be making an obvious point, that audiences enjoy themselves better when they can see and hear the stage. But seeing, within the history of auditorium design, might be a novelty. Many audiences through history have been more able to hear than see the stage. But then the stage is not itself always the main point of focus. There are many accounts of both buildings and behaviours which suggest that parts of audiences like also to look at other parts of audiences – or to prevent that looking (McAuley 2000 does a round-up of this material). For my purposes here the interest is in how the spaces of the theatre impact upon the bodies of the spectators, and indeed produce those spectators. As Beatriz Colomina puts it: 'Architecture is not simply a platform that accommodates the viewing subject. It is a viewing mechanism that produces the subject' (1992: 83; also Sanders 1996).

Some sense of that impact of space on people is contained in Dickens's description of the Britannia. The building itself is 'immense'. This will have an effect on the experience of those inside. In an analysis of medieval cathedrals Tuan suggests that the religious imagination is encouraged by the architecture to soar upwards: 'The body responds ... to such basic features of design as enclosure and exposure, verticality and horizontality, mass, volume, interior spaciousness, and light' (Tuan 1977: 116). In some seats in the immense building of the theatre spectators will feel at the centre of things, able to see all around them, both stage and audience. Others, Dickens's 'common people', will feel themselves to be at the edges of this immensity. In a lighted auditorium they are not sitting underneath the main chandelier but in a dark space. Enclosed, not spacious, darkened. Add to this that they were 'put away' rather than 'in possession'. Architecture, as Tuan says, refines sensibility about space, and it can naturalise ideas about social organisation and hierarchy. The 'common people' in the dark are the dispossessed not the possessors of the theatre space.

But they have brought into their dark space a bodily, and psychic, experience of spaces outside the theatre. For those 'common people' who went to the theatre regularly the theatre building is one spatial experience in a series which would also include home and workplace. Home would be cramped, with small rooms putting pressure on bodies together. For those in factory work their bodies would be subjected to a different form of pressure deriving from the clear divisions of labour and the ongoing activity of the machines, each spatially embodied in the architecture and layout of the factory. In particular, suggests Hetherington, the most significant point of control was the factory door or gate: 'The door becomes one obligatory point of passage within the factory as a whole', and as the place of entry and exit the worker here was subjected to greater surveillance than at the machine (1997: 135–6). In contrast to this an audience entered the theatre on very different terms, and once inside, and put away into its dark space, it was much less available for surveillance and its comings and goings were more casual.

In this series of spaces the factory may seem the most ordered. Yet Hetherington wants to stress that its spatial arrangements were actually heterogeneous. This is part of his general attempt to identify 'heterotopic' spaces where 'the processes of social ordering were tried out' (1997: 18). While the factory seems rather dubious, the theatre is a very obvious candidate as a heterotopia. Dickens's 'common people' may feel put away, but they were less under surveillance. Furthermore, they were in a crowd. Tuan (1977) suggests crowds generate their own thrill. In the 1850 audience people were crammed together in a space they frequented regularly but in groups not necessarily defined as 'home' or 'family' (Dickens notes a large number of precocious 'young girls'). The interrelations between bodies were governed neither by domestic nor factory-machine protocols. Being on the edge of the immensity can feel like being freed from responsibility.

As Dickens noted, the architecture can not only position the focus of attention but also organise the singlemindedness with which it is attended. This, says theatre architect Iain Mackintosh, is its chief purpose – 'to provide a channel for energy' which flows each way between performer and audience (1993: 172). But while Dickens assumed that everyone would want to focus on the stage, that enterprising theatre manager Marie Wilton had other ideas. In the period after her acquisition of the Queen's Theatre in 1865 she made (or, her own self-advertisement aside, continued to make) strategic use of soft furnishings in order to mould the behaviour and composition of the audience. Seats were modelled on domestic armchairs, with antimacassars. There were curtains and the floor was carpeted. Such furnishings implied assumptions about security, class identity and behavioural codes in public. The changes coincided with another development of the 1860s, the spread of an idea imported from France, the restaurant (Chaney 1993: 73). This sort of entertainment allowed for the dissemination of a general way of being in public modelled on the behaviour codes of a particular class. The object of focus was the enactment of respectability.

Wilton, with her husband Squire Bancroft, heavily underscored this in the theatre through seating arrangements that demonstrated social stratification. This, as much as the stage, was the architectural focus of attention. And its effect was intended to make one class comfortable at the expense of another: the antimacassar as repression. The increasingly elaborate classifications of the auditorium might themselves be seen as a device for shaping the audience's sense of itself. The model I am using here is drawn from Mark Wigley's work on Alberti's text on domestic architecture:

> There is a 'natural' relationship between the system of classification, the spaces, and that which is being classified. The wife learns her 'natural' place by learning the place of things. She is 'domesticated' by internalising the very spatial order that confines her.
>
> (1992: 340)

Audiences can learn to discover themselves in the new spatial order. A process of internalising gives access to a new way of enjoying and feeling good about oneself. Bourdieu says that 'taste' is 'the source of the system of distinctive features which cannot fail to be perceived as ... a distinctive lifestyle'. It is a classificatory system 'which is the product of the internalization of the structure of social space, in the form in which it impinges through the experience of a particular position in that space' (1989: 175). Taste enacts whether it is moved by necessity or luxury. Thus 'common people' who afford entry to middle-class theatre might become the staunchest defendants of the values they now share. Outside the theatre, the 1860s was offering new spaces where mixed audiences might feel enabled to buy in to shared values: the department store arrived.

To feel 'at home' in a place goes deeper than subscribing to its rules. It is to feel that it exists for one's use, that one is centred in it, that it has been waiting – as if incomplete – to be filled by one's presence. As Steve Pile says: 'a sense of a solid shared world and a stable sense of ourselves within that world is seen to be essential for our psychic and physical survival' (1996: 12). In a sense the space is telling us who we are. But we are never one thing. Self-definition is process. Nigel Thrift speaks of 'personality' as 'a continuously negotiated and renegotiated expression of social and economic relations that vary ... according to locale and region'; but also 'the study of person-ality involves ... the study of *socialization* as a process of domination *and* resistance' (1983 43).

If much of the history of the auditorium is one of dominated bodies, it is also, famously, one of resistance. The theatre building is, historically, a site of riot. When the audience returned to the newly rebuilt Covent Garden in 1809 they found the ticket prices had been put up. So for nearly three months they rioted each night in the theatre, trying to wrest back control of the pit, 'their' space. Although the activity was sustained by organised radi-cals, for it to have started at all implies that an audience doesn't always will-ingly occupy the space that has been made available to it (Baer 1992). Even in 1880 in the leading comedy theatre, the Haymarket, there was some first-night consternation that the refurbishment had abolished the pit. Audiences, then, arrive at the theatre not simply with assumptions about conventions of watching a play but with the spatial experience of the rest of their lives.

So there needs to be a notion of the auditorium that keeps three elements in view. It is the site of a particular sort of practice – occupying a seat that has been paid for in the company of others to watch an entertainment. It is bound by rules for its use and the values inscribed into its fabrics and furnish-ings – offering, for example, a picture of a society which is both stratified and well organised. It is a place of entertainment, that produces and satisfies expectations – encouraging the emotions with which different groups and individuals embark on and sustain what for them will be a good night out.

These three elements of the auditorium space are intended, I hope not too clumsily, to be the equivalent of Lefebvre's tripartite model for the production of space: spatial practice, representation of space, representa-tional space (1992: 38–9). To illustrate the distinction between *representation* and *representational* I shall return to Dickens. He approved of the Britannia because the auditorium was 'well lighted, well appointed, and managed in a business-like, orderly manner in all respects' (n.d.: 178). Above all it made provision for all the audience to see the stage, so they 'were very attentive': 'the general disposition was to lose nothing, and to check (in no choice language) any disturber of the business of the scene' (n.d.: 179). These arrangements presumably contributed to the Britannia's reputation as a theatre which was suitable for the whole family to visit (just like the all-seater football stadium). So, even though the theatre was crammed to capacity, the crowd in its attentiveness was self-policing: it silenced interruptions; learning to be managed. For, in Dickens's opinion, 'a love of dramatic representation' is 'an inherent principle in human nature' (n.d.: 179).

The orderly auditorium sustains an ideological assumption: that open access to art will lead to appropriate, well-managed, behaviour. The properly planned theatre begins to look like what Lefebvre calls 'abstract space'. This space is associated with the development of capitalism, when labour becomes dissociated from social life, abstracted. Abstract space is 'Formal and quantitative, it erases distinctions, as much those which derive from nature and (historical) time as those which originate in the body (age, sex, ethnicity)' (Lefebvre 1992: 49). So despite the differences articulated in entry price and auditorium position the audience will respond as a coherent attentive entity. The working class exposed to the art it wants to see will become self-policing. It will indeed fall harmoniously into a place in a regime that may be described as 'business-like'.

What is pleasing about the architecture of the Britannia is that, at a time when the auditorium would be expected to be lit throughout the show, it has got rid of the dark spaces. This takes us back to Lefebvre:

> The *representation of space*, in thrall to both knowledge and power, leaves only the narrowest leeway to *representational spaces*, which are limited to works, images and memories whose content, whether sensory, sensual or sexual, is so far displaced that it barely achieves symbolic force.
>
> (1992: 49–50)

Dickens's essay on the people's amusements is an attempt to welcome the new, and to consign to the past, make a memory of, the dark spaces.

Now Lady Audley first started sharing her secret with an auditorium in which there was quite a lot of dark space. It was done in 1863 at the Royal Victoria Theatre, the old Royal Coburg, which had a reputation as a 'blood and thunder' house, with an audience principally drawn from the working-class homes in the area of the New Cut, Waterloo. Although the gallery of the Vic, which held between 1500 and 2000 people, was famous for its crowdedness, its heat and its smell, there had been relatively recent attempts to improve its facilities and regulate behaviour. Nevertheless, observers report boys on each other's shoulders and a mob on the landing on tiptoe. To someone below, the end of it was lost in shadow (Fagg 1936; Roberts 1976; Rowell 1993; Davis and Emeljanow 2001). And this gallery seems to have exerted an influence – at least on middle-class visitors if not on the theatre as a whole. For, while Davis and Emeljanow note that interior divisions 'separated out spectators according to income and social preference' (2001: 40), John Hollingshead, who visited in the 1840s, observed how the gallery hauled up 'large stone bottles of beer from the pit, and occasionally hats that had been dropped below' (quoted in Davis and Emeljanow 2001: 10). In itself it imaged the intermingling of youthful, dirty, excited bodies, but it did not stay in itself – it reached into the space below.

So the theatre's reputation could be said to be based not simply on its class ambience (which was more mixed than people like Dickens admitted), but on the conjunction between class and spatial arrangement. In Lefebvre's terms, the sensory and sensual had not been sufficiently brought into orderly illuminated rows, disciplined by the soft furnishings of knowledge and power. The theatre space, in its 'representation', fails fully to sever the connection with the working-class lives outside it. The experience and history of those lives find their representational space. So the audience, although in a different place from their labouring and domestic lives, are nevertheless not fully subjected to a wholly separate theatre domain. This is what, presumably, has bearing when in front of these indistinct subjects a drama of an upper-class lady is played.

Gestures of distinction

The image of her class position is in part an effect of spatial organisation, and in particular of gesture.

The first appearance of Lady Audley is framed by a repeated observation about her class background. Before she comes on we are told by Luke, the drunken gamekeeper, that she used to be a governess, 'a teacher of French and the *pianny*' (Hazlewood 1972: 237); after she has exited, her maid Phoebe (who is Luke's cousin and betrothed) repeats the observation that by marriage 'from a poor governess she has become mistress of Audley Court' (p. 41). In between the audience see Lady Audley showing her elderly husband his estate, entertaining him with morris dancers and dealing with his sulky daughter (from the first marriage). It is she who mainly commands the space: she leads her husband onto the stage (and later pats his cheeks); she hears the approaching morris dancers, whom she has organised; she moves across the stage to deal with Alicia, the daughter. She commands the stage just as, by implication, she is not only at home in but controls the country-house domain.

And it is not just space which she controls. The opening gesture of showing her husband his own grounds moves on to her furnishing him with his loved 'rural sports' – as it were sustaining the culture natural to those grounds. The third element in the sequence, her dealings with Alicia, is a performance of poise and emotional control in the face of Alicia's jealousy. At this juncture Lady Audley is set up as the guardian of aristocratic decorum, actively maintaining its cool. So by the time she exits these three elements have been schematically linked together to construct something which Bourdieu would call 'habitus', which is defined by 'the capacity to produce classifiable practices and works, and the capacity to differentiate and appreciate these practices and products' (1989: 170). Lady Audley displays all the customary ease of her upper-class position. But she is also in control of it – governing but no longer a governess.

The story will of course confirm that she can't maintain this upper-class ease, that she is always, underneath, the interloper. But Hazlewood's version of the tale is not interested in encouraging any uncertainty or ambivalence about this matter. In Braddon's novel the actual admission by Lady Audley that she murdered her first husband comes very late on; the novel is constructed as a detective narrative. Hazlewood shows the murder in the first act. So that thereafter when Lady Audley assumes her upper-class habitus it is seen as a constructed performance, built out of modes of carrying the body, interacting with others, occupying space. We definitely know she is a murderer, but that action does not prevent her deploying herself spatially in a way which signifies command and control.

In her spatial deployment as an aristocrat Lady Audley is doing within the fiction what a performer would do in order to create a fiction. When a performer takes an upper-class role she apes the body manner and gestures of that class. In a fashionable theatre, particularly towards the end of the century, the performer might herself be a fellow-traveller of that class. In a less fashionable theatre, the actor-manager would certainly have class aspirations. But a performer who was merely employed, even as a star, in one of the poorer theatres would not be considered as being really upper class. But that doesn't mean that she was the same as her audience. She is dressed in fine clothes, she is brightly lit, she moves in spaces that are higher and wider than working-class rooms. The inhabitants of those rooms may well be bearing on their bodies the signs of a hard life – depletion of energy, physical decay, dependency on alcohol, 'going to pieces'. The performer's body may itself be decayed, and alcoholically dependent, but it is produced for presentation, and acquires specialness from that production.

The application of this to *Lady Audley* has to be conjectural, for we know very little about the production or about its star, Mary Daly. But we do know that she is required to make 'large' gestures, ones involving breaches of everyday assumptions regarding the position of arms in relation to body, such as gesturing above the head. The staged female body will have a relationship (albeit unconscious) to bodily norms established for, and experienced by, women in the audience. A majority of the audience was presumably local, from around the New Cut. Those who were 'common people' in this area might be engaged in dressmaking, engineering, bookmaking, the shoe trade (Davis and Emeljanow 2001). The 1860s saw rapid expansion in both engineering and service industries (food, clothing). Possibly women were using their bodies to sew and prepare food. This would have involved them habitually in a very different gestural range from the extensions into space that Lady A's body could presume to make.

But at that time, in this theatre, the specialness is always framed, is always stagey. Thus the performance of upper-class ease by someone who is not of that class has about it a quality of provocation. Unlike real, 'natural', upper-class ease, this is a fiction, a mask, and masks can be ripped off. And those high and wide spaces are not really the spaces of the bourgeois, the open boulevards and high-ceilinged first-floor salons – the spaces which confirm the power of those who move through them. On stage, in a poorer theatre, those spaces are merely quoted, schematically evoked, flattened, painted. So they are in no position to confirm the authority of the body that moves through them. But nevertheless, they are not cramped like the theatre galleries and tenements.

Talking aside

There is, then, an instability around the enactment of 'distinction' in the poorer theatre. In the case of *Lady Audley's Secret* the instability is doubled within the fiction, as I noted in the first scene. Where her class lifestyle is most actively managed is the place of greatest insecurity. This comes at the moment when Lady Audley deals with Alicia. The two women are more or less the same age, but all sorts of other factors distinguish them. Alicia is 'vexed', and angry with her horse. Lady Audley shows sympathy, for the horse. Alicia's aggression has to be managed, as does Sir Michael's teasing: the stage direction requires that Lady Audley smiles. The two women greet each other as step-daughter and step-mother, but Lady Audley treats Alicia as younger – 'there, there, now go and banish that frown from your brow' (Hazlewood 1972: 241).

The differences are visually encapsulated: Lady Audley dressed as the hostess; Alicia in her riding habit, and thus not properly dressed for dinner in the country house. The dialogue between the two women, being watched by Sir Michael and Phoebe, is itself framed. It is a demonstration of decorum, a demonstration made more obvious by arranging that both parties are upper-class women, one an interloper, the other jealous. The decorum is a means of fighting a battle; and, given their sex and class, the only means available. So its rules are watched very attentively. Which means that they are being fixed on by us in the audience. The play is establishing a shared language, particularly about use of body and space, with its watchers.

But even as it teaches the framework of decorous rules, it punctuates them with three asides. Lady Audley has the first one, in reaction to Alicia's remark about secrecy: 'What does she mean by that?' (p. 240); Alicia's asides separately express contempt for Lady Audley and her maid. None of them tells us much that is new – we can already see they don't like each other. But their function is less to do with information than with production of space.

Asides assume, in their many and various ways, an interaction with an audience which differs from that in the non-aside. The gesture of speaking aside does not necessarily have anything to do with the distinction between truth and fiction, but it does – in a pretty fictional way – invite the audience to pretend that they can enter a sort of parallel world. In this parallel world they get their own special access to a character. That access is enabled by Lady Audley when her first aside is framed as a question to which the audience can supply – silently or not – the answer. The melodrama aside seems designed for a labile audience. While the character here loses control of the management of decorum, the performer does another bit of management, offering the audience a role in relation to the action, positioning them.

So in its first scene the play sets up some rules for use of the stage space. They are rules for the management of interaction of characters – the aspiration towards decorum. They also establish the separation from its audience of the playworld as one bound by upper-class propriety. In this way the audience understands what the – as it were – proper use of the stage space consists of. Movements will be planned, managed, non-clumsy. Suvin (1987) calls this 'dramaturgic' space, separating it from the 'empiric' space of the stage and auditorium. It is a separation between the visual and the tactile. The audience is physically absent from but psychically present in dramaturgic space.

That psychic presence makes the separation less clean-cut than Suvin wants it, I think. Phenomenology suggests that audiences vicariously 'live' or experience the play through the act of watching, for that act has kinaesthetic effects which can affect the 'tactile' space. The opportunity for such engagement is vividly activated in the opening scene of *Lady Audley*, when, as soon as it has positioned the audience by and entrained their bodies into the demonstration of decorum, it then produces the parallel space of the aside. In this space the audience perceives, and kinaesthetically adjusts to, the gesture of turning towards them and opening the body

[giving vent to secrecy]

which is the conventional marker of speaking aside.

Fictionally marked as a chink in the decorum, the aside feels physically like a rupture of it, as if a new space is created somewhere between the stage and the auditorium. Lefebvre calls this a 'third space' when he describes the operation of all theatre as an interplay of separate elements (actors, audience, characters, text) that enables bodies 'to pass from a "real", immediately experienced space (the pit, the stage) to a perceived space – a third space which is no longer either scenic or public' (1992: 188). For Lefebvre this third space is that which is classically theatrical.

But to start to wonder what 'classical' might denote here is to see that there may be different ways of passing from the 'real' into the perceived, third space. A sensationalist play such as *Lady Audley* could be said to invite a physically vivid living of a third space while producing it so self-consciously as to make it deliberately fragile. In this way, I would suggest that the engagement with the sensationalist performance has a lot to do with the production and management of sensational space.

'Look out behind you'

You offer the audience a space and tell them that it is a managed illusion. You encourage them to learn the rules and then start breaking them.

Part of the spatial activity of the body, along with gestures and asides, is its relationship to scene. There is a difficulty here, however, because so little seems known of this production, but I shall make some cautious conjectures. The opening scene is 'The Lime Tree Walk', famous to readers of the novel as the place where the murder happens. The lime trees form an avenue leading up to the Hall, which is seen in the distance, stage right. That avenue is stage-centre. Much is probably painted but Alicia has to enter down the avenue. It may be that Sir Michael and Lady Audley also do so, though the stage direction is not specific. The villagers and morris dancers also come on centrally. All other characters first come on from the right.

Out of these two directions of movement, the 'vertical' one – that is, the one going up and down stage – is more prominent than the horizontal. It is marked as an avenue, the lime trees are lined up in perspective; it is also the direction of the one massed entry – the villagers, etc. – of the scene. But while crowding it with bodies may emphasise the direction of movement, it also obscures the effect of those trees. They presumably provide a visual frame for a body when it stands near them, marking it out. The effect will be more available the longer a body remains in place, positioned in the perspective, assimilated into the scenic architecture. Robert and Alicia bump into just such a body when they begin to leave the stage: '*As they go up they meet Lady Audley*' (Hazlewood 1972: 244). Halfway down the vertical axis, framed by the trees, stands the aristocratic hostess. Who we've just heard has two husbands.

Centrally placed on stage, lined up in the perspective, the body occupies a space that might seem to be waiting for it – about it there is something which is, literally, fitting. The picture gives a sense of the balanced, the complete. Yet we also know something she doesn't know, that her first husband is returned. This knowledge makes her an item of narrative curiosity – what will happen when she finds out? She is thus different from us. And the trees frame her, box her in, mark her edges. So perception and knowledge play with one another, giving us something which is both satisfying scenic presence and an object of our attention. None of this is unique to Lady Audley, of course, but in thinking about her we might see how far a whole series of victims and villains have their charisma constructed by space.

As the play goes on that vertical axis regularly appears in the production of the sensational scenes. When Lady Audley's first husband George appears to her, he comes on behind her, from the back. In the next scene she herself appears 'at back' to overhear Alicia telling her father that she dislikes her step-mother. She has an aside: 'Indeed?' (p. 249), and after listening a little longer advances, centre, to join the conversation. The aside calls us into that space *behind* the conversation, and we await a downstage movement. The vertical axis has taken control of the scene. But that axis is not solely controlled by Lady Audley. Alicia uses it, and her first husband enters there unseen. What we learn, albeit unconsciously, is that this axis is a site of contestation of Lady Audley's power. And thus it figures when in Act 2 the drunken Luke confronts her with the fact that he witnessed the murder.

She has a solo speech about her guilt and resolves to silence the whisperings of conscience: 'I am Lady Audley, powerful, rich, and unsuspected, with not one living witness to rise up against me. (*Going up.*)' (p. 251). Enter Luke – by way of coinciding precisely with, embodying, the emotional rising up of all those witnesses in the audience. She commands him to go, then continues up-stage; he lets her know that he knows, and she comes down again. She has a couple of asides, reacting to what he says, and then a solo speech after he leaves: 'shall a boor, a drunkard, a ruffian, hold me in his grasp ready to crush me when he pleases?' (p. 252). The passage between the two solo speeches takes us from defiance of living witnesses to the resolution to destroy them. It also extends the effect of that vertical axis, by reaching it into the audience.

Having gone up-stage and been brought down again she then looks out into the audience, challenging ruffians to hold her in their grasp. The extension of that vertical axis takes it into virtual space, something addressed by the performers as if it were real, taken as close up to the edges of the real as possible. She asks the audience a question, which makes space for an actually vocalised answer; she has them envisage the body being grasped – penetrating the stage–auditorium divide; and her challenge to 'ruffians' plays perhaps on the gallery's self-image. The excitement here possibly derives from activating tensions within spatial perception. Tuan says that 'Seeing has the effect of putting a distance between self and object' (1977: 146). In other sensory respects distance is elided in the experience of the show in that spectators literally rub up against one another and are all in the immediate present of the sound (both musical and vocal). Distance is not wholly assured. Thus, while use of the vertical axis in pictorial space can be watched by spectators, at the transformation of the pictorial into the vividly virtual they are challenged to become participants, positioned on – or, rather, by – the line that is the key site of contestation of Lady Audley.

Towards the end of the solo speech she sees Robert coming: 'let me again resume the mask, which not only imposes on him, but on all the world' (p. 252). That final phrase is of course a challenge to the audience. They know the real Lady Audley is not the woman who sits trimming flowers, but the woman who moves up and down that vertical axis. By responding to her line, they acknowledge their place in relation to that axis – indeed, they confirm that, imaginatively, emotionally, they are positioned on it. Locked by the play's production of space into the space of the play.

This spatial production of the audience may help to explain one of the most famous emotional moments of both melodrama and pantomime. '*George enters at back, and comes down silently to her side.* Where can he be now? Still in India no doubt' (p. 245). Not in India, but BEHIND YOU! The audience is provoked to shout because it knows something more than the character. The basic mechanism is that one character asserts control in relation to another but that other is outside or evading the scheme of control. Lady Audley could apprise herself of her danger by just turning round and seeing what the audience sees. She has failed to retain full control of the space in which she speaks. In the same way she arranges for George to lose control of the space he is in. She asks to be left alone, so he goes up-stage and turns his back; then, responding to her simulated faintness, he leans over the well to dip her handkerchief in water. And she creeps up on him from behind. George becomes vulnerable when he ceases to look at the space around him. That's the moment that excites the audience. They can see what he can't see; but, more than that, they can see what they want him to see. They are doing the looking for him. Through their perception they feel they have a control of the space. If something then is allowed to happen which should not happen, the confidence of that control is threatened.

Arguably this sort of thing only works well with nineteenth-century proscenium-arch stages, as opposed to a seventeeth-century amphitheatre. For the audience has itself become entrained in a mode of looking (Crary 1999). This entrainment is sometimes associated with a mode of passive consumption. But passivity is not what the 'look-out-behind-you' moment produces. An audience shouting at and physically thrusting towards that stage may well be engaged in consumption, but it's a consumption of a fairly active sort. For this moment challenges the sense of control through perception. The audience become vulnerable to bodies that escape the control, bodies which literally creep up closer. In these moments an audience pays its money to find out what it can't have, to be vicariously exposed to risk. Even in an auditorium where there are no dark spaces, the relationship with the bought, but above all with the seen, is made incomplete.

Ascending the rope

And it's a form of spatial incompleteness which structures the play's final scene. Here Lady Audley drags on Phoebe, who is then freed from her grasp by Robert. At this Lady Audley recoils, for she thinks she had killed him. He accuses her, she asserts her wealth, and then attempts to stab him. He takes the dagger, she defies anyone to accuse her, and Luke is brought in. He is about to accuse her when Robert prevents him, to protect Sir Michael's name. Luke falls back apparently dead; Lady Audley has a triumphant aside; and Alicia brings news of her father's death. At this news Robert accuses Lady Audley himself; Luke revives to confirm the story; and then George himself walks on. Confronted by this string of men rising up against her – as if from the dead – she begins to go mad, talking 'vacantly'. In her madness she imagines she sees in front of her another resurrection – Sir Michael. All these men who had seemingly been put away press themselves into space that had been hers. She dies in front of the assembled company, in the same setting where the play opened – the lime tree avenue.

The narrative comes to an adequate end in the focus on her demolition. It is given its sense of fullness not only by the revelation of the real truth but also by the physical filling of the stage with the bodies of the resurrected men. Alongside their sober, balanced, manly accusations (and equally manly for-giveness), the woman does her manifestation of histrionics. Alongside their repeated gestures of pointing, her hands greet a non-existent person and then hold her own head. Theirs are functional gestures, bringing order to a public sphere, carrying narrative to its conclusion; hers are functionless ges-tures, proceeding from the chaos of a private mind, conspicuously redun-dant, treacherous, actorly.

What had so pleasurably positioned the audience in relation to the staged action – their avenue, as it were, into the third space – was Lady Audley's organisation of movement. Significantly there is only one entry from the avenue in the final scene (Alicia with news of her dead father). The others enter from left and right. Lady Audley's deep movement in relation to virtual spaces is replaced by lateral busyness and pointing gestures. The ending seems to enact, in front of its jostling urban audience, the removal of a space which is personal, a space in which an individual body can be centred and powerful. What sends Lady Audley mad is the undeniable presence of others. In her vacant look we see someone who cannot inhabit the space she is in. In a sort of refusal of the inevitable contingency of the world, she des-perately asks not to be touched.

'The history of social change', says David Harvey 'is in part captured by the history of the conceptions of space and time, and the ideological uses to which those conceptions might be put' (1989: 218). Theorists of the emer-gence of modernism argue that, for example, cinema, telephones, cars all alter the experience of space and time (see Chapter 4 and Singer 2001). Experience is something different from conceptions. As both these chapters have argued, conceptions of time and space have to do with the rhythm and space of the body. They in turn shape social organisation. Submission to 'collective rhythms' of work or religion is often required in social groups, Bourdieu observes, because 'the temporal forms or the spatial structures structure not only the group's representation of the world but the group itself', which leads to the 'organization of the existence of the men and the women in accordance with different times and different places' (1977: 163).

In his account of the 'badlands of modernity' Hetherington considers the Palais Royal which, in its spatial facilities and arrangements, 'allowed new forms of sociality to come into being' (1997: 17). Thus it helped to define ideas about social ordering and contributed to the process of cultural development. In so far as all spatial arrangements articulate and impact upon bodily practices, the theatre too must be seen as a site of negotiation around spatial and social identities. Within the circumscribed frame of 'sensation' drama, the organisation and manipulation of space played a part in generating the emotional response. But it is reasonable to suppose that, if this localised argument holds true, it can be extended to all forms of theatre. For they are all materially based in bodies arranged in specific spatial relationships. And for theatre, unlike some other sites of spatial negotiation, there is a doubling in that the material organisation of space and time – in the activity, say, of theatre-going – contains within it an imaginary organisation of space and time – in the fiction. An audience is in two sets of bodily relationships. The particular spatial organisation of the watchers, the particular shapes of the imaginary spaces on stage, and the particular relationship between these two – the 'third space': all three of these particulars, taken together, may be said to articulate a sense of a particular moment in an always changing society.

In which, for example, to great acclaim, Lady Audley goes mad. But while she loses her personal space a much more fortunate heroine down the road at the Surrey Theatre in February 1864 is retrieved from the mine which is flooding with water and brought up by the hero in the mine shaft's basket. Except that the basket gets trapped. So the hero cuts it loose and, with the heroine in his arms, climbs the rope. The curtain falls as they approach the surface. 'It is this new "sensation" ... that will make the fortune of the piece,' said *The Times'* reviewer: 'it is when the figures ... are seen ascending the rope that the grand distinctive "hit" is made, of which people will talk when the intricacies of the plot have faded from their memory' (Knight 1997: 300). Narrative in the sensation drama is overshadowed by the big moment, the startling effect. For literary readers this organisation of the relationship between narrative and moment constitutes the frivolity of sensation drama. Time is compressed – the speed at which Lady Audley goes mad vexes seminars-full of student readers. And space is wildly extended: in April 1861 Jeanne, in *The Idiot of the Mountain*, is trying to eavesdrop. She 'is suspended from the branches of a tree which grows on the opposite side of the chasm, and almost reaches the rude dwelling' (Knight 1997: 286). But lightning strikes the branch and she falls into the abyss. In that moment of sensation the audience is not only encouraged to cathect the momentary, as against the sequential narrative, it is also learning about, playing with, versions of time and space (see also Virilio 1994).

It was not Jeanne's plunge but her suspension on the branch that called for comment: 'It should be remarked that the interior of the cottage and the exterior landscape are both shown at once, and that a complicated action is carried on with immense skill and with excellent effect' (Knight 1997: 287). The lightning and branch-breaking must have been reasonably complex, but it is the juxtaposition of scenes that the reviewer notes. Similarly the point of almost arrival at the surface from the mine in 1864 was the 'hit' moment. These are not the same thing, and they're also different from Lady Audley's murder and madness. But if there is a link it may lie in the interest in bodies which are not securely framed and centred. Two people ascending in a basket might be centred, but that fragile rope indicates they are not secure. Lady Audley may celebrate her controlling position after the murder, but she is overseen by Luke, behind her.

There are repeated effects in this material which, while most certainly not unique, nevertheless give the sensation drama of the mid-nineteenth century a particular texture. The aside, the 'look-out-behind-you' sequence, the villain's space: with whatever different outcome, these all pertain to a negotiation around personal space. Of course delineation of personal space in drama is nothing new. But what is specifically being produced as excitement here is something that arises out of risky eavesdropping, perilous rescue, a maintained secret, all organised spatially by means of the various features I have already noted. Instead of the heroically centred body, these plays generate for their populous urban audience the excitement of ascending the rope. Rescued from the depths, but never finally reaching the top.

And also perhaps 'the sharp discontinuity in the grasp of a single glance, and the unexpectedness of onrushing impressions'. That's Georg Simmel (1997: 175), about 25 years later, describing the experience of metropolitan life. It's an effect that *Lady Audley* seems to begin spatially to articulate.

Part III

Beyond integrity

Part II dealt with the organisation of the performing body in time and space, and, through the agency of that body, the negotiation of the audience's relationship to time and space.

In the Introduction I noted that the engagement between performing and watching bodies is both grounded in bodily matter and at the same time historically variable. Historians of gesture and performance have shown that the body looked and sounded different at different times. To this are added changes in perception, which imply that even where a gesture or performing mode remains constant, it may well have struck watchers differently, had different value placed upon it, had a different relationship to its surroundings.

The proposition that the relationship between body and surroundings changes can take us into a new phase of argument. Much of the work on gesture and performance techniques tends to assume a similar basic definition of the body, with its capacity for intentions and thus interiority. In Part I we were mainly concerned with bodies that were produced, and thought about, as individually autonomous, so that they could be differentiated from one another in schemes of value. A different tradition of thinking about, and producing, the body sees it not as a casing for an inner life, mind or soul, not as something autonomous, not contained within its own integrity. We began to encounter this different body in circumstances where it seemed to be either caught up in a rhythm larger than itself or a function of space. An individual body capable of becoming part of a group body. Not integral to itself, integrated into something else.

The chapters which follow explore a variety of theatrical body practices which, in their various ways, have an interest in, or fascination with, bodies that spill beyond proper limits, are disorderly or excessive, that interlock with non-bodies, that lose autonomy, that assimilate to surroundings. This territory is perhaps more unnatural, in almost every sense, than that of the preceding parts. While the focus remains locked onto bodily practices, I often seem to be reading against the grain or making strange interconnections. This is necessary, I think, because some of the body practices here have either been regarded as marginal and improper or have never been focused on as practices.

The principle of historical specificity is still respected. But before engaging with the case studies which follow, I want to suggest a more generalised overview. In these chapters, and in the book as a whole, there are repeated examples of an interest in body defined in relation to setting and to objects. The relationships change at different points of theatrical practice, but the three main terms are constant. Body is defined in relation to what it makes and the circumstances in which it finds itself. Relationship with found circumstances, the setting, may threaten or support the body's life; use and corruption of things made, objects, may work to transform or reinforce these circumstances. Body work, the function of the body, how it works, is also deeply to do with the work the body does, and has to do.

In its imagining of bodies the theatre is pondering over, and fantasising about, the elements that are crucial not simply to the definition of the body but also to its survival. This work of imagining is part of the process that facilitates the survival. To bodies repressed, anxious, alienated, worryingly decentred it offers fantasies of fullness, completeness. It doesn't need to be a dream of heroism and productivity but of a relationship with settings and objects that is not governed by terror.

Order without necessity, pleasurable dissipation, bodies promiscuously overflowing their borders.

6 Strutting, bellowing, muscles and noise

In 1601 Hamlet offered his famous advice to the actors: 'o'erstep not the modesty of nature. For anything so overdone is from the purpose of playing'. In 1996 the Italian director Romeo Castellucci informed his audience: 'I believe that the ancients have invented the theatre because of an elementary need of complexity; just like the violence against nature of the grafting, the pruning' (1997: 4).

This chapter describes some of the sorts of performing body that apparently deviate from the proper 'purpose' of performing. And it explores the particular ways in which such a body is felt to be inappropriate – overstepping, immodest, doing violence to nature.

That body is responsible for a number of theatrical sins: Going over the top. Ranting. Being melodramatic. In short,

Overacting

While it happens quite regularly that one generation of actors experiences the previous generation as overdoing it, there are moments in theatre history when the fuss about overacting seems particularly pronounced. One of these occurred at the turn of the sixteenth into the seventeenth century.

In one of his attacks on the theatre Ben Jonson describes the fictional heroes 'of the late Age, which had nothing in them but the scenicall strutting, and furious vociferation, to warrant them to the ignorant gapers' (1947: 587). His contemporaries shared his sense of an old-fashioned style. They called it 'stalking', with, as one put it, 'high-set steps' (in Gurr 1963: 98). The key physical quality is focused on the legs, which are in motion, taking large steps, which are high or stiff – moving with a conspicuous muscular control. All which has its effects on the hips and carriage of the torso. It was a very literal 'overstepping' of the modesty of nature.

This was supposedly accompanied by a vocal production which is loud and emotionally coloured – 'furious'. The voice does not speak so much as make sound, not serving the words but vociferating. Calling attention to the muscular production of sound – 'his wide-strained mouth' (Hall in Gurr 1963: 98). The style, as polemically summarised, amounted to 'a stalking-stamping Player, that will raise a tempest with his toung, and thunder with his heeles' (in Gurr 1963: 101). Or as Hamlet pithily puts it: 'strutted and bel-lowed'. Through the descriptions of the movement and sound the constant, and defining, characteristic is that this leg-centred movement and a vocal sound which goes beyond the needs of verbal delivery always come in combi-nation. It's like Arnie's Austrian accent which always comes with his body-built physique, so that in the line 'Hasta la vista baby' we seem to hear the muscles.

This mode of acting was associated in many people's minds with the late Elizabethan star, Edward Alleyn. And although Alleyn played a variety of parts – and indeed was celebrated for his ability to be so various – it is his playing of one part in particular that seems to be a defining moment of strut-ting and bellowing. That part brought him to fame and was much imitated – Marlowe's Tamburlaine. It's this fictional hero, along with Tamar-cham, that Jonson so disapprovingly recalls from 'the late age'. But despite the dis-approval of sober modern folk such as Jonson, Tamburlaine had enormous impact. If we look at his first appearance we can see some of the textual mechanisms that produce the strutting and bellowing phenomenon.

Fetching stations

Tamburlaine, a shepherd, leads on stage a woman of high rank and her two lords, together with their treasure (*Tamburlaine* Act 1, scene 2). Tamburlaine and his two companions have captured them. He waves aside the letters from the local ruler giving them safe passage. He notes the woman's beauty and tells her she will be his sexual partner. He then takes off his shepherd's clothes and dresses himself with the captured armour and curtle-axe. He not only speaks most but presents himself as spectacle. He has freedom of the stage vocally and physically.

The strutting and bellowing don't automatically guarantee impact. They could simply look loud. What gives them their force is a sort of fullness. The sound is more than is necessary for a stage dialogue. It goes beyond the person and the conversational exchange, almost becoming a scenic event – the strutting player 'will raise a tempest with his toung'. Tamburlaine's voice, uninterrupted, fills the scene – not just with sound, but also because it coin-cides with, gives form to, what the audience looks at. And because the legs in movement are central to the technique the strutting body inevitably covers a lot of ground. Andrew Gurr quotes a pamphlet from 1597 which describes someone who 'fetcht his stations vp and downe the rome, with such furious Iesture as if he had beene playing Tamberlane on a stage' (1963: 98). The strutting actor is everywhere on the stage, or, rather, he freely avails himself of the stage space. For this mobility is power, the assertion of a right to walk where one will. Jonson called Alleyn's version of it 'scenicall strutting'. Which, as an image of power, has taken a long time dying – wealthy characters in relatively recent movies still stride decisively around large, wealthy rooms. So too, back in 1587, Tamburlaine fills the space around him.

Or, to be more precise, I should say that Tamburlaine produces a space that is filled by him. My thinking here is influenced by Henri Lefebvre's account of gestures: 'Organized gestures, which is to say ritualized and codified gestures, are not simply performed in "physical" space, in the space of the bodies. Bodies themselves generate spaces, which are produced by and for their gestures.' Then, in what could work as a gloss on 'fetching stations', he goes on: 'The linking of gestures corresponds to the articulation and linking of well-defined spatial segments' (Lefebvre 1998: 216). A similar point can be made from an acoustic standpoint:

> Auditory space has no point of favored focus. It's a sphere without fixed boundaries, space made by the thing itself, not space containing the thing. It is not pictorial space, boxed in, but dynamic, always in flux, creating its own dimensions moment by moment.
>
> (Carpenter and McLuhan 1960: 67)

Clearly there are boundaries for the Tamburlaine actor – the stage, the auditorium. And his space is also pictorial. But that sense of dynamism, of going beyond boundaries, is perhaps glossed by the contemporary description of raising a tempest with the tongue.

While the deep sense of Tamburlaine filling the space may derive from the characteristics of gesture and sound, these are focused by two specific engines. The first of these is the relationship between a particular acting body and a particular dimension of stage. Always present in production, in *Tamburlaine* a physically big performer had his size emphasised by a relatively small stage (the Rose stage was 11.2m by 5m; the Globe 15.08m wide, the Fortune 13.11m by 8.38m). The second engine of spatial production is the dramaturgy. The spatial arrangements of the stage are explicitly organised by Tamburlaine, and they centre on him. The potential symmetry of the stage, three bandits, three captives, has at its heart the impropriety of a male shepherd leading a 'female' aristocrat. When he puts on the illicitly obtained armour the gender difference is toughened, the shepherd masculinised into soldier, male power no longer compromised by class inferiority. His speech dominates the soundscape of the stage and sometimes its only rationale is to articulate his desires. It promises the audience future spectacles and describes a reality they do not yet see. The speech, in dominating the stage, speaks a fantasy but establishes itself as an instrument of power. So too, his costume transformation is theatrical not social, but even as fancy dress it asserts a right over the others on stage. In its own self-organised transformation scene the Tamburlaine body is both present for itself and able to access hitherto unseen spectacle. It is theatricality as both illegitimacy and desirable power. Thus the strutting and bellowing body has the effect of being larger than an ordinary body because it fills the scene.

The discipline of daring

Marlowe's dramaturgy seems to script the impact of strutting and bellowing. Despite the invitations from contemporary commentators to view it as purposeless, excessive, mere noise, it may be necessary to consider this mode of overacting as a technique with very distinct features.

The voice that vociferates produces sound in excess of what is needed to articulate the words. A muscular discipline would be required to guarantee not only supplies of breath but also sustained control over rhythm and pitch. There was a high degree of mobility. The attacks on sawing the air and violent gesturing suggest a regular habit of muscular extension. Those high-stepping, stalking legs would, in particular, have demanded discipline and stamina. In short, this body has to do a lot of physical work in performance, where the muscles tensely maintain a relationship between size and control.

Such foregrounded physicality is usually not acknowledged as an English mode of performing. In the 1590s Thomas Nashe dismissed Italian *commedia dell'arte* as a form much inferior to English acting, which supposedly affected an audience by means of emotional involvement (Nashe instances audiences weeping at the wounded Talbot in Shakespeare's *Henry VI*) – though the effect may well have been produced by 'heroic' acting in a heightened mode. *Commedia dell'arte* was an improvised form based around the interactions between stock personas. As I describe in Chapter 2, the performer would specialise in a particular persona. This was not an effect constructed by a dramatist's text but an entity developed out of the performer's body. What distinguished one persona from another was not only a costume and a set of habitual attitudes, but a stance, a way of moving, an embodying of those attitudes. Later on several of the personas wore distinctive masks. But the facial mask is simply a continuation of what is already happening, namely that the body is constrained – by a costume, a characteristic prop, above all by an organisation and tension of the muscles. Out of that shaping, that de-naturalising, of the body a 'self' appears. The consciousness responds to the tensions and shapes of the body, sees itself as it thinks it looks, inhabits that image.

If instead of the angled shoulders and twisted hips that are regularly associated with *commedia* one envisages stiffened, high-stepping legs, then strutting comes into view as a similar instance of a persona organised by musculature. Certainly, in his work on muscles, Bulwer moves seamlessly from descriptions of groups of muscles to their characterisation: 'the Arrogant paire or the Muscles of Disdainfull Confidence' work with 'the Insulting or Bragging paire or the Muscles of Insolent Pride, and fierce Audacity' (in Greenblatt 1997: 234). Contemporaries of *commedia* were also clear that it required special sorts of vocal production. It was a deliberate mixture of dialects and degrees of vocal 'perfection' (Clivio 1989). Different personas were marked by different vocal qualities. Thus Perrucci said that a performer of *zanni* 'should be ridiculous in the tone of his voice, which ought to be excessively shrill, or out of tune, or raucous' (quoted in Richards and Richards 1990: 137). The Capitano delivered 'highly rhetorical rhodomontades' (Perucci in Richards and Richards 1990: 150). Not only does this deliberate production of vocal 'excess' and the highly rhetorical sound rather similar to vociferation and the delivery of high-sounding terms. It also works by a similar process of relating sound to body shape. If this analogy holds true, then Nashe's comparison between Italian and English modes can be seen as an effective obliteration of something in-between, a physical – as it were masked – English mode.

Strutting was by no means, however, an improvised form. Indeed, when they are printed, most of the strutting parts look so wordy as to be 'undramatic'. One of the editors of a classic 'ranting' part – Herod – calls it monotonous. Yet if this is a predominantly physical mode then the size of strutting speeches may have a particular function. They create the conditions for the display, they give the necessary space for the body to be taken over by particular muscular rhythms and regimes of breathing. Seen on the page, of course, it is very easy to lose any sense of the large physical performance, of the body producing the ranting/strutting part. Yet it had to be highly mobile, flying into rages, fetching its stations across the stage. So by way of trying to become even more precise about the mechanisms of strutting, and in the process trying to resituate the body into the highly verbal text, let's take a look at a play that was custom-made for Alleyn.

Greene's (1970) *The Historie of Orlando Furioso* written after 1592 derives itself from *Tamburlaine*, with some mad stuff *à la Spanish Tragedy* thrown in. It is useful for the purpose here because Greene had a formula in his head that he thought he was copying. Alleyn played Orlando, a mere county palatine of France, who turns up among a set of international princes to sue for the hand of Angelica, daughter of Marsilius. She chooses Orlando; the others set about attacking Marsilius and Orlando fights them off. Wicked Sacrapant decides to break up the marriage; contrives to make Orlando jealous, which sends him mad. After being cured, he again saves Marsilius; then sets about fighting the twelve peers of France, who have turned up. But he's recognised and they end happily ever after.

Orlando is first presented in a formal scene where the princes offer their power and wealth to Angelica. The first four make speeches of about 15 lines each, full of nouns of chivalry and treasure, names of mythic gods and exotic places. Orlando then delivers a speech twice their length which begins by asserting that he is no king, though princely born, and ends by offering to fight single-handed any competitor to show what he will do for Angelica. And whereas all the others have finished with the refrain 'I loue, (my Lord); let that suffise for me', he says: 'I loue, my Lord;/ Angelica her selfe shall speak for me' (Greene 1970: lines 127–8). When she chooses him, it is taken as an insult by the princes, who express contempt for Orlando's status – 'a stragling mate'. Marsilius also annoys them by upholding his daughter's choice. Their anger foregrounds a set of qualities clustered around Orlando: lower status, youth, personal choice, individual merit as opposed to rank.

And these qualities inhabit one of Orlando's favourite words: 'dare'. He ends the scene with it, challenging the others: 'see what we dare,/ And thereon set your rest' (lines 236–7). It reappears, more intensified, at the play's end when, describing himself as a 'common mercenary souldier' (line 1342), he dares the 'proudest' of the twelve peers of France to fight. The contrast in levels of rank is enacted literally in the second scene of Act 1, when Orlando arrives outside the walls of Rodamant's castle. In answer to his challenge, a sleepy soldier appears on the walls, and tells him to go away. Orlando dares him or his master to come out of the gates. In the next scene we see his victory, of course. But that's a much much shorter scene. It's the business of making the challenge against huge odds, doing the daring, which gets the attention, for, as Lefebvre suggests, gestural systems embody ideology (1998: 215).

As Orlando shouts his lines at the castle wall, we know – because we've seen *Tamburlaine* – that, for all its size, the castle will be defeated. The soldier, up on the tiring-house wall presumably, is given height but no authority by the play-house architecture (see also Dillon 1999); the strutter who is fetching his stations around the stage below is closer to the audience, while his voice is probably amplified by the canopy he stands just at the front of. As Tamburlaine did before him, Orlando can line up his body with the architectural arrangements of the space, even while he calls attention to himself. A competent audience will expect that an inversion of relations between high and low, body and building, will happen. But it hasn't happened yet. The image is of 'conventional' power relations – lord's castle with 'stragling grooms' oustide. On one hand the dominant version of order, the way things are outside the theatre; on the other, the possibility of releasing the potency of the body, producing disruption.

The soldier assumes power that's to do with 'height' – rank, building, fixity; Orlando actively produces a new centre which depends on none of these. Neither state is at the moment fully achieved. Because the audience is being drawn, attracted, to each state, the scene, even without being busy with action, has the feeling of mobility. That quality of mobility inhabits most of the activity of 'daring', which presumably also had its typical physical mannerisms. Orlando has to look upwards at the soldier; elsewhere he metaphorically looks upward. Lisa Ullman, writing in a different context, notes that the labile, asymmetric body looks like one ready for change (Laban 1988: 125). The business of daring seems to involve presenting yourself to another, displaying your (physical) qualities, while simultaneously calling them towards you, beckoning them out. An upward-looking displaying, offering and beckoning. That's why the legs need to be tensed, to display that torso and push it upwards. And the steps which tease the others, studiedly moving into their hierarchic space in a way which invites, dares, challenges, those steps need to be not so much large as deliberate, high.

So the question needs asking, why might this body be monstrous?

Herod

To begin to answer that, let's go back to one of the archetypal, and earliest, ranters.

The authors of the medieval cycle plays seem to have found their ranting Herods in the Bible. But what is a passing reference to anger there becomes a bravura performance on the scaffolds and trestles and carts in, for instance, *Magnus Herodes* (Skey 1979/80; Staines 1976). Herod is enraged because he has heard news that a baby has been born who people say is a king. He can't bear to have his own authority questioned, so he resolves to kill what threatens it, babies. Up to this point the task of the Herod actor is to sustain and modulate the elements of aggression, anger, passion. When he first appears, in the Wakefield version of the play, he has been warned that people are chattering about this new king. So he turns directly to the audience and says 'Stynt, brodels [scoundrels], youre dyn – yei, euerychon!' (Cawley 1964: line 82). From here he has to get increasingly angry.

This is organised by a series of threats to the audience, not just telling them to shut up but threatening them physically. The favourite threat is to break bones (which includes braining and breaking necks). It is given extra size (and indeed likelihood) by the sword that the performer would carry. The size has to include height, for the language of breaking presupposes beating and hitting rather than cutting and thrusting (though there is one reference to cutting up flesh), and beating requires a raised arm. But there's another prop. Herod wears a crown. And, through all the threatening, it needs to stay on his head. This means that he is caught between physical wildness and constraint. And that is the engine of the performance.

In the first half of his opening speech (seven nine-line stanzas) he threatens the audience. Halfway through the crown is mentioned, together with his increasing anger. This has its own characteristic image: 'What dewill! Me thynk I brast for anger and for teyn [annoyance/grievance]' (Cawley 1964: line 118). There then follow three stanzas promising violence to others. The climax to this section, and to the speech as a whole, is that, on hearing that the three kings have gone, he falls into a rage – 'We! Outt! For teyn I brast!' (line 148) – and begins calling his knights ratbags and scum, and, of course, beating them.

The text livens things up by suggesting other markers of the exertion. One of his knights accuses Herod of gnashing his teeth; then later he needs to pause to take a drink; and later again he pauses to 'pant' (Doob 1974). While keeping his crown on, the Herod performer has to suggest a passion that comes from the guts:

> Now thynk I to fyght
> For anger.
> My guttys will outt thryng [burst out]
> Bot I this lad hyng [hang];
> Withoutt I haue a vengyng,
> I may lyf no langer.
>   (Cawley 1968: lines 238–43)

Later he claims his heart is palpitating, his internal organs driving him to violence against others. He beats so that he doesn't burst. Which means that as the internal disturbance increases so there is a prospect of ever wilder activity to allay it. It will eventually come to baby killing, but before he gets there he beats his knights and tells his counsellors to throw their books away.

The audience is encouraged to see these actions, as their recipients do, as improper and an outrage. For Herod is showing disrespect to the established social hierarchy, to rank and book-learning. The sight of these noble folk being insulted and beaten is a topsy-turvy image (and for some audiences lots of fun). And it's the sort of image that has been labelled 'carnivalesque', inverting order. Except, of course, that this carnivalesque is being produced by a king. Except – again – that this king is being driven not so much by defence of his crown as by his internal organs, what Bakhtinians so modestly call lower body stratum perhaps, his guts. Herod's is a rule against rules, a sort of triumph of the gut.

Although cited by early modern critics as the precursor to Tamburlaine's strutting, Herod is a different entity. The threats and beating gestures, though large, are different from stalking. And there is a different relationship with the physical and ideological context. Herod is an amateur performer on a temporary or movable platform, doing a performance that happens once a year at this time. Tamburlaine is a professional in a custom-made theatre. But the Herod performance foregrounds a set of characteristics which were then applied, rightly or not, to other strutting performances. That set of characteristics combines a body at bursting point with the disruption of appropriate decorum, all marked, by the biblical narrative, as ungodly.

Tear-throats

The Herod part scripts the characteristic fusion of large bodily action and sustained vocal noise. In his case it is much more vocally messy, with its staccato shouts, than Tamburlaine's blank-verse fluency. But bellowing remains, as much as strutting, a sign for monstrous excess, both physical and ideological. To find out how, I'll take each element in turn, starting with bellowing.

Let's return to Greene's Orlando, and his opening speech. It seems to be a highly static, wordy suitor scene. Like the others, Orlando talks of where he's from, the reputation of Angelica and the journey he's made. But whereas their speeches string together lists of nouns, and specifically exotic-sounding proper names, his speech rapidly organises itself by a refrain, as he lists the various things that 'might well haue kept me backe'. For a reader or listener this device gives the speech a more distinctive shape than the others. The refrain is not so much an ordering device, however, as a spectacle of the ability to order. Look closely and you'll find a chunk of the speech has worked itself loose from syntactic coherence:

> Swift Fame that sounded to our Westerne Seas
> The matchles beautie of Angelica,
> Fairer than was the Nimph of Mercurie,
> Who, when bright Phoebus mounteth vp his coach,
> And tracts Aurora in her siluer steps, etc.
>
> (Greene 1970: lines 97–101)

The main verb has vanished. But that's unimportant alongside the major task, which is to produce the sound of high eloquence (Jean Howard makes a similar point about Shakespearean dramaturgy when she suggests that in some circumstances the content of a speech matters rather less than its event or sound). The particular sense here is of marginal importance (we know it'll be stuff about the size of the world and Angelica's beauty). The general sense, on the other hand, is to do with the important spectacle that I've already noted – that this is not just high, but organised.

Orlando demonstrates the ability to order. He accompanies this with the common rhetorical trick that denies rhetoric: 'I list not boast in acts of Chiualrie' (line 119). Yet it's the longest of these speeches and, with its refrain, the most ornamental. But its work is to deny ornament and to produce not so much communication (narrative, poetry) as a spectacle of vocal power – high, ordered, straight. And the other part of its work is to choreograph the body: the refrain does not just institute a particular insistent pattern of breathing, but it makes audible, measurable, the vocal power that differentiates each new repetition of the refrain. It foregrounds the body in the speech, which is why it feels appropriate that Orlando ends with a physical challenge.

This sort of speaking could be said to be noise, which Jacques Attali, borrowing from information theory, defines as 'the term for a signal that interferes with the reception of a message by a receiver, even if the interfering signal itself has a meaning for that receiver' (Attali 1985: 27). If you expect speech which holds the mirror up to nature, then speech which calls attention to itself as production will feel like noise. Speech blocked by the body. A similar sort of effect, but using different means, was performed on the melodrama stage. Dickens describes the speech of a character called Michael the Mendicant, who confesses to having wrongly attacked another: 'I ster-ruck him down, and fel-ed in er-orror!' (Dickens n.d.: 175). This sort of delivery is often referred to as syllabification, speaking every syllable available. But it's more than that, since extra syllables are being squeezed out of words. The distortion testifies to the force behind it. Language is being forced to say more than it is capable of, and it is heard not so much for what the words communicate as what their break-up communicates. The melodrama voice instrument does to words what the music does to the body, stretching and shaping to express something which is beyond everyday utterance. The forceful distortion again foregrounds the body in the speech, in that the vocal equipment is conspicuous in its effects. And in the case of Michael the Mendicant, much to the huge pleasure of the audience, the rest of his body is as active as his voice: he 'cried out, "What! more bel-ood!" and fell flat' (Dickens n.d.: 175).

In their separate ways the bellowing rhetoric and the syllabification make murky the transparency of language. To quote de Saussure, the verbal sound here 'is not a mould in which thought must necessarily fit, but a plastic substance' (in van Leeuwen 1999: 125). The message is clear long before the pattern of rhetorical accretion has stopped; 'blood' would mean the same thing if it were only one syllable. So one has to listen to something extra, something that seems to overwrite the message. The effect is rather like that which Barthes finds in French and German songs, an effect caused 'by the very friction between the music and something else, which something else is the particular language (and nowise the message). The song must speak, must *write*' (1977: 185). This writtenness is a sort of thickening up of the texture so that it cannot be taken as mere lyric expressivity, what Barthes (1977) calls 'expressive reduction'. He has got to this point by adapting a pair of terms from Kristeva, allowing him to distinguish between 'pheno-song' ('structure of the language being sung, the rules of the genre ... the composer's idiolect', etc.) and 'geno-song':

> the space where significations germinate 'from within language and its very materiality'; it forms a signifying play having nothing to do with communication, representation (of feelings), expression; it is that apex (or that depth) of production where the melody really works at the

language – not at what it says, but at the voluptuousness of its sounds-signifiers, of its letters.

(Barthes 1977: 182)

The presence of melody is not always required. Buh-lur-uudd-duh. Vowels spawn clusters of writhing unmentionable sounds.

Barthes' reflections on song are an attempt to get at what he calls the 'grain' of the voice, the materiality of the body heard in the voice. He invites us to listen to a Russian church bass. What we hear

> is directly the cantor's body, brought to your ears in one and the same movement from deep down in the cavities, the muscles, the membranes, the cartilages, and from deep down in the Slavonic language, as though a single skin lined the inner flesh of the performer and the music he sings. The voice is not personal: it expresses nothing of the cantor, of his soul; it is not original (all Russian cantors have roughly the same voice), and at the same time it is individual: it has us hear a body which has no civil identity, no 'personality', but which is nevertheless a separate body.

(Barthes 1977: 181–2)

In the same way, perhaps, when the melodrama performer explores words for their vowels, when he produces from one vowel a range of new sounds, you seem to hear the muscles of the stomach contracting, noises not so much from the windpipe as the digestive tract. Noises you'll hear in the dark rooms of sex clubs. For the strutter the words are differently organised (and in 1590 pronounced differently), so a different range of sounds is produced. But the Orlando actor can't do his first speech as a continuous shout. The technique of accretion, the refrain that builds at each repetition, requires steady intensification while still keeping in place the effect of echoed sounds. Those sounds begin to join up in memory across the speech, each new iteration nagging more persistently. Instead of dwelling on single syllables the voice pushes its way through elaborate syntactical structures. This may not have the effect of coming from deep down. It doesn't require that sort of gravitas. It's more full of energy, a hammering persistence rather than unravelling depth. Contemporary audiences had a name for those who did this sort of delivery, and that name clearly places the physical body in the sound: 'tear-throats'.

The sound of the tear-throat is monstrous because it breaks rules. In his treatise on manners from 1576, Della Casa advises that one 'eschewe ye pompe, brauery, & affectation, that may not be suffred and allowed to inrishe an *Oration*, spoken in a publike place' (in Smith 1999: 246). Similarly, in his advice on proper conduct Guazzo advises that the voice 'ought to measure its forces, and to moderate it selfe in such sort, that though it straine it selfe somewhat, yet it offend not the eares by a rawe and harshe sownde' (Smith 1999: 256). Within this code of manners the raw and harsh bellowing voice is an offence. But its cultural monstrosity perhaps goes further. In a discussion of the 'pointing' of texts designed to be read aloud, Smith notes a shift from 'physiological' punctuation based on where a speaker draws breath to 'syntactical' punctuation based on Latin grammar. What the punctuation 'rationalizers' wanted to do, he says, 'in effect, was to shift the site of speech from the thorax to the brain', part of a larger process of separating mind from body, on the model of Descartes (Smith 1999: 239). Bellowing tends to foreground the bodily activity of speech. And its monstrosity can perhaps also be seen within an even wider frame. The musicologist John Shepherd suggests that '*the very fact of music*, based as it is on the physical phenomenon of sound, constitutes a serious threat to the visually mediated hegemony of scribal elites' (1991: 159). Tamburlaine dismisses their letters. Bellowing is like music in so far as it is sound in excess of what is needed for communication of words, and it is certainly a physicalised sound.

Bellowing was, of course, a theatre phenomenon. And this perhaps adds one further element to its monstrosity. Smith notes that puritans lamented that theatre attracted more people than did preaching: theatre 'engendered, through sound, a subjectivity that was far more exciting – and far more liber- ating – than those created by oratory, conversation, and liturgy by them- selves' (1999: 270). Within the early modern soundscape, a theatre in full swing would have been a major irruption. This coincides, perhaps, with a sense that through theatre those who were 'masterless men', the actors, were achieving wealth and fame. The deliberate disordering of the soundscape is, perhaps even more than 'rough music', a sign of the disordering of social relations. The bellower was claiming to himself the right to generate the loudest noise, to dominate acoustic space, whereas the loudest noise is meant, Schafer argues, to be sacred noise (1994: 179). The loud voice 'claims most territory', and as such is a 'factor in the system of social distance': it is 'able to create imaginary social relations between what is presented or repre- sented by a sound and the listener' (van Leeuwen 1999: 125, 27). The actors, much to the disapproval of some, performed, in every sense, a disruption of social relations. To this we shall return.

Noise

The other party in that disruption was the audience. As I noted in passing above, the early modern auditorium was a noisy one. The typical audience for strutting was conspicuously excited, absorbed in what it watched, possessed by it, 'ravished'. So too the melodrama audience, in its different space, yelled at its villains.

Now, although Hamlet somewhat snottily remarks on clowns who set 'barren spectators' laughing just at the point where the play is discussing some 'necessary question', it was frequently the case that the script itself was designed to produce noise. So too melodramatists wrote in lines they called clap traps. It was a very old technique. One of the first things the Wakefield Herod does is to tell his audience to shut up. That audience has already been cued. We know Herod is a baddy. Opposition to Herod expresses itself in chatter about the new baby, Christ. It is perhaps morally sound not to let yourself be quietened by this monarch, and, being a play, shouting at kings is allowable and fun. So the opening of Herod's first speech is organised as a sort of duet with audience. He repeatedly tells them to keep quiet and threatens beating or worse if they do not. In the staging arrangements of a cycle play it would be quite possible for the Herod actor to get reasonably close, particularly if his reach is extended by a sword, to anyone – 'May I se hym with eyn' (Cawley 1964: line 102) – who is talking. So there's some risky fun in the mutual challenges here. And in a culture regularly exposed to Herod figures audiences start to look for this fun whenever a performer begins to rant at them.

But, when Herod starts, the performance is relying on more than its own formal devices. It is playing off what an audience might well be bringing with them. Clearly his crime is peculiarly nasty and resistible, the systematic killing of babies. But that crime also images another death of serious and abiding religious importance, the death of Christ. Added to this spiritual iniquity there's the worldly nastiness. The Wakefield dramatist, among others, draws into the invention of Herod references to local magnates (and presumably performers could have done likewise). So there are various sorts of deep fear and anger that can be tapped into by the formal mechanisms in order to produce noise. The crowd, crammed into town on the festival day, is being worked up. But it goes on within a safe framework. The noise that is released is also controlled. The effect of Herod presumably unites this crowd – in one voice, so to speak – against an acknowledged biblical enemy, on the side of the good. And it contrasts with other moments in the cycle, such as the crucifixion, where Christ is quiet, transcendent; where an audience is invited to watch in silent awe.

Herod's noise, with its close connection to violence, fits alongside Attali's definition: 'noise had always been experienced as destruction, disorder, dirt, pollution, an aggression against the code-structuring messages. In all cultures, it is associated with the idea of the weapon, blasphemy, plague' (Attali 1985: 27). And because noise is connected with death, it 'is a concern of power; when power founds its legitimacy on the fear it inspires, on its capacity to create social order, on its univocal monopoly of violence, it monopolizes noise' (1985: 27). So in most cultures, says Attali, noise also 'lies at the origin of the religious idea' (1985: 27). Chaos precedes the formation of the world; the voice of God can be terrifying. In the face of this threat human culture sets about controlling noise by organising it.

This is the work of music. It can produce dissonances, and then dispel them; introduce the threat of noise, then harmonise and rhythmically order it. The primitive terror of violence in society is dealt with by ritualisation, as sacrifice. Music, in its capacity to eliminate dissonances 'to keep noise from spreading', operates like ritual sacrifice which keeps violence from spreading. Thus, 'the production of music has as its function the creation, legitimation, and maintenance of order. Its primary function is not to be sought in aesthetics ... but in the effectiveness of its participation in social regulation' (Attali 1985: 30). This effectiveness, in Attali's story, will later on be limited by the distance music moves from ritual sacrifice as it is taken into a society of exchange and commodity.

Cultural pollution

Music is Attali's central concern, but we have already encountered a different mode of organising noise. Herod's role in the cycle plays could itself be said to provoke anxiety and disorder, as part of a scheme that will then promote security and order. There is a ritual context to the ranting. For the cycle plays happen at one particular time of the year, on a religious feastday. They involve the community in a network of customary roles and practices. The story enacted is a religious one, with its own internal scheme of analogies and contrasts. Herod's speech has a place alongside other noise makers and against, pre-eminently, Christ. The occasion of ranting triggers recognition of, and draws on, aspects of the violence, the noise, of real medieval lives, and then organises that noise into a theatrical turn with a precise place in a ritualised event.

That ritual event changes its nature, is less contained by a religious frame, in the early modern period. When Alleyn strutted and bellowed he did it for money. The context to his bellowing was secular, his story 'worldly' as opposed to biblical. It did not fall into place in a scheme which ensured it would be followed by a transcendental Jesus. The organisation of noise would thus seem to be less clearly functional. But there needs to be caution about replicating Attali's pessimistic narrative of the commodification of music. For around the emergence of strutting there still seem to be real fears about social noise.

In their history of the Queen's Men, Scott McMillin and Sally-Beth MacLean argue that the company opposed itself to the development of blank verse by Kyd, Marlowe and Shakespeare. Marlowe, for instance, produces a text concerned with activity, 'what characters do rather than what they are, and his language generates a sense of that activeness at every turn' (McMillin and MacLean 1998: 123). This was the sort of linguistic urgency that energised Alleyn. The Queen's Men, by contrast, performed in a way that would encourage the recognition of allegorical meanings, seeking to give concrete demonstration to ethical or political abstractions. The performance speaks its message in 'the accent no ear can misunderstand'. This theatrical 'literalism' differed substantially from the blank-verse dramatists, and, by McMillin and MacLean's persuasive account, the Queen's Men staged this difference in their play *Selimus*. '*Selimus* demonstrates the degeneration of a world of rhetoric into a world of violence' (McMillin and MacLean 1998: 158). A text that begins with the traditional Queen's Men's rhymed iambics then moves into blank verse and then ends in death by strangulation – a concrete assault on the body through its sound-production system. The blank verse of an Alleyn, far from using sound to tame noise, apparently returns noise to violence.

The play images that violence as strangulation. But there is present another sort of violent noise, the noise that interferes with what the eye and ear clearly understand, the noise that disturbs allegorical reading, that challenges scribal culture. The effect of strutting and bellowing is to ravish the audience. As Jonson put it, someone like Alleyn did not 'speake to the capacity of his hearers'. By which he presumably meant, as did Hamlet, that he played below the level that would suit an intellectual audience. Alleyn's strutting clearly produced a response – hairs raised on the back of the neck – but it was a response that did not depend on intellectual engagement for its pleasures. That means, in a society where intellect was increasingly linked with education and literacy, and where both of those were linked to the ability to *afford* education, that Alleyn's noise may be said to be an example of what Carla Mazzio describes as 'aggressive orality', 'a response to the movement of representation away from the body' (1997: 69). In this respect it might be associated with those who could be described as less conspicuously literate, the 'meaner sort of people'.

A sense of 'aggressive orality' is produced by the Alleyn narratives we have looked at. Tamburlaine began as a shepherd-bandit and assumed high office by conquest. Greene, we remember, in constructing a Tamburlaine-like vehicle for Alleyn, felt that the gestus of daring was a crucial element. The strutting performance dares against those who are nominally superior. At this point the part and the performer begin to blur together. Daring parts were acted by those who, in the early days, had the technical legal status of masterless men, socially vulnerable apart from the patronage of their aristocratic masters. As I noted above, the loud voice may play a part in the imaging of social relations. The noise of the bellower thus connects, perhaps, into some quite deep social fears. One of these might be the ever-present idleness and riot which the city fathers feared in their urban workforce; another centres on the upstart glamour and youthful enterprise of those who seemed to have no respect for inherited position and degree.

So rather than follow Attali's continuous line of musical degeneration through forms of commoditisation, stage 'noise' could perhaps be viewed as a series of disturbances of theatre's organisational poise. The repeated worry about the racket of melodrama performance could then be seen as another instance where noise has to be thought of in terms of real violence – in this case the disturbance, or more often the potential for it, of the metropolitan underclass. Quite early in the nineteenth century this violence penetrated theatre space in the Old Price riots at Covent Garden in 1809 (Baer 1992). That episode was a politically orchestrated – as it were – challenge to more than just theatre managers. In the nightly assemblage of rattles, songs and rowdy dancing, noise confronted dominant order.

The nineteenth-century solution to this was to attract more of the middle class into the theatre, partly by furnishing the theatres like middle-class spaces and partly by espousing as dramatic values such things as 'nature' and 'realism'. It was a strategy that Hamlet would probably have recognised. Certainly it has been argued that the King's Men seemed to want to teach the Globe audience to behave differently from those in other amphitheatres such as the Red Bull, where the audience was characterised as citizens of the 'meaner sort' (Wilson 1993). If they were to get the full theatrical pathos of the closing moments of the tragedy, the Globe audience needed to share Macbeth's sense that an adequate image of futility was that of a player that 'struts and frets his hour upon the stage', where 'sound and fury' signify nothing. In Hamlet's preferred sort of drama, on the other hand, playing has a purpose. Overacting distracts from the purpose of playing. It engenders too much local noise, which also produces social noise.

A dark and shady grove

Alongside the sound is the fury. So far I have concentrated on the monstrosity of bellowing, partly because there were models to hand which would enable me to show how it might be conceived as a form of cultural pollution. But now let's have a look at the strutting body that makes that noise.

Hamlet, Jonson and their contemporaries regarded stalking and gesturing as an offence to the modesty of nature. Hamlet tells the Players not to wave their arms around in big gestures. Instead of strutting they are to speak trippingly. The aim is to hold that mirror up to nature. So too Jonson advises. When he attacks the playing of the fictional heroes of 'the late age' he sets up a contrast with the 'true Artificer' who 'will not run away from nature, as hee were afraid of her; or depart from life, and the likenesse of Truth; but speake to the capacity of his hearers' (1947: 587).

Alongside the invocation of nature an adjective appears: 'the true brood of Actors … Keepe naturall unstrayn'd Action in her throne' (Carew quoted in Gurr 1963: 95). Strutters, we recall, strain. This means that good acting has to appear to be unstrained. Conspicuous muscular exertion is invented into a sign of bad art. And it reappears meaning the same thing at another theatrical period concerned about overdoing it. In the 1860s the playing of the American actor Edwin Forrest was described as 'common and vulgar'. What this amounted to is described by an eye-witness from 1863 as Forrest's 'muscular school; the brawny art; the biceps aesthetics; the tragic calves; the bovine drama; rant, roar, and rigmarole' (quoted in Walker 1999: 27).

A later critical assessment of Forrest argued that the reason he caused controversy was because 'absolute harmony can never exist between the antagonistic systems of muscle and mind. Forrest was an uncommonly massive and puissant animal, and all of his impersonations were more physical than intellectual' (in Walker 1999: 27). That confident ability to separate the physical from the intellectual is a result of culture not anatomy. For instance the mind–body split announced by Descartes was not so well established when John Bulwer was thinking about gesture. He saw muscles as the only means by which the soul can express itself. As Stephen Greenblatt says, muscles are 'the link between the soul – "being otherwise very obscure" – and the known world' (1997: 232). Or, as Bulwer put it, 'the almost *motions* of the Affections & passions ... outwardly appear by the operation of the *Muscles*' (p. 232). Yet not everybody shared this view. In the anatomical mappings of the body, heart and brain and various sorts of viscera all played key roles. In the passage of vital spirits around the body they travel, said Helkiah Crooke, through 'the darke and shady grove of the Muscles' (quoted in Paster 1997: 112). To this way of thinking, muscles are not a centre of soul or identity or vital forces, they are opaque.

Bulwer concentrated on muscles that communicated, muscles that caused the significant expressive movements of the body, those of hand and head. This leaves less clear the status of muscles that do actions which don't directly communicate, such as in the movement of legs. Now it may be the case that, for the early modern audience, strutting was notable not simply because it involved conspicuous muscularity in general but because it involved legs in particular. Histories of fashion suggest that different parts of the body become invested with interest or desire, as it were cathected, at different periods. It may also be possible to show that different parts of the body play a role in characterising different social and sexual groups (although I am not about to do that here). For the strutting player, as Shakespeare puts it in *Troilus and Cressida*, his 'conceit/ Lies in his ham-string' (1.3.153–4). This is in a society where, some years later, the commentator on manners, Richard Brathwaite, observed that Stuart aristocracy 'no longer relies on legs as supporters ... but "learns to pace"' (Brathwaite quoted in Ravelhofer 1998: 253). Barbara Ravelhofer concludes that 'Such learning ends in the loss of male/female distinctions' (1998: 253). A different way of describing decadent behaviour was put by Vaughan, who attacks 'cavaleers' who 'trust most impudently in the hugeness of their lims and in their drunken gates' (in Bryson 1990: 152). Each writer is using the legs as the key indicator in the process of social typification. So too, more neutrally, does Dekker, invoking a London street: 'Chapmen (as if they were at Leape-frog) skippe out of one shop into another: Tradesmen (as if they were dauncing Galliards) are lusty of legges, and neuer stand still' (1885: 51). The activity is not registered by arms or hands. As Brathwaite put it in 1631, 'It is no hard thing to gather the disposition of our heart, by the dimension of our gate' (1970: 82).

Bulwer's work on muscles was, suggests Greenblatt, haunted by a pair of demons. The first of these he identifies as 'involuntary or nonsignificant movement ... twitches, tics, swellings' (Greenblatt 1997: 235). The archetype of involuntary muscular movement is the male erection, which Bulwer found paralleled in the movement of facial muscles: 'the Muscles of the Face are filled with Spirits after the same manner as a certain member directly opposite unto it which importunately sometimes looks us in the Face, which being filled with Spirits growes stiff and is extended' (Greenblatt 1997: 234). Laughter and erections: these are both examples of unwilled and uncontrolled muscular movement. And both are present in the sort of theatre which people like Hamlet criticised. Clowns encourage laughter, and strutting, with its muscular, daring, vaunting male body, is like erection.

Stiff and extended, the strutting body didn't only foreground muscles, but it behaved like muscles which, unbidden, importunately look us in the face. Muscles working beyond the control of brain and soul. It was a mind-less art.

Incarnations of vanity

But its cultural monstrosity has other causes as well.

When in 1612 Thomas Heywood advised actors 'not to vse any impudent or forced motion in any part of the body, no rough, or other violent gesture' (1941: sig. C4r), alongside the concept of force another adjective has sneaked in: 'impudent'. Force is associated with, measured by, disrespect for hierarchy. Good actors keep unstrained action 'in her throne'. But the strutter 'vaunts his voyce upon a hyred stage'. That which is hired owes its place to money rather than natural hierarchy. There is something out of order about strutting. It's not a matter of those who were classed with vagabonds taking the parts of kings – true 'natural' actors did this as well. But strutting had something immodest about it.

Certainly some of the famous strutting narratives told of challenges to high authority by those who were less high. But the immodesty goes deeper. By enacting strain, by displaying muscular exertion in movement and sound – indeed by demonstrating the capacity to produce – the strutter called attention to himself as actor. Here the relationship of force and impudence can be repositioned. It's not so much that if you've got the muscles you might get uppity, but that when you get uppity we particularly notice the muscles. It's as if hierarchic disrespect comes with a certain sort of body.

In Greene's *Orlando* a technique central to the activity of daring is the displaying of the body. It's a trope repeated in what look like apostrophes to mythic gods and landscapes. But they're apostrophes that turn out to be calls for attention – all you elements and gods, see me feeling/doing this. Apostrophe, reaching up and out, is also a calling in towards the self. The strutter produces himself as the looked-upon, just as the voice establishes social relations. It's a gesture of power. Apostrophe as instruction. In this way delivery of the lines organises the musculature (look up, reach out, beckon, display) and establishes it not just as the object to be looked at but also the agent of powerful looking, which Herod set up. The audience is in turn fixed onto that body by its narrative centrality, then by the body's poise, by the microtechniques of the dare, by the persisting engrained voice. Its concentration is thickened up, intensified, made visceral. It is fixated there. Becoming the object at which the impudent male looks back.

It is as male self-display that it seems to be critiqued in 1609. In Act 5 scene 3 of Fletcher's *Faithful Shepherdess* the characters who had spent the night in the forest are returning home at dawn, being met by the Priest of Pan. Amarillis enters, in flight from the Sullen Shepherd; she is concealed by the Priest and they both watch as the Sullen Shepherd enters. He stands and addresses the off-stage Amarillis, telling her to wait, and advertising his own attractiveness: 'Turn again, and see/ Thy shepherd follow, that is strong and free'. His poetry describes his own body and he physically displays himself during the speech. He appears to be in sole occupation of the stage, directing the audience's look at himself (see/free), while his voice alone fills the otherwise silent air. It's a mode of occupying the stage that might be likened to Tamburlaine. But the role is neither as free nor as physically central as he imagines. He is watched by the hidden, disapproving Priest and Amarillis. The youthful male watched by age and womanhood. The audience, aware of the hidden watchers, is now positioned so that its look at the active male body is distracted. Far from seeming potent and central, that body now looks arrogant. It is display without function. Playing without purpose, as that Danish student put it.

And his opinion has a long historical legacy. In dealing with strutters modern commentary has to sort its way through two sets of discourses – that of, say, the seventeenth century and that of its own cultural moment. To encounter that second one, let's come forward to look at a familiar late twentieth-century body. Describing the body-builder, States says the body 'is put to no use: it becomes nothing else, it presents nothing beyond its own grotesque possibilities. ... the muscleman's display is the incarnation of vanity' (1985: 122). One place it performs is in action movies. In a survey of the discourses around these Yvonne Tasker quotes typical hostile criticism of the 'baroque muscles' as 'largely non-functional decoration' (Tasker 1993: 78). Such criticism in more theoretical language is exemplified by this from Barbara Creed, describing muscle stars as 'simulacra of an exaggerated masculinity, the original completely lost to sight, a casualty of the failure of the paternal signifier' (1987: 65). And this body attracts another label: 'it is difficult not to see the engorged muscular physique as a giant potent penis, and difficult not to think that that is precisely what it is *supposed* to be' (Ian 1996: 194). The terms begin to be familiar.

When it enters the movies the built body also has another set of values laid over it. Commentators on sci fi movies note a fascination with the 'armoured body' (Lorentzen 1995). The reference here is specifically to Nazi culture, which has generated a body discourse that intensively works over the familiar terms. Right at the start Mumford in 1934 attacked mass sports where the 'surrogate manliness and bravado are the surest sign of ... a pervasive death wish' (1934: 304). More modern commentary has focused on the marching, with its goose-step producing the 'superfluously vigorous, erect strutting Nazi' (Bosmanian 1971: 162). Conceived as a way of seizing control of the streets, this sort of muscular display was a clear performance of aggression. Indeed, in general, the political culture of Nazism encouraged explicit exhibitions of embodied ideology which McNeill describes as 'expressions of muscular loyalty' (1995: 147).

When the armoured body slides into association with the built body, the one haunting the other, it gives an ethical grounding to what seems to be already a deep tradition. Noting that body-builder movies are dismissed as 'dumb movies for dumb people', Yvonne Tasker comments that 'cultural (class) power is associated with an articulate, verbal masculinity, an identity that is played off against a masculinity defined through physicality' (1993: 98, 107). The audience for Forrest's melodramatic biceps aesthetics wept 'good hearty tears'. The audience for the newer star, Edwin Booth, was 'refined', 'cultivated', 'intellectual' (Walker 1999: 27). Back further, strutters were mocked by the newer, smarter men of theatre. There seems to be a repeated trope.

That trope, and the values in it, are naturalised culturally by being presented as opinions on good and bad acting. We have seen Jonson's views. In the modern period too there is a very strong sense that the musclemen are bad actors and the films uncomplicated vehicles which allow Stallone, Schwarzenegger, van Damme to show their stuff. But it's worth pausing to ask what exactly is being 'acted' here. Dyer describes the labour that goes into the production of the effect of a built body (1999: 148–55). The performance is not only underpinned by rigorous training regimes, it is also a performance of the quality of 'physicality'. This is often emphasised by narrative. The structure of *Universal Soldier* (1992), for example, produces the two musclemen as an excessive pairing, oddly like Orlando quite unnecessarily fighting the peers of France, just for the sake of display. Schwarzenegger has most recently demonstrated an ability convincingly to perform the language of North American politics. It's not quite like the way he talks in action movies. The minimal and simple lines given to the body-builder star are, perhaps, as precise in their construction and effect as the blank verse made available for bellowing.

When Barba and Saverese review world-wide performing techniques they comment that in the west 'the search for realism, or better, naturalism, and psychological rather than physical bases for action have gradually destroyed a heritage of rules fixing performer behaviour' (1991: 192). In the context of a search for naturalism the strutting body seems excessive, an example of bad acting. It is certainly not allowed as part of a heritage of rules based on physical performance. Indeed, the refusal of its cultural legitimacy as a mode of performance is a thoroughly entrenched position. For that search for naturalism seems also to stand in for, and help to articulate, an antipathy to a range of other things. Such things as a body that is 'unnaturally' built, a body as deliberate simulacrum, physical impudence, a body displayed for its own sake, physicality as power.

Cacophany

Something else besides the strutting body is effaced from the tradition. It's that audience body which is shouting, weeping, consuming, smelly – the body of amphitheatres, melodrama houses, 'popular' art. The body which is noisy. The forms of theatre that set themselves against strutting and ranting are the ones that want to organise noise out of existence. In doing so, they could also be seen to be denying one of the basic activities of theatre, which faces violence in order ritually to dispel it, which risks and organises noise. The silenced theatre is a theatre which has also tamed the body, made it respect limits, given it second place to mind, and ensured that it is always functional – like a proper labour force.

The body is regulated by its duty to carry the signs, to be purposeful, to become both meaningful and natural and, naturally, transparent. How, within the particular culture of the west, might a theatrical practice return to an insistence on the sheerly physical thereness of a body, a body released from the tidiness of signification?

Early on in the performance, for example, an actor might introduce an endoscope through one of his nostrils. On a screen behind him, while he speaks, you can look at the interior of his body, descending with the camera to the entry to the vocal cords. You watch as the words you hear are made.

This scene comes from Romeo Castellucci's production of *Giulio Cesare* (1996). In his notes to that production, Castellucci says that he doesn't believe in 'the simple theatre, in the pure theatre'. Instead he looks to rhetoric 'as to a hard mother who teaches me the art of the theatre' (1997: 4). 'Rhetoric accepts and reveals the corruption of the theatre: it looks at the theatre in a pitiless and knotty way: it enhances the true face of the theatre which is just that of falsehood, corruption' (1997: 2). He chooses to do Shakespeare's *Julius Caesar* because it is a play about rhetoric, with incorporated quotations from the Roman historians. But it is as much Roman theatre as Roman history that Castellucci looks back to. For him Roman theatre is more focused on the body than is Greek theatre; it is not so much literary as literal.

> The Roman theatre doesn't avail itself of the sublimity of the word, but it is a literal text, for it shows and executes 'literally' ... Once again, rhetoric is involved: in rhetoric what is important is the fusion between word and body: the word "Made Flesh" or the "literal" body are the same thing.
>
> (Castellucci 1997: 5)

In the forum scene Mark Antony is played by a laryngectomised performer. This, says Castellucci, is 'a prophet of a new voice', a voice which is 're-born' (1997: 6). For the audience the famous 'Friends, Romans, countrymen' is heard afresh, not because it is a new interpretation of the lines but because we hear the sound as production. We hear the words being made by and in the body. Sound levels are often kept just at the threshhold of audibility. This is as difficult to deal with as sound which is too loud – it is as interfered with, as noisy. The concentration is on the work of that voicebox as much as on the poetry of the speech. And the difference of what we are hearing becomes more marked as, through the loudspeakers, comes the recorded sound of a very Anglicised Brando doing the same speech. Fluent, poetic, literary, recorded, recordable voice – disembodied.

'The "cacophany theory". "Caco" means "ugly". And Caco was also a mythical thief' (Castellucci 1997: 11). This is classic Shakespeare stolen and made 'ugly', in that it has become insistently embodied. Words and flesh are fused. That's what we literally see in the endoscopy scene:

> the image seen by the spectator leads to the total coincidence between the word and its vision (the vision of its carnal origin) and produces bewilderment because one doesn't really know which is the prevailing part: if the word spoken or the sight of the letter.
>
> (1997: 7)

Castellucci's attack on 'simple' and corrupt theatre involves, in the 1990s, the exploration of new means of embodiment, the refusal of literariness. It is also a refusal of tidy beautification, of commoditised acting. Castellucci uses people who are non-actors, cast because of their physical qualities, their bodies and voices, rather than their ability to reproduce theatrical formulae. This then produces a different sort of watching, without familiar reference points in conventions of acting. It leads an audience into new, complex areas where response falls outside neatly available categories. 'What is indescribable is what can be seen, what is not important to be said any more. Blood and visions produced in the musical power of the hydraulic organs and war trumpets' (1997: 5).

Castellucci's formula for blood, organs and trumpets sounds a bit like the trumpets-and-drums description of strutting plays. They too could be seen as a theatre of cacophany. So could melodrama. Of course they dealt in different sorts of body, and over time became customary, cliché-ridden – and then simple, rather than complex. But they can also be seen to be positioned in a similar relationship to literariness. For the theatres of cacophany insist on embodying the word, anchoring it in the flesh. They deal in that which is not necessary, in literalness, in excess. Bodies that question their allocated boundaries.

7 Lolo's breasts and a wooden Christ

This chapter is interested in performance practices that take the body into domains in which it becomes apparently de-natured or cyborged. In these practices there is a negotiation between body and non-body, but the terms of that negotiation change in different cultures. Performance, it suggests, has something to do with the relationship between organism and object.

Body gurus

Let us begin with things people will do to their bodies in the interests of being a better performer. This section will look at two examples of bodies trained and manipulated.

One of the performer-training regimes that is currently influential has been developed by the Japanese theatre-maker Suzuki Tadashi. Suzuki's work came to pre-eminence in the late 1970s. Its roots lie in the Japanese classical tradition of *noh* and *kabuki*, mingled with a response to Japanese post-war reconstruction and western existentialism (Allain 2002). Suzuki wants to find a physical language to transcend cultural difference. The way towards that language is through training regimes. These consist of exercises that develop the physical concentration and control of the performer by setting physical targets which are very difficult to achieve.

> At best, ideals of performance should be developed into a practical system; and even if that level cannot be reached, there is certainly no reason to give up trying, and so reveal a total lack of any critical spirit whatsoever.
>
> (Suzuki 1986: 63)

The spiritual authenticity of the work is established, somewhat penitentially, in the struggle with the body's physical recalcitrance.

In his most famous theoretical text, 'The Grammar of the Feet', Suzuki describes an exercise in which the performers pound their feet on the ground in time with rhythmic music. It requires 'an even, unremitting strength without loosening the upper part of the body'. Loss of concentration means an actor cannot continue to the end 'with a unified, settled energy'. That debilitating moment comes about when the actor 'misses the sense of being toughened or tempered' (Suzuki 1986: 9). A sense of physicality is acquired through consciousness of the feet. Whereas in daily life the relationship of the feet to the ground is taken for granted, 'in stamping, we come to understand that the body establishes its relation to the ground through the feet, that the ground and the body are not two separate entities' (Suzuki 1986: 9). As a consequence of the training, then, the actor has a very different sense of her existence on stage from what she has in daily life. The achievement of this difference from the daily in its turn has value within a philosophical position which views modern life, negatively, as sterile and mechanised. The body trained to be outside the daily puts us in touch with 'fundamentals'. The drive is away from the localised, the specific, the culturally diverse, the individual towards the abstracted and universal. This, for Suzuki, is the importance of *noh* performance, although he recognises that modern practitioners such as Grotowski are on the same journey. When *noh* actors appear to inhabit sacred space, it is because of the relationship between their body and space. The traditional fixed arrangements of the *noh* stage have been 'internalised into their very bodies … The actor's body and the space reveal a mutual connection. I call a space which is thus connected to the actor's body a *sacred space*' (Suzuki 1986: 91). The effect of this sacred space is to make a break in the flow of worldly time, reaching to fundamentals.

Those fundamentals can also be found through the stamping exercises. For although they seem to require an actor's excessive concentration on her own body, the stamping also works to call forth the energy of an object that is worshipped and to take that energy into oneself. What gets imaged, especially through the sound of the stamping (which on the *noh* stage creates echoes), is 'a mutual response between actor and spirit' (Suzuki 1986: 14). The actor's body is penetrated, then, by that which is usually outside the body – the 'spirit', the space of the *noh* stage, the ground. So that within the *noh* tradition actors 'create gestures of true dignity and majesty, just as though they had no individual sense of their corporeal being' (Suzuki 1986: 46). And in being free of the corporeal entertain the sacred.

The assimilation of body to non-body is a project to rediscover fundamental values in a world that is mechanised, culturally diverse, individualised. Or, to come at it another way, the exercise which compels awareness of the limitations of the body leads to a fixation on that which marks the limit and lies beyond it. A number of Suzuki's exercises have their rhythm set by the beating of sticks. In her account of participating in workshops, delivered at Performance Studies International 7 (held in Mainz in 2001), Julia Whitworth (unpublished) described the participant's body in direct relationship with normative demands on it. Crucial in this process is the sound of the stick cracking against the floor and cutting through the air. The exercise is undeniably led from outside. The participant is 'at the mercy of the leader' with regard to how long difficult positions are held within a regime which sets 'you against your body, your breath … the floor'. The effect, as Whitworth described it, is 'Pavlovian'. But what could also be observed, as Whitworth herself realised, is that the effect was not confined to the duration of the workshop. Regularly in her account she returned to the beating of the stick – 'which I keep emphasising'. There at an academic conference an ocean away the power of the stick was still inside her body. And that power seemed to speak a master discourse – where Suzuki's 'tyranny' coexists with the participant's learnt understanding of the physical and mental 'purity' of the form.

Purity is an interesting word here. The training seems pure because of the totally focused concentration. But that concentration is produced in exercises, and theories, which promote the assimilation of body and non-body – ground, space, spirit; a mingling rather than a purifying. But a loss of individuality promoted by a loss of physical integrity is not always ideologically marked as 'pure'. Take for example the performances of the late Lolo Ferrari.

Known to most TV viewers through Channel 4's *Eurotrash*, Lolo eventually had her own spot on the programme, 'Look at Lolo'. In this she would demonstrate some simple leisure activity, such as inflating an airbed, throwing frisbees, doing the hula hoop. In the latter sequence she and her constant pair of male companions showed their complete inability to produce the bodily dexterity required to keep the hoop anywhere near the hips. Performing with tanned bodies in swimwear, the three enacted bodily ineptitude. Sequences often ended with the men giggling at each other's efforts while Lolo stolidly presented herself to camera.

That presentation to camera generically fixed Lolo. She had come to fame in the world of media soft porn, where her artificially enlarged breasts were much photographed. With its surgically reorganised face and breasts, Lolo's body was produced as sex object within a heterosexual economy. And it is within that context that the arrangements of 'Look at Lolo' seem deviant – for the men show no desire for her, and her own objecthood is foregrounded through her physical incapacity. Meanwhile, elsewhere on the show female fashion models might appear live with the presenter, Antoine de Caunes, in routines in which he played clown to their sexiness produced as elegance and charisma. Against these figures Lolo was one of the stream of physical eccentrics, the trash of *Eurotrash*. Or she herself was a clown. That conspicuously modified body, the assimilation of flesh and silicon, somewhat disrupted the familiar and daily production of female body as sex object. It enacted unnaturalness. But that was an act that Lolo didn't seem to be fully in control of.

For as the biographical film *Look at Lolo* revealed, Lolo did herself desire fame, and her husband helped her to that fame by suggesting, planning and overseeing the modifications to her body. Those breasts were objects of his invention and pleasure. In the size of those breasts we see the body assimilated to more than silicon – we see perhaps the 'mutual response between actor and' – well, not quite spirit, but a form of masculine desire.

The borrowing of Suzuki's phrase is intended not simply to provoke an exploration of Lolo's penetrated body but to reflect back on the terms of the exploration. For just as the master's tyranny, with its pounding rhythm and its stick, teaches the body to assimilate to that which is non-body – ground, space, spirit – so the husband's desire, and the promise of being extraordinary, transcendent even, may have taught the body to assimilate to non-body in the form of silicon. Lolo's body could be said to be inhabited by the project of her own guru. And that guru also had his drive towards abstraction. Lolo's body was designed to become the perfect female sex object. Or, put more precisely, it was designed to imitate an ideal of body that was in circulation. But which was never real, in any individual, localised way. In a similar way the Suzuki performer reaches for an ideal, losing a sense of individuality to make contact with fundamentals which, again, don't exist in any culturally specific, local form. Each body – in its relations with non-body – may be said to be a copy of that which does not exist, a simulacrum perhaps.

A difference between them is that one is 'trash' and the other is serious. That distinction partly derives from the cultural frames around each. But those frames articulate a set of value judgements. Suzuki training is practised in workshops that foreground effort, liveness that can't be mediated; Lolo is photographed, an identity always mediated, while the pain of the surgery – its liveness – has no discursive presence. The Suzuki performer trains to reach something 'authentic', a set of values more fundamental than today's mechanised, localised culture. Lolo's project to become an ideal female sex object is debased precisely to the extent that it moves away from the individual to the generalised. Values that oppose the mechanised seem to have more seriousness than values that affirm the sexualised body: one is a caricature, the other is not. Lolo's performance practice apparently shows her subjugation to the will of a characteristically masculine power; the Suzuki performer, on the other hand …

Finally, Lolo's silicon implants are really in there. In there in a way which the ground is not in the performer. For all Suzuki's insistence that the ground and the body are not two separate entities, the only way in which they can reach the effect of penetration is through sound and energy. Or, to use another of Suzuki's words, 'spirit'. For the distinction of seriousness between Suzuki's dream of a body penetrated by non-body and Lolo's breasts is a distinction of value between spirit and matter.

Post-human body

The mingling of body and non-body has its own familiar contemporary name – cyborg. But neither the Suzuki performer nor Lolo Ferrari fit very closely with popular notions of cyborg. For those notions tend to be based on experience of sci fi movies, comics and novels – Robocop's human face in a machine body, William Gibson's humans with a range of implants. In turn these fictional encrustations differ from cyborg's linguistic (if not cultural) point of origin. The article on 'Cyborgs and Space', written by Clynes and Kline, originally appeared in *Astronautics* in September 1960. It was a consideration of how the human body would need to adapt to space travel. As Clynes, a concert pianist as well as a neurophysiologist, put it in 1977, cyborg 'denotes how a man may extend his regulatory processes to suit the environment he may choose to live in' (1977: 192). Thus there is no reason why in space travel he should take 'an encapsulated earth environment with him ... rather he should use his intelligence to redesign his bodily regulatory processes, supplementing them with artificial automatic homeostatic devices' (Clynes 1977: 193). Thirty-four years later, using an interesting noun, he explicitly rejected the science fictionalisation of the term, as a 'monsterification of something that is a human enlargement of function' (Clynes quoted in Gray 1995: 47).

But Clynes was fighting a losing battle against the deluge of cyborg-speak. For there is now a large number of entities regarded as cyborg. Indeed, from a point of view that regards cyborgness as a functional dependency of body on machine and the imbrication of body with information systems, then everyone in the developed world is a cyborg. In critical commentary as in popular imagination, however, it is not so much Clynes' human enlargement of function as the body–machine interface which is the object of focus. There is about cyborgs an air of scientificity, where the science feels new. Indeed, it is this newness which for Gray and his co-editors marks the break with previous examples of body–machine interface. If we can look back and see earlier examples of humans using objects as cyborgian, that is because of our own mindset. This mindset has been produced in a world where 'information disciplines, fantasies and practices' have 'transgressed the machinic–organic border', so that there is no longer the clear break between machines and organisms (Gray, Mentor and Figueroa-Sarriera 1995: 5).

Presumably it would be possible to trace a similar conceptual and physiological shift marking the invention of the wheel. But that 'cyborg' needs to be delimited in its application to the present moment indicates its rhetorical productivity. That is to say, we know we have encountered the epistemological break into postmodernity because we can think cyborg. Commentators have noted this metaphoric and ideological potential (King 1989; Penley and Ross 1991; Sobchack 1994; Lupton 1995; Wilson 1995;

Lury 1998). Analyses of movies and prose fiction show the cyborg as a place where, for instance, ideas about nature and gender are foregrounded, if not tested (Springer 1991, 1994; Balsamo 1995; Holland 1995). In Gabilondo's essay on 'Postcolonial Cyborgs' (1995) the cyborg functions as part of a new ideological apparatus, together with consumer culture, in relation to modern capitalism. But when it is treated as rhetorical device, with whatever subtlety, a sense of the involvement of real body within cyborg begins to vanish. However imaginatively engaging they are, however kinaesthetically activated the spectator, filmed bodies, computer-generated images, are not physically present to, inhabiting the same space as, spectators. And where we do encounter, in real space and time, a cyborg we tend not to notice ... the person with contact lenses or heart pacemaker, the woman in the wheelchair or – as Clynes would say – the man on a bicycle (Hogle 1995; Wilson 1995). The rhetorical force of the word cyborg insists on it as a marker of a break. An achieved and naturalised assimilation of body and machine remains merely human – cyborg has, obligatorily, to describe the posthuman.

A physical attempt to produce and inhabit the posthuman body has been undertaken by performance artist Stelarc. In a series of experiments/shows he has exteriorised the interior of his body by inserting a camera, and he has decentred control over his own organism by having his body electronically wired so that operators at remote terminals can initiate the impulses which activate his muscles (Stelarc 1998, 2000; Farnell 2000; http://www.stelarc.va.com.au). The poststructuralist body with no psychic interior, the body decentred across information systems, these are literally imaged. Yet at the same time, as a performer, Stelarc also initiates and organises the experiments in which he risks his own body. He retains his managerial agency, and indeed his star status. Unlike the body kept alive by the pacemaker or the 'dead' donor body with equipment and chemicals plugged into it, Stelarc's posthuman body is the product of a set of stunts which foreground their own scientificity. It is a dramatisation of modernness, with Stelarc as both author and performer.

A way of avoiding the agency that comes with such adventuring is in the performed installation, using the body 'in such a way as to reduce it to the status of a mere component in an economy of artifacts and environment' (Tomas 1995: 257). Employing Roger Caillois' notion of psychasthenia, David Tomas argues that in this art the body's own representational space incorporates object-like attributes and thus 'promotes a simultaneous "*generalization of* [physical/ artifactual] *space* at the expense of the individual" body's subjective autonomy' (1995: 257). Later Tomas takes this beyond art practice to argue that in 'technologically-intensive performed installations machine systems become ... the determining factor in the definition of the body's physical installation' (1995: 259). He goes on: 'A modern fighter plane is a technological breeding ground for a new kind of site-specific "self"' (Tomas 1995: 260; see also Virilio 1991: 96

on the technician as a 'victim of the movement he's produced'). I'd guess that the fighter pilot herself had a self-image that was to do with control, accuracy, quickness – agency. But the image of such a pilot, helmeted, within the controls, like the appearance of the performed installation, suggests an interrelation of body and objects. Once that's said, a problem arises.

For the production of apparent relationship between body and objects has been part of the work of performance for a number of centuries. Betterton's Hamlet (followed by Spranger Barry's and Garrick's) expressed shock by knocking over a chair; the fan of the Restoration actress expressed almost everything (Sofer 2003); Richard Foreman's lighting works to metamorphose 'person to person-object, and, conversely, object to some form of living matter' (Falk 1999: 42). These are clearly 'apparent' relationships – not authentically felt as the installed performer might feel them. But there is another set of sensors in the room, those of the audience. Within certain modes of performance that audience is encouraged to – what? – lose itself, suspend disbelief, get caught up in the action. Or let's put it another way: 'the imaginary of the word and the imaginary of the film or video image' can be taken, says Mark Poster, one step further by 'placing the individual "inside" alternative worlds'. This one step further is 'virtual reality' (Poster 1995: 86). Now although it's not what I think Poster means by 'virtual reality', it is worth asking what sort of reality was being inhabited by the nineteenth-century audience that shouted – and threw things – at the villain. That audience could be said to be having its physiological mechanisms controlled by the discourses working upon it, finding itself physically caught up into an information system, cyborgised.

In putting it that way I am suggesting that much of the discussion of cyborg is an engagement with the mechanisms of performance and, particularly, spectatorship. Stelarc describes an experiment whereby analyses of JPEG files 'provide data that is mapped to the body via the muscle stimulation system … The images that you see are the images that move you' (Stelarc 2000: 123). Alphonso Lingis suggests that this is always the case: 'The apprehension of an exterior objective, as something soliciting the synergic hold of the sensibility, dynamically orients the postural schema' (Lingis 1994: 14). What Stelarc has done is to set up an experiment/performance which concretises a basic, but hidden, neural-physiological process. The effect of the performance is to suggest that this is happening for the first time, and that it happens only as a result of the interface of body and technology – that a cyborg has been born.

The impact of that birth upstages the discussion and staging of body/non-body and virtuality which have occupied phenomenology and performance practice. It is able to upstage because, as we have seen, the cyborg is a marker of the new and its rhetoric is cathected. And this oddly dis-bodied cyborg – with its obliviousness to ordinary bodily processes – is the thing Manfred

Clynes was critical of. He thought it traduced his project of 'human enlargement of function'. That project, adapting the body for space travel, depended on self-regulating 'man–machine' systems. These would function 'without the benefit of consciousness in order to cooperate with the body's own homeostatic controls'. Such capabilities, at their mimimal, are 'demonstrated under control conditions such as yoga or hypnosis. The imagination is stretched by the muscular control of which even the undergraduate at a Yoga College is capable' (Clynes and Kline 1995: 30–1). That control of individual body may be taken further, as de Landa notes, through the widely available historical practice of military drilling, where individuals are taken up into a machinic system, becoming a body of men (1998: 58ff.), the group body I described in Chapter 4.

The bodily discipline that Clynes and Kline had in mind, for 'human enlargement' – and certainly that of the drilled body – seems to be more akin to the training programme of Suzuki than to the techno-acrobatics of Stelarc. But at this point the modern image of the cyborg intervenes, keeping apart the 'modern' work of Stelarc and the performer-training system. Performer training may have everything to do with 'human enlargement' but nothing to do with the production of cyborgs.

As Suzuki would attest, with his attacks on the loss of spirit in the modern world. But, in the widest sense of its application, these two rather unlike performance modes both could come under the word 'cyborg'. The limits of body and the possibilities of its enlargement – hollowed, united with the ground, decentred – are explored by placing the body within an external mechanical, and discursive, framework that takes it over (Haraway 1991). The stick, and its psychic spasm an ocean away, are as much an effect of the remote operator as the electronic spasm. That these things are regarded as separate has more to do with ideas about kinaesthetics than with kinaesthetic experience. The division of terms here is taken from Hillel Schwartz, who mobilises it as part of an attempt to describe the new kinaesthetic of the twentieth century, in which movement expresses bodily wholeness. Kinestructs, or kinaesthetic ideals, differ from kinecepts, or 'central kinaesthetic experiences' (Schwartz 1992: 105).

The kinestructs of Suzuki and Stelarc – and indeed Lolo Ferrari – are separated by ideas about spiritual purpose and modernity. But they are not so clearly distinguished as kinecepts. For it might be that we are now looking at the emergence of a new kinaesthetic. That kinaesthetic can be found in gym culture, in dieting, in 'building' the body – but also in 'personalising' and inhabiting the accessory, the manner of using the mobile phone, the car that is driven and decorated as enhancement of the person. This new kinaesthetic has to do with the experience not so much of alienated mechanisation of the body but instead of the body as something that can be extended beyond 'natural' limits – where that nature is sterile, humanist, not sexy enough.

The cyborg, then, rather than marking an epistemological break, is itself operated by rather older mechanisms. These mechanisms have to do with the activity of performance.

Cyborgisms

In November 1995 Stelarc conducted a performance experiment called 'Ping Body/Proto-Parasite'. His musculature, in Luxembourg, was wired so that it could be viewed, accessed and activated from terminals in Paris, Helsinki and Amsterdam. The body's movements were involuntary but it could trigger the upload of images to a website. Thus the body was moving 'not to the promptings of another body in another place, but rather to Internet activity itself ... stimulated not by its internal nervous system but by the external ebb and flow of data' (http://www.stelarc.va.com.au). The internet activity comes from operators working at a distance – like puppeteers, perhaps. The rods or strings have been replaced by electronic impulses but the model is similar. And for all the 'postmodernity' of Stelarc's work the relationship of the puppet body to the human performer is quite old.

In that relationship the puppet body reveals human limit, offers an ideal of completeness beyond individual human capability. Kleist, in 1810, reported a dancer saying that the puppet exceeds the capacity of a human dancer. For the puppet will never show affectation, which appears when the soul 'is found at any point other than the movement's center of gravity'. And the puppet is 'antigravitational', having nothing of 'the inertia of matter'. None of this can be equalled by man: 'Only a god could compete with matter in this field' (Kleist 1989: 417–18). The puppet's activity embodies mechanical order, efficiency, control. From these qualities human performers have to learn, as Gordon Craig was later to say, if the art of the theatre is to be saved from the decay caused by the attempt to imitate nature. No actor has yet reached 'such a state of mechanical perfection that his body was *absolutely* the slave of his mind' (Craig 1980: 67). The aim, in Craig's famous formulation of 1907, is to become an Ubermarionette.

Craig's views on the actor as a – so to speak – performing machine can be taken to be symptomatic of his cultural moment. The Italian Futurists were also specifically interested in puppets, but in general modernist engagements with the body tended to focus on its capacity either to be machine-like or to learn from the machine – the word 'robot', as Reichardt tells us, was coined by Capek in 1917, from a Czech word meaning 'obligatory work or servitude' (Reichardt 1978: 31; see also Gropius 1961; Wollen 1993; Segel 1995). Meyerhold's explorations in bio-mechanics (1922) apply the 'constant laws of mechanics' to muscular movement (Braun 1969). In Dziga Vertov's film *Enthusiasm* (1931) such mechanical efficacy is shown to derive from the activity and rhythm of productive work, where the body by means of an object transforms nature. These cultural interests, however, already had their industrial predecessors. Meyerhold wanted to maximise the productivity of the actor in the same way as Taylorism promoted a 'scientific' organisation of time and motion, and thus profit, on the factory floor. This seems to have produced its own aestheticisation in the mechanical orderliness and predictable patterning of the female bodies in dance troupes such as the Tiller Girls and then the movies of Busby Berkeley (Theweleit 1992; Wollen 1993: 54ff; Kracauer 1995; see p. 86).

As I noted in Chapter 4, the agitational sketch *Tempo Tempo* (1930) used verse rhythms to image the effects of capitalist factory speed-up on the workforce – and then used the same rhythms to celebrate the effects of the new Soviet Five-Year Plan. The mechanised body, whether of decorativeTaylorism or productive biomechanics, is foregrounded as both an ideological proposition and an ideological naturalisation, depending where you are coming from. It is this ideological foregrounding, rather than the mere conjunction of body and machine, which would seem to be characteristic of the Modernist moment. Under the smiles of the Berkeley girls they work to balance on the movie set's scenic devices. They adjust their performances against the concealed machinery, which is working to produce an image of perfection, which in turn aestheticises the notion of machine.

That concealed engine of perfection has a history in performance that extends well beyond the temporary ideological concerns of modernism. The tragic actor of ancient Athens learnt physical techniques for performing in a face mask and buskins – those boots that gave elevation to the body. The mask, says Lecoq, is 'a sort of vehicle, drawing the whole body into an expressive use of space, determining the particular movements which make the character appear' (2000: 56). The worn objects produce in and on the body particular modes of walking and of looking – looking with the neck and shoulders, balancing, high-stepping. The outcome of these muscular disciplines is the effect of something more than human, the dignity and gravitas of tragedy. Differently positioned objects – say, a neck-ruff and a corset – will produce different muscular disciplines, accentuating the verticality of the body, holding stiff the length of its spine, producing a high centre of gravity, a decorous stillness and stability even while dancing. The outcomes of these particular techniques are the poise and decorum of the courtly body of the European late sixteenth/early seventeenth centuries (Vigarello 1989; Franko 1993; Howard 1998; McClary 1998). Later still there was a more famous – and indeed still current – attempt to elevate the body further, to raise it literally off the ground. With wooden wedges in her shoes the classical ballet dancer of the mid-nineteenth century minimised her contact with the stage to that of a single point (Hammond and Hammond 1979; Foster 1996). Through a training that developed her leg muscles to the edges of 'womanly' delicacy and threatened permanently to distort her feet, she achieved an effect of disembodied female perfection – or femaleness extended beyond the body and hence perfect. The nymph that is more (or less) than human, woman as non-body.

And the ballerina in this sense comes to be almost like Kleist's puppet, transcending the earthbound limits of human physicality. The effect is further enhanced by her appearance as one of a group, where each duplicates the other's movements, in an artform that not only inhibits individualisation through speech but that also insists on similarities of coiffure and costume. The ballerina, barely an independent subject, is – hence – graceful. For in Kleist's terms grace is 'purest' in a body that has either no consciousness or infinite consciousness: a puppet – or god.

Now, the image of a ballerina *en pointe* is not readily categorised as a cyborg. She is, however, an instance of the relationship with that which is non-body, her wedges, which modifies the organisation of body. It seems even less appropriate to associate regimes of performer training with cyborg. But some of these regimes are also not too distant from the automaton as ideal. Barry King suggests that in general actor training is designed to reduce physical behaviours to 'a state of automaticity' (King 1985: 29). But there is a more specific link. One of the leading figures of modern mime, Etienne Decroux, looked towards 'la naissance de cet acteur de bois' (Decroux 1963: 24). He was alluding to Craig's Ubermarionette, who in turn derived from Kleist's discussion of the puppet. But the genealogy comes forward as well. Craig, polemicist for the mechanical actor, was guest of honour at a mime show in 1945 done by Decroux and Jean-Louis Barrault; in 1972 Barrault met, and inspired, Suzuki; who went on to promote a training regime in which 'the actor moves like a puppet to the rhythm of the music' (Suzuki 1986: 11).

The echoes and parallels I have been trying to generate here are intended to suggest that, far from being higher or more developed, the cyborg is a phenomenon that takes its place in a domain familiar from histories of performed practices. It is one instance of ongoing cultural formulations of the relationship of body and non-body (Gonzalez 1995; Hess 1995). Each of these formulations assumes specific terms and practices defining body and non-body. In turn the deployment of these terms and practices has the potential to articulate the specific values operating in a culture. The cultural cathexis of the neck-ruff is a more insistent use of the carriage of the head as a marker of class than that of the neck-tie. So what cultural value might we observe in the accounts of cyborgs? Some suggest that the image of cyborg presents the body as a site of debate (about for example gender). But arguably this is the case for all imaging and discussion of bodies (early modern dance regimes articulated class values). The point is what the debate is about. In the case of cyborgs the focus seems to fall not so much on the limits of the human body – a more Modernist concern, perhaps – but on the possibilities of human perception and definition.

While that may need arguing, the central point for my purposes here is that the cyborg presents for analysis what all performed practices present – namely particular conjunctions of body and non-body, where the specific selection of object and body part may be taken to be a form of cultural and ideological cathexis.

God and puppet

It is the closing days of Easter Week, Granada, 2001. In a shopping precinct that is deserted in the quiet time of siesta there is a whiff of baroque music. Coming around the corner you see a still figure on a small podium. She wears a blue robe, her head veiled in white. The body tilts forward, leaning towards the flowers that stand in front of it. The only sound is the music.

On its own it is enigmatic – not even drawing much of a crowd. But for anyone who has recently visited the Ramblas of Barcelona, or London's Covent Garden, this performance slots into place. It is one of those living statues, a public art form in which the performer remains as still as possible. Those statues that make movement do so as if automata, repetitively and mechanically. And, to encourage the suggestion of statuary, any exposed flesh is painted in the same colours as the costume – total whiteness or a metallic sheen are the preferred effects. It is a form of busking by doing nothing, meticulously. But unlike the singing busker the statue works to generate a sense of enigma, of not properly belonging to the public space it inhabits. For human occupation of public city space tends to involve activity and sound – reading the paper, chatting, crossing the square, looking in shops, making a speech. Statues are part of the environment of the activity. Except when it's a human being behaving like a statue. And then, because it's clearly human, it becomes a performance of control, of sustaining – against the effects of time on the body – the condition of statueness. The willed choice to be as if non-body.

Here, at long last, I need to pause over the word 'non-body'. My use of it is intended to go beyond, or even go round, the word that might seem more obvious – 'object'. The relations between object and body in performance have already been dealt with eloquently by performance phenomenologists, in particular Stanton Garner Jr. That work draws on concerns that cluster around another binary, that between object and subject. In Merleau-Ponty's formulation that binary is firmly oppositional: 'Every object can affirm its existence only by depriving me of mine' (in Garner 1994: 106). For Garner this tense relationship between object and subject is the new thing that comes to be staged by modern realism, with – in his account – Pinter's *Caretaker* (1960) picturing the subject's discovery of its own contingency and de-centredness in a setting full of de-functionalised and randomly assembled objects (Garner 1994: 110–19). So in their relationship to the body the objects have an effect on the subject: body and subject assimilate to one another on one side of the binary, kept there by antagonistic objects.

This model doesn't fully allow for the sense of body extended through, or invested into, objects. Within the phenomenological account these are objects which retain their functionality, being simply equipment for the subject. But that account has also provided the basis for Garner's thumbnail sketch of the development of performance from a time when stage props were properties, belonging to the person, to a time when they become de-functionalised and unsettling. It's an evolutionary history taking us to modern alienation. What that history occludes is the recurrence of various, but always cathected, body–object relations. For the cyborg is also modern. Indeed it is first formulated in the year of Pinter's *Caretaker*. And, while in itself I'd suggest it is simply another instance of the performed cathexis of body and object relations, as a concept cyborg offers us a way of modelling those relations that doesn't come with all the accumulated phenomenological baggage. This focus on body–object cathexes might give us a different sort of history of performance, which I have sketched bits of in the previous section. It also extends beyond mere object the concept of that which is outside but shaping the body. Cyborgism has given us the information system as bodily environment, something which carries the idea of extension and investment in a way which Foucauldian disciplinary discourses do not. So, by this argument, when Decroux famously says 'The more he holds, the less an actor is required to hold himself well', the first part evokes the (alienating) tension between subject and objects. It is the second part of the statement that envisages taking something into the body, discursively incorporating, in order specifically to make a new body. With Craig behind him, Decroux might be said to be envisaging actor as cyborg.

In front of the shop windows, holding herself well, she was much more enigmatic, more exotic, than those objects imitating bodies in the windows themselves. By the next day she had relocated, into the Cathedral precinct. Midday on Easter Sunday: the baroque tune drifted around the monumental stonework. The statue stood, people walked by. But there, so close to the Cathedral, a different context to the performance insisted itself. For all week still figures had been moving around the streets of the city. These figures were all explicitly religious. And all of them had converged at some point on the Cathedral precinct. In that space, now once again emptied of all the concentration and bustle that surrounded those religious figures, the statue stands. By contrast to that earlier activity the statue's customary enigma looks marginal, fading into something small and thin, individualised, laconic, arty – human.

For those other still figures were made out of wood. Painted and garbed, surrounded by candles and flowers, the figures are mounted on platforms which are carried on the shoulders of thirty-two bearers, hidden, but for their feet, under the wooden structure. One such, the day before, had come up the tree-lined street into the Plaza del Carmen. Preceded by hooded penitents bearing crucifixes and candles, followed by a band which features wailing brass and woodwind, the figure of Christ is bent under the burden of his cross. Caught by the wind, the purple drapery on Christ flutters. As the platform rounds the corner, the bearers change the rhythm of their walk. Turning corners underneath the several tons of their load is a work of art, and to display their skill they change rhythm with the band into a *paso doble*. There, moving but not going forward, seized – in-formed even – by the rhythm of thirty-two bodies in unison, the platform sways. And with it, swaying too, 'in the rhythm of the music', its drapery fluttering, the wooden Christ seems to move.

The total effect requires careful organisation and hierarchies of effort. The progress of the procession is facilitated by its administrative minders, with dark suits, shades and mobile phones. The front of the procession consists of penitents in the pointed hoods and robes of their order, adults and children, some barefoot. On a warm day the robes make it hotter. Behind the platform is the band, in uniforms with caps, with the heaviest instruments, the drums, doing most work. Most hidden, but working hardest, are the bearers. Their movement is constrained by the necessity to maintain complete unity among themselves, to liaise rhythmically with the band and, above all, to sustain and manipulate – and to display their capacity to manipulate – that object they inhabit. Weighing on their shoulders is the non-body which is god. We are in a culture of icons. As Baudinet says, 'Transfiguration, *metamorphosis*, this is the name that designates both the glory of the resurrected body and the work of the spectator's gaze on the icon' (Baudinet 1989: 151). The platform is touched reverently as it passes. Yet the non-body's movement depends, as does a puppet, on its bearers. But the bearers' bodies are disciplined by the object, and its non-body, that contains them.

When they have departed from the Cathedral precinct, what is left on Easter Sunday is a woman performing her body as if it were non-body, a statue. The relationship between her and the processions is probably entirely fortuitous, produced by this chapter. And that relationship could be mapped in various frames: independent performer or organised religio-economic brotherhood; secular versus religious; new art or invented tradition (some processions started as recently as the 1980s); individual woman or patriarchal community; solo effort versus group discipline. The mode of embodiment in each case makes meaning or, to use Donna Haraway's (1991: 195) phrase, 'Embodiment is significant prosthesis'.

She uses the phrase in an essay about feminism and the production of knowledge. Inspecting the claims of impassive objectivity and decoding, she argues for a deliberate partiality, for 'situated' knowledges. 'Accounts of a "real" world do not, then, depend on a logic of "discovery", but on a power-charged social relation of "conversation". The world neither speaks itself nor disappears in favour of a master decoder' (Haraway 1991: 198). She offers her survey of explanatory trends in biology as an 'allegory' applicable to the project of feminist objectivity. And adds: 'The boundary between animal and human is one of the stakes in this allegory, as well as that between machine and organism' (1991: 200). In another essay she returns to this boundary. Her particular focus here is the discourse(s) of immunology, but her observations about the delineation of boundary have bearing, I think, on those performance practices in Granada – as indeed elsewhere. 'Organisms are made; they are constructs of a world-changing kind. The constructions of an organism's boundaries, the job of the discourses of immunology, are particularly potent mediators of the experiences of sickness and death ...' (Haraway 1991: 208). Similarly, '"objects" like bodies do not pre-exist as such. Scientific objectivity (the siting/sighting of objects) is not about disengaged discovery, but about mutual and usually unequal structuring' (1991: 208). Insisting on the historical specificity of bodies, she suggests that the object of knowledge is 'an active part of the apparatus of bodily production'. Hence 'Bodies as objects of knowledge are material-semiotic generative nodes. Their boundaries materialize in social interaction' (1991: 208). And, we might now add, these social interactions have to include performance practices.

The history of performance practices shows changing relationships between body and non-body. The particular point of physical contact, and the conceptual terms of the relationship, change historically. The cathexes in a particular culture's performance of body/non-body may tell us something about that culture. But from this point we can now take a further step. If Haraway's account of the delineation of boundaries is correct, it would seem that performance is one of those sites that enable this delineation to take place. Casting our minds back to those performances in Granada, we can see that they draw differing boundaries between object and organism, and that these boundaries pertain to such things as tradition and novelty, individuality and community, secularity and religion. As Haraway says, 'what counts as an object is precisely what world history turns out to be about' (1991: 195). Or, in the more local case of that Spanish Easter Week, the relations of god and man.

8   Dissipation

The room is dark. Over by the staircase there is a glow of light. Someone is descending the stairs. A young woman appears carrying a lamp. Claudine is walking into the opening of Act 2 of Pocock's 1813 play *The Miller and his Men*.

A pair of flashlights probe the darkness. Each beam moves separately over a large shadowy warehouse, searching. Somewhere in the shadows something inexplicable moves. Behind the flashlights two figures, male and female, in long dark coats, only their faces highlighted, looking.

Scenic openings

That second example could be any one of a whole series of episodes of the TV sci-fi series *The X Files*. The two detectives, Scully and Mulder, had as a sort of hallmark the flashlight search sequence. Probing unknown spaces was their specialised business. If that is an *X Files* cliché, the young woman with a lamp is no less so. When, in a play or movie, she moves with her fragile light source into shadowy spaces, we feel that she is taking a risk, about to encounter danger.

And how do we feel this? The single light source creates sharply defined and various masses of shadow. As the lamplight swings around, the shadow appears itself to be mobile. Light and dark play across the body that holds the lamp. That body, although it is bearing light – an agent of illumination – is also caught up into something bigger than itself, the interplay between light and dark. The flashlight beam is never quite wide enough, the lamplight is too feeble, the candle flickers and gutters. The separation between the body and the space it moves through is often blurred, as the light continually gets absorbed into shadow. The body begins to lose its distinctness.

What Claudine finds in the room are the sleeping bodies of the Count and his servant; the fire is nearly out. Then she hears noise, puts out her lamp and hides as her father, who is as sleepless as herself, comes in. He tells us that he wants to solve the mystery of the Miller's behaviour, which 'hangs like a fearful dream' on his mind. As the dawn glimmers he sets off. Claudine reappears, concerned for her father, and exits. The Count's servant starts to talk in his sleep and half-wakes. As he talks, 'A light from the dark lantern borne by Riber is seen passing the window'. Then Riber appears at the door, but quickly steps back, away from the light suddenly caused by the servant stirring up the fire. The servant settles to sleep again. Riber, with his lantern, comes in with the Miller (Pocock 1974: 104–5).

The light changes almost as frequently as the characters come and go. The stage is always shadowy, but lit at different times from a variety of sources – the embers of a dying fire, Claudine's lamp, the glimmer of dawn, a sudden blaze from the fire, a dark lantern. Spectators trained in melodramatic convention might be familiar with such lighting arrangements and patterns. So too they might predict that, in a cottage with a window and a door, something untoward will be seen through that window and someone unexpected will walk through that door. Just as shadows are going to be pierced by sudden lights so openings are going to be filled. When Riber first appears at the door, he doesn't walk in; he steps back. It is a classic melodrama trope: a doorway is a threshold; rather than walk straight across that threshold, the body pauses on it, taken over by the rhythm of the door, which swings open and shut, but is always fixed to the doorpost. And just as bodies will appear in doorways, so at windows lights or faces from outside will peer in. It is as if the melodramatic setting draws bodies into itself. Scenic openings require human bodies to occupy them; bodily movement is motivated by the rhythms of light; the body protects itself by becoming indistinguishable from the setting. Thus the stage set itself appears to be a major protagonist in the melodramatic text. The human body turns into a function of that setting.

That is the proposition from which I begin here. In the previous chapter I looked at the combination of, and boundary between, body and non-body. In this final chapter I explore the removal of bodily boundary. This also involves a notion of loss of depth. The integrity of the body is gone beyond.

While the apparent loss of bodily boundary is now claimed as one of the distinctive features of virtual reality and cybercultures (Featherstone 2000; Stryker 2000), its story within theatre begins a lot further back.

A person's disposition

As a function of setting the body has its musculature disciplined by the requirements of the set. A woman walking with a candle is carrying something delicate. It could go out if a draught catches it. So a degree of stillness and control is needed in the arm muscles. And since the candle or lamp is used for searching dark spaces, the face must look toward where the candle is held. This in turn places constraints on the movement of neck, shoulders, upper torso. They move as a unit. Meanwhile the other arm and the legs have to feel their way. Their job is to move through space while keeping the light source secure. The effect is that of taut concentration combined with tentative exploration: because it's taut, it's determined, but it is also fragile. What begins as a description of movement with a candle ends up being an analysis of mood, emotion, even the character of the moment. These then could be said to be a result not so much of the actor's intention to depict mood or to characterise, but of the interaction between body and scene. Melodrama operates – perhaps indeed initiates – a mode of scenic characterisation.

That claim needs justification, particularly in the face of a later drama that viewed melodramatic method as a trivialisation of the stage. The new 'serious' drama of the end of the nineteenth century – the thesis plays and naturalism – itself took pains meticulously to describe its settings. This is D. H. Lawrence: 'The kitchen of Luther Gascoigne's new home. It is pretty – in "cottage" style; rush-bottomed chairs, black oak-bureau, brass candlesticks, delft, etc. Green cushions in chairs' (Lawrence 1974a: 99). Minnie is preparing her husband's tea. He is a miner, and soon enters, in his pit-dirt. When, on this occasion, he settles to have his tea without washing first, he has to take precautions:

> *Luther:* I s'll ha'e ter ha'e a newspaper afront on me, or thy cloth'll be a blackymoor. (*Begins disarranging the pots.*)
> *Minnie:* Oh, you *are* a nuisance!
>
> (Lawrence 1974a: 101)

We soon see that there is a lot more at stake than the matter of pit-dirt. In Minnie's eyes, Luther is not really good enough for her. Her aspirations above his social class are marked in the way she speaks, in her manners, in her taste – indeed in the furnishings of the room. The threat that dirt will move from Luther onto the furnishings is a scenic concretising of the difficulty between them. Note, however, that, in contrast to my claim about melodrama above, this is less of a blurring of person with scene and more of a conflict between character and setting.

Of course Minnie's kitchen gives insights into her character; indeed it shows how she wants life to be. But it is a source of struggle. So too for Mrs Holroyd, shown at the door of her miner's cottage while we hear the pulse of the fan engine and the chuffing of the driving engine in the pit headstocks. That sound marks the thing that exerts pressure on her, puts limits on her life. Naturalist setting proposes how environment determines character. Contrast with her and Minnie an aristocrat who sits in her conservatory 'and with a pair of scissors seems busily engaged in trimming the flowers in pots on stand' (Hazlewood 1972: 252). She is required to continue trimming flowers throughout the scene that follows. In that scene she is accused of killing her first husband. Surrounded by her flowers, doing her amateur gardening,

Lady Audley maintains the image of an aristocrat. The setting is not her product, it doesn't limit her behaviour, and her work in it is a mere game. She claims it is a 'mask'.

It is a rather suggestive notion. Trimming flowers produces an image of the 'lady-like' body, restrained in its movement, delicate and careful, not distorted by effort. Yet Lady Audley's body can also achieve considerable size of gesture and movement. Her sedentary delicacy is thus an image of a body constrained, brought within limit: a not unviolent image. The scissors, furthermore, are used by a hand that has carried out murder. This knowledge, combined with their constant use during the verbal fencing, gives to the scissors a suggestion of the weapon. But of course they are not a weapon – they would be very much less potent in the 'mask' if they had any association with weaponry. And, although they are used to make cuts into plants, that use is delicate, precise, ladylike. Because she is required to sit, the physical concentration is on hands and fingers, the points where her body mingles itself with flower heads. The woman sits like a flower among flowers, and she cuts at those flowers with a movement that, in its ladylike precision, might be said to make her even more flower-like.

The conservatory, its flowers, the activity of the scissors – all are compelled to Lady Audley's use in establishing her 'mask'. And, being worn by her, they seem to be inhabited by her, becoming extensions of her own body. The scene adds nothing to our knowledge of Lady Audley's character, however. Instead it could be said to emphasise what we already know, to intensify and prolong our exposure to her presence. It spreads her out over the scenic space. The attempt to describe the interplay of flowers and scissors and woman's body offers merely a set of suggestions, possibilities; it is engaging because it is, cognitively, unfixed.

A body's objects

Lady A's scissors are not a tool on which labour is expended for the purpose of transforming the surroundings. By contrast, Minnie works with saucepans to make a meal. Even though the meal is fictional, the pots are really carried to table and really set out with neat precision. Crucial in the interrelationship of body and scene is the role of objects or props.

When Mrs Holroyd does her laundry, the performer's body is required to work on stage. Within the fiction that work is continually necessary: just as Luther needs to protect the tablecloth from pit-dirt, so Blackmore needs to get rid of his swarf before touching the sheets. The work to fend off dirt transforms the environment in a way that expresses the woman's ambitions. Minnie and Mrs Holroyd may imprint their characters on their settings, but those settings are the result, and cause, of labour. And while their bodies are caught up into the routines of that labour there is a sense of plans and ambitions that are frustrated. The work of the body here is separate from, and an imprisonment of, the mind. That's important, because a notion of an autonomous mind can be a device for ensuring the human is distinct from environment.

Lady Audley trims flowers in order to be ladylike, in order, that is, to produce nothing. The trimming is certainly a form of work, but it is not allowed that status. The performer has to orchestrate it in relation to the primary job of maintaining the conversational fencing. The mask of trimming suggests that Lady Audley is mindless, one of those 'silly beings', women. It is intended that there should be no sense of separation between mind and body here. Indeed, for the audience, seeing the disposition of Lady Audley's body in its setting, they are seeing what we also have to call her disposition.

Within the genre of melodrama this is not a strange effect. At its beginnings melodramatists thought of the body as part of the 'scene'. William Dimond recounts that, for political reasons, he removed 'the principal object in my design' – the hero Gustavus Vasa – 'from the foreground, into the perspective' (Dimond 1809: preface). For the melodramatist there was another scenic element besides the 'perspective', the music. Thus Thomas Holcroft directed that music in one part of his *Tale of Mystery* (1802) should express 'first pain and alarm; then the successive feelings of the scene'. At the climax of this scene the heroine shrieks out, 'joining the music, which likewise shrieks' (Holcroft 1802: 21, 22). Holcroft and Dimond themselves may have been working in a tradition. Michael Wilson attributes to pantomime the experiments with 'the assimilation of dramatic situation and subjective landscape'. This was possible because of the literary place, or non-place, of pantomime: 'The aesthetic detachment that effaced literary text allowed a free assimilation of elemental, nonverbal dramatic action to a newly-expressive scenic picture' (1990: 200).

The contemporary context for the melodramatic experiments has been described as 'a new cognitive dispensation', 'a new collective absorption in the increasingly vivid, if also hallucinatory, contents of the mind itself' (Castle 1995: 125). Such concerns are familiar from the works of poets such as Shelley and Keats but before them, feeding directly into melodrama, was the well-established literature of gothic, which posited a whole range of entities existing between human and inanimate domains. The vampire is something neither human nor animal. It is perhaps a human which is always partly in a different region. Anomalous ... 'neither an individual nor a species ... the Thing, which arrives and passes at the edge'. It is, in the words of Deleuze and Guattari, 'a phenomenon of bordering' (1996: 244–5). In its monsters gothic dreams of that which is recognisably human flowing beyond human boundaries, dissipated into the non-human. But never completely, so that what remains is perhaps a supernatural entity, perhaps an effect of light or an accident of music, when that too seems to shriek.

This cultural heritage and its theatrical embodiment linger on in melo-drama. But by the time of Lady Audley the earlier way of doing things was under pressure. The resulting tensions can be observed in the detail of the body's interaction with props and scenic objects. A good illustration comes from Henry Irving's notes for his performance of Mathias in *The Bells*. When he first hears of his prospective son-in-law's professional interest in the case of a Jew murdered some years back, 'Mathias is leaning down picking up coke with tongs, drops coke and looks up. His face is illuminated with the red light from the fire' (Mayer 1980: 57). Shortly after he drops the tongs. A contemporary observer tells that Irving had the stove door hinged on the upstage side, so that when the door was opened red light would fall downstage onto Mathias's face. The business of the tongs is structured as a series: Mathias puts one lump of coke on the fire, picks up a second, drops it, then drops the tongs. The orchestrated combination of lighting and sound effects made it a memorable, and parodied, part of the show (Mayer 1980).

The scenic effect is in tension with another way of acting the narrative of secret guilt. Before this point Mathias had shown signs of agitation at the mention of the Jew, including the famous hallucination (shared by the audi-ence) that he can hear sleigh bells. So the clatter of the dropped coal is heard as a sign that Mathias's body cannot sustain a performance of everyday activity, being disrupted by his concealed secret. The coal tongs are an instrument he can no longer control. In this respect there is nothing weird or supernatural about the relationship between body and setting. It is the light-ing effect that is strange. For, although the light source is naturalised – expli-cable – coming as it does from the open stove door, the red-lit face acquires special status. Unlike the tongs, this sign is not generated by the guilt within Mathias. It comes from outside, as if the setting, however inanimate, is point-ing him out. That hint of something like super-nature is fleeting, caught up into the more naturalised tongs sequence, readable merely as a sign of guilt. This is a self-consciously psychological melodrama, with a climactic focus on mesmerism. So although it retains its melodramatic use of music and lighting it is also specifically shaping the relationship between body and setting in order to locate the presence of mind. That presence is marked, brought into being, by the awkward misfit between body and setting. While the red light on Mathias's face does not suggest the autonomous presence of mind, the dropped tongs clearly do.

Plenty of previous plays had showed mind. All those soliloquies where people tell their thoughts, those asides. In some plays people get gripped by their own histories, horrors of the past resurface. But we see those horrors because they bend and twist the body in front of us. What is in the mind is in the body, and is usually spoken about as well. Mathias's handling of the tongs, by contrast, produces a sense of the body at odds with the mind. He is intending to carry out a normal daily activity, but is disrupted by something unbidden from within. This awkwardness with regard to objects, and perhaps setting, is a feature which Stanton Garner (1994) identifies as characteristic of the modern stage. Earlier on, he says, objects were subordinated to character/actor; they belonged – props are properties. They connected character/actor and *mise-en-scène*: 'By extending and physicalizing the body's operation on its material environment, props situate the body more firmly within it' (Garner 1994: 89). This relationship between body and object was changed within the practices of naturalism and realism: the development of the furnished box set, the use of authentic contemporary objects on stage, the fashion for antiquarian accuracy.

> As stage objects proliferated and asserted an increasing density, manipulability gave way to an independence from – and eventually, an antagonism toward – the human subject's attempt to appropriate and humanize its spatial surroundings. It is an easy jump from *Hedda Gabler*'s scenic claustrophobia to the cluttered junkshop of David Mamet's *American Buffalo*.
>
> (Garner 1994: 91)

Although Garner's account of the changes in the status of stage object produced by different modes of drama is correct and full of insight, Mathias's trouble with tongs preceded *Hedda* by about 20 years. To Garner's account it may be useful to add a sense of changing ideas with regard to the body, and mind, that are staged. For a larger cultural history, as well as a theatrical history, can be observed in the various sorts of relationships between staged body and objects. Lady Audley and Minnie Gascoigne differ in their handling of objects. Not only are the plays arguing for different understandings of human identity and history, in which, for Lawrence, work is central, but they also have different understandings of what the body is, especially in so far as it relates to objects – is delimited by, or inhabits, them. This relationship is precisely nuanced.

Woman, rat, fire, woman

In his analysis of how human activity produces and relates to the space which surrounds it, Henri Lefebvre pauses to reflect on the activity of tools 'which are separate from nature and responsible in severing from nature whatever they impinge upon, but which are nevertheless extensions of the body and its rhythms' (1992: 213). The key word for my purposes in this chapter is 'extension', that set of mechanisms whereby the body is taken out into scenic space. Objects fit alongside light and sound as the agents of this mediation. Lady Audley's scissors feel like a very different bodily extension from Minnie's saucepans, with a very different degree of separation from 'nature'. In trying to get at the complexity of the relationship between body and scenic space, together with the production of 'mind', I have noted some contrasts between melodrama and naturalism. I shall try to summarise these through analysis of two examples.

In the second scene of Lawrence's *Widowing of Mrs Holroyd*, Mr Holroyd brings home two women from the pub. As he goes into the scullery to get a drink, a rat runs into the kitchen and under the sofa. The two visitors clamber to safety – one onto the table, the other onto the armchair near the table. Mrs Holroyd herself is on the sofa, with her legs under her. Mr Holroyd begins to move cautiously towards the sofa. The distribution of the bodies in the stage set establishes a difference between the sexes, with the women all off the ground, scared. But that distribution is more tightly organised yet. The armchair and table are to one side of the stage; the sofa, according to Lawrence's directions, is against the back wall in the centre. The women visitors, on the edge of losing their balance, are slightly comical: they are put to one side both physically and tonally. The serious business is then focused onto the central area of the stage, where husband faces wife, and where wife faces downstage, towards the audience, while the husband is seen from the back. As he gets nearer the sofa, he stoops gradually lower, to look underneath it. Mrs Holroyd, watching 'fascinated', is bunched up. Then, as he gets very close, she suddenly screams out and her gesture changes: 'Leaning forward on the sofa, as far as she dares, she stretches out her arms to keep back her husband, who is about to kneel and search under the sofa for the rat' (Lawrence 1974b: 159). Her gesture is intended by the character to prevent her husband making himself vulnerable to attack by the cornered rat. But the organisation of the stage picture says something a little different. A woman, terrified and yet fascinated, watches a hunting male as he comes towards her. As he lowers himself to her level, she screams and stretches out her arms – in a gesture which both fends him off and yet opens up her body towards him. She is leaning on the edge of her balance, he is about to kneel. The audience's view of the scene looks from the direction of the hunter towards the hunted. And what that look discovers is that the woman who earlier expressed her disapproval of her husband's behaviour is yet physically dependent on him. And how that look discovers this truth is very like the shape of sexual aggression where the woman is the object to be looked at and penetrated.

The setting disposes its characters in a physical hierarchy, sorts out subject from object, lines up the bodies according to a sexual logic that it suggests is deep and 'natural'. Through its organisation of viewpoint it lines up the viewers according to the same logic. As the central axis of the stage suddenly becomes emphasised, so the off-centre women's bodies become more trivial. Viewing comes to feel orderly in its concentration on depth rather than a distracted scanning from side to side. Cutting out the superfluous comic female flesh, that centralised concentration depicts a fundamental difference of male and female. It is as if the stage is stripping down to the essence of the family circumstances and the reality in which normal grown adults find themselves fixed: an Oedipal stage, so to speak. The channelised viewpoint establishes this as true; the audience gaze is invited to follow the male as he penetrates the stage depth, as he asserts his mastery. It is looking made phallic.

The second scene is from *Lady Audley's Secret*. The stage shows two rooms in a pub: in one room two men, one of them very drunk, talk. There is a candle on the table and stairs leading to a hayloft. The other room is empty, and through the window there is a 'moonlight perspective'. During the scene two women enter the empty moonlit room. Lady Audley has come with Phoebe to see Luke, who is blackmailing her. It is he who is drunk in the next room; the other is Robert Audley, who suspects the Lady's secret. Phoebe passes through the connecting room to rouse Luke from sleep; Robert then asks her to show him to his bed. Once they have gone, Lady Audley also goes through the connecting door and looks at the comatose Luke. She is joined by Phoebe, who says how worried she is to leave Luke in this state in case the house burns down. Lady Audley suddenly gets an idea; asks Phoebe to leave her alone with Luke; peeps in at the door of Robert's bedroom, then locks it:

> takes up candle – goes to hayloft – looks into it and enters it – The reflection of fire is seen within – she re-enters, and places candle on table – locks the door which parts the room in centre, and exits, L. door. The fire grows stronger, and Luke wakes up.
>
> (Hazlewood 1972: 262)

There are more doorways in this scene than anywhere else in the play. Lady Audley, alone among the characters, goes through all of them (whereas Luke goes through none). Once she has entered, at each of the three doorways she first looks through, hovering on the threshold before doing anything further (in the case of Robert's room, she locks the door rather than going into the room). Nobody but her goes into the space leading to the hayloft. She has crossed every threshold the stage offers. When she crosses this last it is in 'silence' (that is to say, with accompanying music, but no words). In fact, Lady Audley is more quiet in this scene than any other. She speaks in a hushed voice so as not to be heard by Robert, spends considerable time peeping, does the climactic action, and, without talking, exits. There is a third element which distinguishes the scene: it is in an interior at night, and there are specific directions as to the use of flame (which is not required anywhere else). It begins with two light sources, a candle and moonlight. Luke tries several times to light his pipe from the candle, fails, and falls asleep. Robert then lights his cigar. At this point the two women enter the next room. When Robert goes to bed, Phoebe lights a second candle for him, making the room brighter than before. She re-enters without it. Then Lady Audley takes the candle into the hayloft, making the room darker than it has ever been. Thereafter the glow commences, and gets brighter, while she, having returned the candle, exits – back through that silent, moonlit, first room.

It is as if the quality of that first room – night and silence – pervades the other, following through the doorways Lady Audley, who brings silence and darkness. She also becomes associated with flame (but not light). The original candle was both a light source and a potential flame source. Luke could not use it, Robert merely lit his cigar, but Lady Audley, going much further than her enemies, sets fire to the house. To do so, she takes away a light – and returns with flame. Her association with fire is so complete that, at the climax of the scene, where hitherto there might have been a speech of triumph from her, there is now a scenic effect instead. The way is paved for this by the construction of a relationship between her body and the scenic space – the exploration of and pauses in doorways – and by a rhyme between her body and scenic space – her silence and darkness repeated by that moonlit room.

In these two scenes the audience is invited to look differently, and their look is differently valued. Lawrence has it truth probing. His scenic arrangements are produced as revelatory of the deep 'truth' in the representation. Hazlewood's scene suggests nothing deeper about Lady Audley.

Superficial performance

If the effects do indeed derive from a relationship between her gestures and appearance and the scene, then what is important is not her interior but her exterior. Her 'secret' deed is anticipated. The thrill is to watch it being carried out, unstoppably. The scene has no secret to reveal, it is most interesting at its surface. So now let's press further with thinking about surface. This might require 'an altogether different way of understanding the body in its connections with other bodies, both human and nonhuman, animate and inanimate' (Grosz 1994: 165). The connections between woman's body, aristocratic dress and flame, for instance.

One way of understanding those connections is supplied by the work of Deleuze and Guattari, and it's from a summary of their thinking by Elizabeth Grosz that the quotation above is taken. Grosz goes on to say that Deleuze and Guattari focus on bodily connections

> linking organs and biological processes to material objects and social practices while refusing to subordinate the body to a unity or a homogeneity of the kind provided by the body's subordination to consciousness or to biological organization. Following Spinoza, the body is regarded as neither a locus of consciousness nor an organically determined entity; it is understood more in terms of what it can do, the

things it can perform, the linkages it establishes, the transformations and becomings it undergoes ...

(Grosz 1994: 165)

As the mention of Spinoza implies, Grosz sees Deleuze and Guattari working within a tradition of philosophies of the body, taking their place alongside Nietzsche, Foucault, Lingis. For all of these thinkers, by Grosz's account,

> the body is seen as a purely surface phenomenon, a complex, multifaceted surface folded back on itself, exhibiting a certain torsion but nevertheless a flat plane whose incision or inscription produces the (illusion or effects of) depth and interiority.

(1994: 165)

The body is a social object, a text to be marked by institutions, regimes of discipline and pleasure. But it is also 'as a receptive surface on which the body's boundaries and various parts or zones are constituted, always in conjunction and through linkages with other surfaces and planes' (1994: 116). The same point is made, slightly more polemically, by Brian Massumi: 'There is no interiority in the sense of a closed, self-reflective system. There is only multileveled infolding of an aleatory outside, with which the infolding remains in contact (as a dissipative structure)' (1999: 80). The outcome of this way of thinking is that 'consciousness is a by-product, perhaps even an epiphenomenon, of the inscription of the body' (Grosz 1994: 137). Thus, in his reflections on 'Savages', Alphonso Lingis discusses scarification: 'These cuts and scars on the face of the Yoruba are the clawmarks of Azagu, but they are not just zones of his body destroyed by the totemic leopard, for they are his pleasure and his pride and his very identity' (Lingis 1983: 36).

Within this tradition, the work of Deleuze and Guattari is large and complex, but one of their major contributions is towards a sense of the body as something which, far from being contained and coherent and whole, is always drawn towards a system which is fractal. The body of the baby is experienced as a set of random and various intensities, reacting to and connecting with stimuli around it: 'Some of the body's vibrations resonate with its surroundings and are amplified. Some clash with them and are muffled' (Massumi 1999: 75). This multiplicity is then prevented and organised 'by a process of *application* (a channelizing overlay of social categories) centering on the family. Deleuze and Guattari call that process "Oedipus"' (Massumi 1999: 77). The process reinforces that tendency in the body that pulls away from the fractal towards wholeness, 'conventionally expressed as authorized social categories to be in or conjoin with (man/woman, husband/wife, boss/employee, and so on)' (Massumi 1999: 78).

In this element of their work the viewpoint of Deleuze and Guattari seems to tie in with that of feminist thinking about the body as derived from so-called 'French feminism':

> Women have ... a different relationship to their bodies than men. Recognition of this fact necessitates a more 'fluid' notion of female embodiment, one modelled on Irigaray's conceptualisation of feminine desire, and a self that exists not by repulsion/exclusion, but via interpenetration of self with otherness ... Boundaries ... are 'essentially' masculine products that seek to 'contain' women's corporeal 'flows'.
>
> (Williams and Bendelow 1998: 120)

The problem with this version of the idea is that it tends to settle back rather comfortably into binarised categories, of women and men, with a fair bit of essentialism thrown in. Women may flow beyond male boundaries, but this notion itself sets and respects boundaries – where male and female are single categories, whole entities, yet bound for ever into a binary division, one symmetrically inverting the other. Deleuze and Guattari, by contrast, strive to push into a world of potentialities, where bodies are not necessarily whole, where connections are made across supposed category boundaries. This 'desire to escape bodily limitation' – whatever the sex and species of the body – leads to 'becoming' (Massumi 1999: 94).

In one of their examples Deleuze and Guattari discuss a masochist who is treated by his master as a horse: she puts a bit in his mouth, controls him with reins and a riding crop. But the masochist is not to be understood as imitating a horse. The relationship is one, rather, of 'exchange and circulation'. They explain:

> Horses are trained: humans impose upon the horse's instinctive forces transmitted forces that regulate the former, select, dominate, overcode them. The masochist effects an inversion of signs: the horse transmits its transmitted forces to him, so that the masochist's innate forces will in turn be tamed. There are two series, the horse's (innate force, force transmitted by the human being), and the masochist's (force transmitted by the horse, innate force of the human being). One series explodes into the other, forms a circuit with it: an increase in power or a circuit of intensities.
>
> (Deleuze and Guattari 1996: 155–6)

Involved within this circuit the masochist may be said to be 'becoming-animal': he doesn't literally turn into a horse, or even imitate a horse; the horse isn't real, nor does the horse turn into a human being. But between these two separate entities something new is possible – facing the 'great dissipative outside', led to a '*supra*personal level ... a beyond of mutation and monstrosity' (Massumi 1999: 95, 96).

This process of 'becoming-animal' can be repeated across a range of possible (and impossible) connections. As Grosz puts it: 'Becoming-woman desediments the masculinity of identity; becoming-child, the modes of cohesion and control of the adult; becoming-animal, the anthropocentrism of philosophical thought'. The process takes us, of course, beyond what is even thinkable: 'Deleuze and Guattari produce a radical antihumanism that renders animals, nature, atoms, even quasars as modes of radical alterity' (Grosz 1994: 179; see also Braidotti 1994: 112). If one can manage to hang onto 'becoming-atom' as a possibility, then it's a piece of cake – as it were – to conceive of Lady Audley in the fire scene as a body 'becoming-scene'. What that formulation gives is a sense of a circuit of intensities between the body and the flame. To see the fire as a metaphor, an image for Lady Audley's passion, is to reduce it, to de-materialise it as an effect in its own right. To see her merely as a user of fire is to keep her contained within the boundaries of function, intention, planning. She becomes instead something onto which the force of fire is transmitted, thereby gaining an increase in power.

It might be more precise to describe Lady Audley as 'becoming-flame'. My preferred formula, 'becoming-scene', is useful because it has more general application across a range of melodramatic bodies – bodies caught up into the play of light, watched through gauzes, dissolving into mists. But it is not a phenomenon of all performance. For the form in which a body enters an exchange with something other needs to be regarded as specific to a culture, if it happens at all. For instance Deleuze and Guattari, shortly after their masochist example, describe 'courtly love'. It

> does not love the self, any more than it loves the whole universe in a celestial or religious way. It is a question of making a body without organs upon which intensities pass, self and other ... The field of immanence is not internal to the self, but neither does it come from an external self or a nonself. Rather it is like the absolute Outside that knows no Selves because interior and exterior are equally a part of the immanence in which they have fused. 'Joy' in courtly love, the exchange of hearts, the test or 'assay': everything is allowed, as long as it is not external to desire or transcendent to its plane, or else internal to persons.
>
> (1996: 156)

The mechanisms of exchange of hearts and the test are specific to a particular medieval cultural formation. But on the melodrama stage there was a repeated enactment of a state that was neither 'internal to the self' nor coming from 'an external self', that moment at which a character realised their implication in a logic of events, the moment they called *apprehension*

(Shepherd 1994). Similarly, as I'm arguing here, there is a connection – a contamination – of surfaces of body and setting. So that when we look at the flames 'produced' by Lady Audley they're clearly exterior to her, otherwise she'd be burnt, but in her connection with them we also envisage her interiority. Flagrant conflagration. A hot lady.

The flames are also exterior in that they are the products of the stage technicians. Lady Audley is something acted in front of an audience. Which makes her different from the masochist discussed above, or Lingis's Yoruba, in that she is a fiction from whom the performer is separable (if not wholly separate). In this respect it might seem inappropriate simply to transfer to this example the various insights drawn from philosophies which address the construction of real identities and pleasures. But Deleuze and Guattari seem to feel there is no problem extending their analytic framework to a work of fiction. They pause over *The Waves*, by Virginia Woolf – 'who made all of her life and work a passage, a becoming'. Each of the seven characters in the novel 'with his or her name, its individuality, designates a multiplicity (for example Bernard and the school of fish). Each is simultaneously in this multiplicity and at its edge, and crosses over into the others' (1996: 152). So, alongside various modes of human organisation and culture, there are also individual artworks that take their readers/spectators into the domain of 'becomings'.

If this is true, then we need to ask what the readers or spectators get out of it. What is the feeling from looking at someone else's becomings, reading an account of someone else's scarifications? Some people assume that these things have special effects. For if you look at Lingis's account of 'Savages' in his book *Excesses* in the British Library, you have to read the book in the Rare Books room, where it must never be left unaccompanied on a desk, and has always to be returned to staff other than the usual book-issue staff – presumably to avoid standing in the queue, where the book might once again have the chance of plugging itself into random neighbouring bodies.

Lost in space

In order to think about the possible response to becomings in the theatre I plan to draw on the work of someone who seems to pull in a very different theoretical direction. After that I shall return us to Deleuze and Guattari and put melodrama into a larger cultural narrative.

In 1938 Roger Caillois published an essay, 'Mimicry and Legendary Psychasthenia' (Caillois 1984), based on a pair of essays from 1934 and 1935. It was in large part an exploration of camouflage among insects; but from here Caillois moved on to reflect upon the relationships between body and space as constitutive of identity. These reflections in their turn had their influence on the psychoanalytic rethinkings of Jacques Lacan – which heads off in a direction rather different from that of the authors of *AntiOedipus*. Camouflage, as Caillois saw it, is often highly risky (make yourself too exactly like a leaf and you might be eaten by one of your fellows). Rather than being fully functional, it is a luxury, and a dangerous one at that. In fact the drive to play dead, to become assimilated to the space around you, amounts to a psychic step backwards. Tempted by space, the creature agrees to the blurring of the boundaries which make it distinct. In taking on the characteristics of the space around it, it loses its self. We are a long way here from any celebration of becomings.

For that celebration very largely depends on the psychic and social circumstances of those watching the becomings. Caillois' own horrified fixation on the habits of the female praying mantis, which destroys the male during sex, indicates how far he is attracted into a mechanism that promises to shore up his own wholeness, boundedness. And clearly that will be the case for some audiences – there were, after all, many that came to think of melodrama as trivial and improper and excessive, deviant. Audiences are persuaded to enter a series which has spectator at one end and performer at the other. Kinaesthesia, empathy, mimesis, identification lead into various states of 'becoming-character'. While this is true of most forms of drama, melodrama makes the operation more contentious, risky, laughable perhaps, because in becoming-character the audience is taken into a domain of becomings. When Lady Audley assumes her 'mask' – her camouflage, if you will – in the conservatory, she doesn't lose herself into its space. Instead there is a sort of blurring of boundaries: she disposes herself among, into, the flowers, and the floral setting in its turn comes to be emotionally imbued – flowers as wealth, ornament and danger. It's not so much a loss of self into space as a *self-ing* of space. There is a correspondence of animate and inanimate, brought about through a coincidence of textures, performance registers, tones. We can see how such things might be planned technically by recalling Henry Irving's notes with regard to light and sound effects. The various surfaces, linked into circuit, engender something in excess of, larger than, the constituent elements.

When an audience watches it learns how to read and evaluate the rules, moods, functions of the space, the 'world', in which the characters exist. This is a major way that it imaginatively enters the fiction. Now where those character bodies are made to dissipate, to enter circuits with the inanimate, then boundaries blur. The clear organisation of spatiality, that which also gives the audience its own sense of place, gets masked. And at this point the spectators become like those insects who find themselves tempted by space. Or rather they become like those human psychic casualties whom Caillois goes on to discuss, for in conditions of 'represented space', where the living creature is no longer the origin of the coordinates which give it its bearings, but is 'one point among others', in these conditions 'it is dispossessed of its privilege and literally *no longer knows where to place itself*. Where the 'feeling of personality' is 'considered as the organism's feeling of distinction from its surroundings', for schizophrenics 'space seems to be a devouring force. Space pursues them, encircles them, digests them' (Caillois 1984: 28, 30). Possibly like finding oneself – or losing oneself – in a 'pit of darkness, a trap of temptation, profligacy and ruin, triumphantly yawning night after night'.

That is from Charles Kingsley, not a schizophrenic, but a *spectator in the wrong theatre* (in Roberts 1976: 26). At the Old Vic. For there the jumble of humanity crammed into the gallery to watch *Lady Audley* might literally seem to be selves without distinct individual place. Their uproar at the climaxes of a play might indicate how closely they were drawn into, assimilated by, its intensities. It was a very different mode of viewing from that encouraged by the society comedies at the Prince of Wales's in the 1860s, or, more obviously, those self-aware dialogues among the fashionable for the fashionable that Wilde produced at the end of the century. Alongside these plays, and especially the committed realism of the New Drama, melodrama was regarded as trivial, superficial; the audience uproar was seen as a response to the shape of the fiction, not to the deep issues of the day.

But let's resist the lead of the New Drama, look at what the melodrama audience was enjoying and then reflect on its relationship to the performance. In his description of a visit to a melodrama, Dickens notes how the audience applauded enthusiastically at the entrance of a particular character, and then cheered loudly when after a soliloquy he '"went off" *on his back*' (Dickens n.d.: 176). This response is only partially to do with the enacted story – it is generated more by expectation and appreciation of particular performance 'turns'. The whole of the part of William in Jerrold's *Black-Ey'd Susan* (1829), which made T. P. Cooke into a star, is structured as a series of turns, requiring Cooke to move quickly between comic earnestness, heroic fighting, weeping and sentimental story-telling. This, at the level of the narrative, repeats the mode of performing speeches, which would be delivered as a series of 'points'. Julia Walker defines the term: '"point" is understood to be the actor's use of his/her body to "underline" the meaning of the text. ... such underlinings seem to be fully separable from the actor's overall interpretation of his/her role' (1999: 16). Points were responded to, and applauded, as performance events in themselves. So that the speech becomes a series of intense moments, rather than a whole entity; the character is effective as a series of turns, interesting the audience in what the body can *do*, rather than in its interiority. It's a way of watching that produces a heightened here and now, a buzz without a product.

For a commentator such as Dickens what was strikingly apparent about the melodrama audience, apart from their uproar, was their insistent bodily presence. He notes that they have their food and their drink with them, and that they smell. Watching the play is in circuit with a whole set of other orificial pleasures. It might be compared to a different form of entertainment, the sort of sex 'where the egos are multiple and superficial, surface effects. They form at the couplings, where an excess potential develops. A mouth, it is adjustable. It can couple on to a nipple – or a bottle, or a thumb ...' Such couplings may be contrasted with that sort of sex where in an 'air-conditioned bedroom, is an entity: a man, a woman. A phallic machine, coupled on to a womb. The subject ... which is affected by it all and contented with it all, is a unit, a transcendent selfsameness' (Lingis 1983: 35–6).

I have reached across to Lingis's description of sexual couplings because it may offer a model for thinking about the response to melodrama. But also, and before it does that, it takes us into a larger narrative which subsumes melodrama.

This narrative is that of the development of a new way of thinking and looking in the late nineteenth century. It has shaped both attitudes to and representations of bodies. It also shaped notions of pleasure. The different sorts of body and pleasure are contrasted by Lingis. In his reflections on 'savages', the inscription – the incisions and scarifications – on the flesh 'extends the erotogenic surface, produces a place or a plane productive of pleasurable torments, of voluptuous moments of subjectivity'. By contrast, German nude beauty is

> surface and depth one. It is the organism. A functional whole, coded from the inside. And it is male, female. Human. Phallic. That is, the whole body organized, for the other. Which other? Alterity itself, the transcendent, the beyond? ... Oh no, here we are *en famille*. For a mummy, for a big daddy.
>
> (Lingis 1983: 43)

The contrast between what I am calling dissipation and integrity is organised, enabled, by a conceptual model.

That model has been popularised, indeed naturalised, by psychoanalysis. It is the model which sees an Oedipal stage as natural to every individual's development towards adulthood. The working out of 'correct' relationships with regard to the mummy and the big daddy. For Lingis, as for those who have influenced him – Deleuze and Guattari – the Oedipal stage is far from natural. Instead it is a coercive mechanism, which validates certain organs (inventing them as the 'sexual' organs) over others and ideologically insisting on wholeness and depth: 'it is a categorical overlay, an overpowering impositon of regularized affects ... experienced by the overcoded body as a physical constraint' (Massumi 1999: 94). And it serves an economic purpose. That German beauty, says Lingis, is 'civilized nudity. It is also capitalist nudity' (1983: 43).

Detecting the truth

So far I have moved between becomings, bodily blurrings and pleasures of skin and surface. These are all on one side of the opposition between dissipation and integrity. Such has been the historical dominance of integrity, however, that these dissipated modes have been barely recognised as either practices or pleasures. They have been masked by a form of theatrical pleasure which developed alongside the philosophical shifts that were to produce psychoanalysis and related outlooks.

I think we can see the tensions arising from these new theatrical interests and pleasures flexing themselves in Hazlewood's *Lady Audley*. In Act 2 Robert Audley confronts Lady Audley, to get her to admit to her crime. He observes that her eyes are dull, that she regularly falls into deep reflection, that her levity of manner is forced and 'unnatural'. In short, he thinks that by close observation of her body he can penetrate the surface and see through to the reality beneath, her 'secret', much as Lawrence's play probes Mrs Holroyd. But what Robert sees so medically does not precisely coincide with what is offered for the audience to see. Prior to this scene she has charmed her husband, manipulated Alicia, expressed confidence in herself, suddenly been confronted by Luke, been 'staggered' to find that he knows everything, and then planned to get rid of him too. None of this is the levity of manner she affects in front of Robert, but nor is it the relapse into deep reflection that he claims to observe. Instead, it is a performance full of sharp changes, with a consequent effect of energy. And the scene in which he attempts to brand her as the guilty creature which is at odds with its environment is precisely that conservatory scene where she blurs with her setting.

While Robert is offered as someone who believes that you can get to the truth by close scrutiny, like a doctor or detective, the stage refuses to produce Lady Audley as the detective's object. She is not something where the surface always expresses – symptomises – the reality, the guilty depth. In this respect Hazlewood's dramatisation deviates from Mary Braddon's novel, written in 1862, which is governed by a narrative of detection. What is uncovered here is not simply a crime. It is the narrator, rather than a detective, who periodically tells us about Lady Audley's 'glittering' eyes, who notes symptoms of a strange nervous energy: 'an unnatural crimson spot' burned in each cheek, 'an unnatural lustre' gleamed in each eye. For the novel means something different by the 'secret' than does the play. In the play it seems merely to be the murder, which is kept secret. In the novel, the secret is a biographical history of madness, a mad mother. Criminal detection is coupled with medical diagnosis; against her madness, Robert's 'calculating, frigid, luminous intellect'. The truth of Lady Audley's crime is the truth of her body, which is specifically set apart from its setting: 'her eyes glittered with a light that was not entirely reflected from the fire' (Braddon 1987: 313, 345, 298). That body's surface, in the detection mindset, will inevitably declare the real truth of its psychic depth.

In being shaped as detective narrative Braddon's novel was perhaps more up-to-the-minute than Hazlewood's play, for detection was the newly emerging genre. Tom Taylor's *Ticket-of-Leave Man* is often credited with being the first detective play in 1863, because it features a detective, but it was certainly preceded by numerous prose narratives, if not plays, structured as detection. This generic emergence is connected by Paul Virilio, in his schematic history of perception, to the influence of the French Revolution's preoccupation with lighting: 'revolutionary journalism aims to *enlighten* public opinion, to make revelations, to delve behind deceptive appearances'. It is assisted in 1836 by mass circulation, and in 1848 'the *serial novel* takes off' (Virilio 1994: 35–6). The detective has a luminous intellect.

This shift in perception gives a context for understanding what Irving was doing in *The Bells*. As we have seen, he constructed a stage picture in which Mathias's body was placed in circuit with sound and light effects. But in part these effects can be read as pathological symptoms of hidden guilt. The depth breaks surface when he cannot properly control the coal tongs. On the other hand, the red light falling across his face has no such clarity with regard to depth. In the final scene, where Mathias's crime is spoken aloud in open court – as it were seen clearly for what it is – that court is a dream, Mathias is mesmerised within the dream, and the whole thing is played behind gauze. The hesitation between depth and surface here seems to have a contemporary parallel in North America. Edwin Booth played Hamlet in 1870 and 1881. At the ghost's revelation of murder, in 1870 Hamlet grasped his cloak, and then fingered his throat 'as if his cloak choked him'; in 1881 the cloak was dropped 'quite unheeded' (Walker 1999: 23). The interior has learnt to be separate, to be an interior.

The fashion for detection in the 1860s and 1870s seems not only to offer a new theatrical pleasure but to invent a particular way of regarding the body. Lady Audley's glittering eyes betray the madness deep within. It is not just that surface and depth are one, but that the surface will always express the depth. Out of this culture emerges those philosophies of the body which, in Elizabeth Grosz's phrase, deal with 'the ways in which the psychical interior has made the body its forms of exteriority' (1994: 115). Most influential of these philosophies was psychoanalysis, which had its own fascination with detective fiction, focusing on one story in particular, that of the mythic Greek Oedipus. In its use of the Oedipus narrative psychoanalysis instituted a particular way of thinking about the body and identity. This is why it figures so strongly for Lingis in his articulation of the relationship between dissipation and integrity. Its relevance to us here is that it is accompanied by developments in theatre practice which in their turn shape ideas about proper practices and pleasures.

The ecstatic body

Detective dramas gave way towards the end of the nineteenth century to naturalism. Its stage pictures claimed to be accurate renderings of the surface of everyday life, but they also consolidated the construction of something else, the permanent presence of depth concealed beneath surface. Much of the mindset of naturalism lives on, repeating its truths about bodies, repeating the idea that bad art is superficial.

But despite the influence of naturalism and psychoanalysis another way of thinking was available. Nietzsche, first of Grosz's philosophers of 'surface', was writing through the 1880s. And in 1907 Edward Gordon Craig argued for a theatre that was against the reproduction of nature, and against acting as impersonation (Craig 1980: 70–1). He told actors: '*if* you could make your body into a machine, or into a dead piece of material such as clay … and *if* you could put aside Shakespeare's poem – you would be able to make a work of art' (Craig 1980: 153). His designs for the stage make of the human body a scenic element, subject it to the larger organisation of light and monumental shapes – as in his sketch called 'Electra' where groupings are arranged in relation to, and in the shadow of, verticals, while the central figure makes impact not just because of its centrality but because of the fabric that spills off the body into a long train. 'By means of your scene you will be able to mould the movements of the actors' (1980: 26).

The son of Ellen Terry, who was leading actress for Henry Irving, Craig was brought up on melodrama. Coming from a more machinic modernism Fernand Léger had very similar ideas in 1924: he attacks ballet in favour of acrobatics and suggests it would be better if dancers 'accept the role of "moving scenery" … The individual has disappeared. He becomes a moving part of scenery' (1973: 39, 40). Léger was principally a painter, and much of Craig's theatre thinking was done as designs rather than productions. While contemporary theatre staged depth and bodily integrity (and still does today), body as surface was (and is) more often found in two-dimensional forms. Even here, however, the narrative drive tends towards character revelation and detected truth. In the earliest series of *The X Files* the detection narrative, given licence by its sci-fi genre, no longer always led towards clear truth. The conclusions were undecideable as between what really happened and what appeared to have happened. But in general, while detection narratives contain passages of uncertainty, inexplicability, those moments of lost bearings, of characters becoming-scene, are felt as lapses from control and wholeness, to be put straight by revealed truth.

By contrast, in a form largely free of narrative demands, the music-video body is often pleasurably a surface without depth. From a random (and perforce dated) sample, in the video of the Venga Boys' *Kiss* the bodies were seen under water, written over, replayed on video, under strobe lighting, in close-up, in different costumes between shots. This, it could be argued, is a dance track and the job of the video is to find a personality for the sound rather than for the makers of the sound (Goodwin 1993; see also Cubitt 1993). To convert technology into party, to subject the bodies to the higher demands of the rhythm. By contrast Alice Deejay's *Back in My Life* was produced more as 'atmospheric', expressive, monochrome. The setting is a sea shore. But it's not used as narrative. Instead appropriate expressive images are generated by mingling the setting and the bodies. We see faces blurred in spray from water. In shots of a rocky coastline there are dancers. They move within the textures of the rocks and the sea-spray, a 'moving part of the scenery'. On the beach the figure is semi-transparent – we see through her. Part human, part landscape. Body-becoming-setting.

Lingis calls German bodies not only 'civilized' nudity but 'capitalist' nudity. In *Back in My Life* it may be a different sort of body, but it is hardly much further from capitalism. The objective of the pop video is to sell the song by producing it as visual image, creating an atmosphere for the particular song while respecting and enhancing the 'personality' of its singer(s). And unlike the theatre of melodrama this is a mode from which, at the point of consumption, the human body in the artefact is literally absent. It is consumed either in the individualised home, or as a sort of wallpaper in pubs and clubs.

Clubs. The dance club takes us back into a space, not perhaps of theatre but certainly of performance. Participants watch and dance for themselves and others (Malbon 1999) – and indeed in the work of a performance group such as Blast Theory the terms of clubbing performance are adopted and explored. The music video in a club may be one of a number of projections. Video projection, lights, lasers play onto the surfaces of the space, rendering the original architecture fluid, altering its rhythms and points of focus. In the dance culture which developed in the early 1990s another crucial element was MDMA, sold (if you were lucky) as Ecstasy. This worked on the mind and body in conjunction with dance tracks designed with the drug in mind:

> Today's house track is a forever-fluctuating, fractal mosaic of glow-pulses and flicker-riffs … Experienced under the influence of MDMA, the effect is synaesthetic – like tremulous fingertips tantalizing the back of your neck, or like the simultaneously aural/tactile equivalent of a shimmer. In a sense, Ecstasy turns the entire body-surface into an ear.
>
> (Reynolds 1998: xxvi)

The separation between mind and body is undetectable. The body is experienced as a surface traversed by 'tingly rushes' (1998: xxvi). This surface makes couplings with the sounds, continually rediscovering new collocations of intensity. Individual dancing bodies merge into a 'collective' body which 'includes technology (in the form of music, lighting and drugs), and, therefore is perhaps best understood in terms of mind/body/technology assemblage' (Pini 1997: 124).

Writing about the rave, Pini argues that 'subjectivity is restated in terms which do not reproduce traditional distinctions between mind and body, self and others, physicality and machine' (1997: 119). For many people Ecstasy and dance culture were very different from a form of leisure structured around the search for sexual partners: 'the libido had actually been sublimated into a completely different form. People weren't going out on the pull' (Reynolds 1998: 44). And even if they were, 'The "ecstatic dancing body" produced within this configuration represents a form of sexuality which is difficult to define in terms of clear-cut desire' (Pini 1997: 119). The libidinally extended, tingling, body surface is not to be entrained into the closed unit of man, woman, phallic machine. As Lingis says elsewhere, 'The moments of subjectivity, of pleasure tormented with itself … are all on the surface' (1983: 36). The effect of early dance clubs, such as the Ramplings' Shoom in Southwark, did something new to one's sense of self:

> the Shoom scene was not about being seen, but about losing it – your cool, your self-consciousness, your *self*. Quoting T. S. Eliot, Gray describes the fruit-flavoured smoke as 'the fog that both connects and separates. You'd have these faces looming at you out of the fog. It was like a sea of connected alienation.'
>
> (Reynolds 1998: 39)

Or as one of Pini's interviewees said: 'your boundaries are just so stretched out, it isn't you any more' (Pini 1997: 120).

While music videos might seem to be little more than the marketing devices of an industry, their visual tricks with body surfaces occur in a culture where the sensitising of body surface is part of a pleasurable loss of self. It is in this respect that the lived practice of dance culture makes genuine challenges to dominant culture's assumptions about sex, sexuality, modes of connecting with others. Characterising this as 'nomadic' subjectivity, Rosi Braidotti says: 'Nomadic shifts designate … a creative sort of becoming; a performative metaphor that allows for otherwise unlikely encounters and unsuspected sources of interaction of experience and of knowledge' (1994: 5). The challenges of dance culture went through a period of being politically articulated when dancers, in the face of physical opposition by police, toured the countryside, demanded the right to party. To hang on to connections within the alienation.

When Louise Gray describes Shoom with its faces looming in the fog, the connected alienation, she could almost be describing one of the melodrama houses or even an amphitheatre in full voice. There too, in the gatherings of intensity, produced perhaps in the scene of 'emphatic proximity, intensive interconnectedness' (Braidotti 1994: 5), blurring the audience–performer distinction, caught up by the dark spaces of theatre and rhythms of performance, there too the audience may be said to lose itself. And as such constituted a disturbance to those who were troubled about the maintenance of good order in London. The various guardians pointing the way to a satisfactory modernity rebuked the noise of the public theatres. That dedicated, intelligent liberal, Dickens, was pleased that the reconstructed Britannia Saloon was well lighted, orderly. He noted complete families were in the pit at the Vic, like a nursery. Male, female, phallic machine. Empty fields guarded by policemen.

And on the other side of this order the crammed pit, dark spaces, sweaty dancefloors. People losing themselves in the scene, in the fog. Bodies without depth. Superficiality. Dissipation.

Notes

1 Script as a discipline of the body

1 Bryan Turner had made a similar point about Foucault in the first edition of *Body & Society* (1984).

2 See Elam (1980) on texts. 'Like Meyerhold, reflexologists, and behavioral psychologists, Brecht believed that the mere imitation or copying of appro- priate gestures and expressions could bring about desired mental states' (Kalb 1998: 27).

3 I am trying not to assume a culturally non-specific performance technique. We don't know much about Restoration modes of performing, but in addition to Roach's point (quoted earlier) about inhibition and decorum we can assume a certain quality of formality. My guess is that this might make a performer rather more sensitive to the offered possibilities for formally organised embodiment.

4 Compare this summary of the French political philosopher Bossuet writing in the 1670s: 'The paternalistic monarch, whose mastery of the realm depended on his mastery of the self ... did not allow whims, resentments, or desires to confound his intelligence or weaken his resolve' (quoted in Merrick 1998: 23). See also Muchembled (1991: 137): 'The "modernisation" of gestures manifests itself in a repudiation of everything that is too animal in man. As in Molière's *Tartuffe* (1664), it involves a minimum of hiding, not only "that breast I would not know how to look upon" but also the exercise of one's natural functions.'

2 Theatre and bodily value

1 Stallybrass suggests that Bakhtin is caught into an 'essentialist problematic' (1987: 137); the historian of food, Stephen Mennell (1995), points out that it was the upper classes which gorged themselves, the gaping orifices were on the bodies of dukes and bishops.

2 The problems with inferring 'real-life' performance practices from paintings are spelled out by West (1991). Howard (1998) tends to efface the impact of visual convention when she reads a woodcut of dancing couples in order to infer how the country dancers are less classically restrained than the courtly pair, whereas it can also be argued that bent bodies and physical closeness are shorthand graphic markers for countryfolk and clowns.

3 Wright argues that this episode recalls 'the late Gothic device of the pedlar and the apes' (1984: 134). Rose (1984) links propriety of dress and the coherence of society.

3 The wrong dog (an account of significant inaction)

1 Greenblatt links *energia* with 'the capacity of certain verbal, aural, and visual traces to produce, shape, and organize collective physical and mental experiences' (1988: 6); the energy I am talking of is less textual, more connected with productive process, and felt more as 'flow'.

Part II Introduction

1 An example of the theoretical development of the idea is Michael Taussig's reflection on Freud's 'ideational mimetics': 'in which ... bodily copying of the other is paramount: one tries out the very shape of a perception in one's own body; the musculature of the body is physiologically connected to percepts' (Taussig 1993: 46; see also Sullivan 1992 for a Lacanian model).

Bibliography

Albright, A. C. (1997) *Choreographing Difference: The body and identity in contemporary dance*, Hanover, N.H.: Wesleyan University Press.

Allain, P. (2002) *The Art of Stillness: The theatre practice of Tadashi Suzuki*, London: Methuen.

Andrews, R. (1991) 'Scripted Theatre and the *Commedia dell'Arte*', in J. R. Mulryne and M. Shewring (eds) *Theatre of the English and Italian Renaissance*, Basingstoke: Macmillan.

Ansorge, P. (1975) *Disrupting the Spectacle: Five years of experimental and fringe theatre in Britain*, London: Pitman.

Armstrong, W. A. (1954) 'Shakespeare and the Acting of Edward Alleyn', *Shakespeare Survey* 7: 82–9.

Arnheim, R. (1956) *Art and Visual Perception: A psychology of the creative eye*, London: Faber & Faber.

Artaud, A. (1970) *The Theatre and Its Double: Essays*, trans. V. Corti, London: Calder & Boyars.

Astington, J. H. (1986) 'Eye and Hand on Shakespeare's Stage', *Renaissance and Reformation* 10: 1.

Attali, J. (1985) *Noise: The political economy of music*, trans. B. Massumi, Minneapolis: University of Minnesota Press.

Ayckbourn, A. (1979) *Absurd Person Singular*, in *Three Plays*, Harmondsworth: Penguin.

Baer, M. (1992) *Theatre and Disorder in Late Georgian London*, Oxford: Oxford University Press.

Bailey, P. (1996) '"Naughty but Nice": Musical comedy and the rhetoric of the girl, 1892–1914', in M. R. Booth and J. H. Kaplan (eds) *The Edwardian Theatre: Essays on performance and the stage*, Cambridge: Cambridge University Press.

Bakhtin, M. (1984) *Rabelais and his World*, trans. H. Iswolsky, Bloomington: Indiana University Press.

Balsamo, A. (1995) 'Forms of Technological Embodiment: Reading the body in contemporary culture', in M. Featherstone and R. Burrows (eds) *Cyberspace/ Cyberbodies/Cyberpunk*, London: Sage.

Barba, E. and Saverese, N. (1991) *A Dictionary of Theatre Anthropology: The secret art of the performer*, London: Routledge.

Barker, C. (1977) *Theatre Games: A new approach to drama training*, London: Eyre Methuen.

Barthes, R. (1977) *Image-Music-Text*, trans. S. Heath, London: Fontana.

Baudinet, M.-J. (1989) 'The Face of Christ, the Form of the Church', in M. Feher, with R. Naddaff and N. Tazi (eds) *Fragments for a History of the Human Body: Part one*, New York: Zone.

Beckerman, B. (1962) *Shakespeare at the Globe, 1599–1609*, New York: Macmillan.

—— (1970) *The Dynamics of Drama: Theory and method of analysis*, New York: Alfred A. Knopf.

—— (1990) *Theatrical Presentation: Performer, audience and act*, ed. G. Brim Beckerman and William Coco, London: Routledge.

Benjamin, W. (1973) *Illuminations*, trans. H. Zohn, ed. H. Arendt, London: Collins/ Fontana.

Bennett, B. K. (1983) 'Strindberg and Ibsen: Toward a Cubism of time in drama', *Modern Drama* 26.3: 262–81.

Bevington, D. (1984) *Action is Eloquence: Shakespeare's language of gesture*, Cambridge, Mass.: Harvard University Press.

—— (1998) '*The Tempest* and the Jacobean Court Masque', in D. Bevington and P. Holbrook (eds) *The Politics of the Stuart Court Masque*, Cambridge: Cambridge University Press.

Bishop, T. (1998) 'The Gingerbread Host: Tradition and novelty in the Jacobean masque', in D. Bevington and P. Holbrook (eds) *The Politics of the Stuart Court Masque*, Cambridge: Cambridge University Press.

Blacking, J. (1987) '*A Common Sense View of All Music': Reflections on Percy Grainger's contribution to ethnomusicology and music education*, Cambridge: Cambridge University Press.

Bogart, A. (1995) *Viewpoints*, ed. M. B. Dixon and J. A. Smith, Lyme, N.H.: Smith & Kraus.

—— (2001) *A Director Prepares: Seven essays on art and theatre*, London and New York: Routledge.

Bogue, R. (1989) *Deleuze and Guattari*, London and New York: Routledge.

Boling, R. J. (1996) 'Stage Images of Cressida's Portrayal', *Essays in Theatre* 14.2: 147–58.

Bosmajian, H. A. (1971) 'The Persuasiveness of Nazi Marching and *der Kampf um die Strasse*', in H. A. Bosmajian (ed.) *The Rhetoric of Nonverbal Communication*, Glenview, Ill.: Scott, Foresman & Company.

Boucicault, D. (1987) *The Corsican Brothers*, in *Selected Plays of Dion Boucicault*, introd. A. Parkin, Gerrards Cross: Colin Smythe.

Bourdieu, P. (1977) *Outline of a Theory of Practice*, trans. R. Nice, Cambridge: Cambridge University Press.

—— (1989) *Distinction: A social critique of the judgement of taste*, trans. R. Nice, London: Routledge.

Bradby, D., James, L. and Sharratt, B. (eds) (1980) *Performance and Politics in Popular Drama: Aspects of popular entertainment in theatre, film and television 1800–1976*, Cambridge: Cambridge University Press.

Braddon, M. E. (1987) *Lady Audley's Secret*, ed. D. Skilton, Oxford: Oxford University Press.

Braidotti, R. (1994) *Nomadic Subjects: Embodiment and sexual difference in contemporary feminist theory*, New York: Columbia University Press.

Brathwaite, R. (1970) *The English Gentlewoman*, New York: Da Capo Press.

Braun, E. (ed.) (1969) *Meyerhold on Theatre*, London: Eyre Methuen.

Bremner, J. (1993) 'Walking, Standing, and Sitting in Ancient Greek Culture', in J. Bremner and H. Roodenburg (eds) *A Cultural History of Gesture*, Cambridge: Polity Press.

Brissenden, A. (1981) *Shakespeare and the Dance*, London: Macmillan.

Brown, J. R. (1953) 'On the Acting of Shakespeare's Plays', *Quarterly Journal of Speech* 34: 477–84.

Bryson, A. (1990) 'The Rhetoric of Status: Gesture, demeanour and the image of the gentleman in sixteenth- and seventeenth-century England', in L. Gent and N. Llewellyn (eds) *Renaissance Bodies: The human figure in English culture c.1540–1660*, London: Reaktion Books.

Burns, E. (1972) *Theatricality: A study of convention in the theatre and in social life*, London: Longman.

Burroughs, C. B. and Ehrenreich, J. D. (eds) (1993) *Reading the Social Body*, Iowa City: University of Iowa Press.

Burt, R. (1998) *Alien Bodies: Representations of modernity, 'race' and nation in early modern dance*, London and New York: Routledge.

Butler, J. (1990) *Gender Trouble: Feminism and the subversion of identity*, London: Routledge.

Caillois, R. (1961) *Man, Play, and Games*, trans. M. Barash, New York: The Free Press of Glencoe.

—— (1984) 'Mimicry and Legendary Psychasthenia', trans. J. Shepley, *October* 31: 17–32.

Campbell, O. J. (1925) '*Two Gentlemen of Verona* and Italian Comedy', *University of Michigan Publications* 1: 49–63.

—— (1932) 'The Italianate Background to *The Merry Wives of Windsor*', *University of Michigan Publications* 8: 81–117.

Cannon, W. B. (1942) *The Body as a Guide to Politics*, The Thinker's Forum 15, London: Watts.

—— (1953) *Bodily Changes in Pain, Hunger, Fear and Rage: An account of recent researches into the function of emotional excitement*, Boston, Mass.: Charles T. Branford.

Carpenter, E. and McLuhan, M. (1960) 'Acoustic Space', in E. Carpenter and M. McLuhan (eds) *Explorations in Communication: An anthology*, Boston, Mass.: Beacon Press.

Carter, A. (1999) 'Dying Swans or Sitting Ducks? A critical reflection on feminist gazes at ballet', *Performance Research* 4. 3: 91–8.

Castellucci, R. (1997) *Cacophany for a Staging: Giulio Cesare*, Cesena: Societas Raffaello Sanzio.

Castle, T. (1995) *The Female Thermometer*, New York and Oxford: Oxford University Press.

Caudwell, C. (1937) *Illusion and Reality: A study of the sources of poetry*, London: Macmillan & Co.

Cawley, A. C. (ed.) (1968) *Magnus Herodes*, in *The Wakefield Pageants in the Towneley Cycle*, Manchester: Manchester University Press.

Chaikin, J. (1972) *The Presence of the Actor: Notes on the open theatre, disguises, acting and representation*, New York: Atheneum.

Chaney, D. (1993) *Fictions of Collective Life: Public drama in late modern culture*, London and New York: Routledge.

Clivio, G. P. (1989) 'The Languages of the *Commedia dell'Arte*', in D. Pietropaulo (ed.) *The Science of Buffoonery: Theory and history of the* commedia dell'arte, Ottawa: Dovehouse Editions.

Clubb, L. G. (1980) 'Shakespeare's Comedy and Late Cinquecento Mixed Genres', in M. Charney (ed.) *Shakespearean Comedy*, New York: New York Literary Forum.

Clynes, M. E. (1977) *Sentics: The touch of emotions*, London: Souvenir Press.

Clynes, M. E. and Kline, N. S. (1995) 'Cyborgs and Space' in C. H. Gray, H. J. Figueroa-Sarriera and S. Mentor (eds) *The Cyborg Handbook*, London: Routledge.

Colomina, B. (1992) 'The Split Wall: Domestic voyeurism', in B. Colomina (ed.) *Sexuality and Space*, New York: Princeton Architectural Press.

Craig, E. G. (1980) *On the Art of the Theatre*, London: Heinemann.

Crary, J. (1999) *Suspensions of Perception: Attention, spectacle, and modern culture*, Cambridge, Mass.: MIT Press.

—— (2001) *Techniques of the Observer: On vision and modernity in the nineteenth century*, Cambridge, Mass.: MIT Press.

Creed, B. (1987) 'From Here to Modernity: Feminism and postmodernism', *Screen* 28.2: 47–67.

Csikszentmihalyi, M. (1975) *Beyond Boredom and Anxiety: The experience of play in work and games*, San Francisco: Jossey Bass Publishers.

—— (1979) 'The Concept of Flow', in B. Sutton-Smith (ed.) *Play and Learning*, New York: Gardner Press.

Cubitt, S. (1993) *Videography: Video media as art and culture*, Basingstoke: Macmillan.

Cunnar, E. R. (1993) '(En)gendering Architectural Poetics in Jonson's *Masque of Queens*', *Literature Interpretation Theory* 4: 145–60.

Daly, A. (1992) 'Dance History and Feminist Scholarship: Reconsidering Isadora Duncan and the male gaze', in L. Senelick (ed.) *Gender in Performance: The presentation of difference in the performing arts*, Hanover, N.H.: University Press of New England.

Davis, J. and Emeljanow, V. (2001) *Reflecting the Audience: London theatregoing, 1840–1880*, Hatfield: University of Hertfordshire Press.

Debax, J.-P. (1995) '"God Gyve You Tyme and Space": Toward a definition of theatrical space in the Tudor interludes', in J.-M. Maguin and M. Willems (eds), *French Essays on Shakespeare and his Contemporaries*, London: Associated University Presses.

Decroux, E. (1963) *Paroles sur le mime*, Paris: Gallimard.

Dekker, T. (1885) *Seven Deadly Sinnes of London* (1606), in *Non-Dramatic Works*, vol. 2, ed. A. B. Grosart, London and Aylesbury: private circulation.

de Landa, M. (1998) *War in the Age of Intelligent Machines*, New York: Zone Books.

Deleuze, G. and Guattari, F. (1984) *AntiOedipus: Capitalism and schizophrenia*, trans. R. Hurley, M. Seem and H. R. Lane, London: The Athlone Press.

———— (1996) *A Thousand Plateaus: Capitalism and schizophrenia*, trans. B. Massumi, London: The Athlone Press.

Dennis, A. (1995) *The Articulate Body: The physical training of the actor*, New York: Drama Book Publishers.

Denny, N. (1974) 'Aspects of the Staging of *Mankind*', *Medium Aevum* 43: 252–63.

Desmond, J. C. (1998) 'Embodying Difference: Issues in dance and cultural studies', in A. Carter (ed.) *The Routledge Dance Studies Reader*, London & New York: Routledge.

Dessen, A. C. (1977) *Elizabethan Drama and the Viewer's Eye*, Chapel Hill: University of North Carolina Press.

—— (1980) 'Shakespeare's Patterns for the Viewer's Eye: Dramaturgy for the open stage', in S. Holman (ed.) *Shakespeare's More than Words can Witness: Essays on visual and nonverbal enactment in the plays*, London: Associated University Presses.

Diamond, E. (1997) *Unmaking Mimesis: Essays on feminism and theater*, London: Routledge.

Dickens, C. (1982) *Dombey and Son*, ed. A. Horseman, Oxford, Oxford University Press.

—— (n.d.) 'The Amusements of the People' 1 (30 March 1850), in *Miscellaneous Papers*, London: Cassell.

Dillon, J. (1993) '*Mankind* and the Politics of "Englysch Laten"', *Medievalia et Humanistica* new series 20: 41–64.

—— (1999) 'Tiring House Wall Scenes at the Globe: A change in style and emphasis', *Theatre Notebook* 53: 163–73.

Dimond, W. (1809) *The Hero of the North*, London: Barker.

Donald, J. (1995) 'The City, the Cinema: Modern spaces', in C. Jenks (ed.), *Visual Culture*, London and New York: Routledge.

Doob, B. R. (1974) *Nebuchadnezzar's Children: Conventions of madness in Middle English literature*, New Haven, Conn. and London: Yale University Press.

Douglas, M. (1996) *Natural Symbols*, London: Routledge.

Dovey, K. (1999) *Framing Places: Mediating power in built form*, London and New York: Routledge.

Dukes, A. (1926) *Drama*, London: Thornton Butterworth.

Dyer, R. (1999) *White*, London and New York: Routledge.

Elam, K. (1980) *The Semiotics of Theatre and Drama*, London: Methuen.

Elias, N. (2000) *The Civilizing Process*, trans. E. Jephcott, Oxford: Blackwell.

Elyot, T. (1907) *The Boke Named The Governour* (1531), introd. F. Watson, London: J. M. Dent.

Erickson, J. (1995) *The Fate of the Object: From modern object to postmodern sign in performance, art, and poetry*, Ann Arbor: University of Michigan Press.

Fagg, E. (1936) *The Old 'Old Vic': A glimpse of the old Theatre, from its origin as 'The Royal Coburg', first managed by William Barrymore, to its revival under Lilian Baylis*, London: Vic-Wells Association.

Falk, F. (1999) 'Setting as Consciousness', in G. Rabkin (ed.) *Richard Foreman*, Baltimore, Md. and London: The Johns Hopkins University Press.

Farnell, R. (2000) 'In Dialogue with "Posthuman" Bodies: Interview with Stelarc', in M. Featherstone (ed.) *Body Modification*, London: Sage.

Featherstone, M. (2000) 'Post-Bodies, Aging and Virtual Reality', in D. Bell and B. M. Kennedy (eds) *The Cyberculture Reader*, London and New York: Routledge.

Featherstone, M. and Burrows, R. (eds) (1995) *Cyberspace/ Cyberbodies/ Cyberpunk*, London: Sage.

Feher, M. with Naddaff, R. and Tazi, N. (eds) (1989) *Fragments for a History of the Human Body: Part one*, New York: Zone.

Feldenkrais, M. (1949) *Body and Mature Behaviour: A study of anxiety, sex, gravitation and learning*, London: Routledge & Kegan Paul.

Fergusson, F. (1953) *The Idea of a Theater*, New York: Doubleday Anchor Books.

Filmer, P. (2003) 'Songtime: Sound culture, rhythm and sociality', in M. Bull and L. Back (eds), *The Auditory Culture Reader*, Oxford: Berg.

Fletcher, J. (1970) *The Faithful Shepherdess*, in Beaumont and Fletcher, *Select Plays*, intro. M. C. Bradbrook, London: Dent.

Foreman, R. (1992) *Unbalancing Acts: Foundations for a theater*, ed. K. Jordan, New York: Theatre Communications Group.

Foster, S. L. (1996) 'The Ballerina's Phallic Pointe', in S. L. Foster (ed.) *Corporealities: Dancing knowledge, culture and power*, London: Routledge.

—— (1998) 'Choreographing History', in A. Carter (ed.) *The Routledge Dance Studies Reader*, London and New York: Routledge.

Foucault, M. (1979) *Discipline and Punish: The birth of the prison*, trans. A. Sheridan, New York: Vintage.

Frank, A. W. (1996) 'For a Sociology of the Body: An analytical review', in M. Featherstone, M. Hepworth and B. S. Turner (eds) *The Body: Social process and cultural theory*, London: Sage.

Franko, M. (1985) 'Renaissance Conduct Literature and the Basse Dance: The kinesis of *Bonne Grace*', in *Persons in Groups: Social behaviour as identity formation in Medieval and Renaissance Europe*, Binghamton, New York: Medieval and Renaissance Texts & Studies.

—— (1993) *Dance as Text: Ideologies of the Baroque body*, Cambridge: Cambridge University Press.

—— (1995) *Dancing Modernism/Performing Politics*, Bloomington: Indiana University Press.

—— (2002) *The Work of Dance: Labor, movement, and identity in the 1930s*, Middletown, Conn.: Wesleyan University Press.

Frisch, H. (1987) 'Shakespeare and the Language of Gesture', *Shakespeare Studies* 19: 239–51.

Frith, S. (1998) *Performing Rites: Evaluating popular music*, Oxford: Oxford University Press.

Gabilondo, J. (1995) 'Postcolonial Cyborgs: Subjectivity in the age of cybernetic reproduction', in C. H. Gray, H. J. Figueroa-Sarriera and S. Mentor (eds) *The Cyborg Handbook*, London: Routledge.

Garner, S. B. jr. (1994) *Bodied Spaces: Phenomenology and performance in contemporary drama*, Ithaca, N.Y. and London: Cornell University Press.

George, K. (1980) *Rhythm in Drama*, Pittsburgh: University of Pittsburgh Press.

Glennie, P. and Thrift, N. (1996) 'Reworking E. P. Thompson's "Time, Work-Discipline and Industrial Capitalism"', *Time & Society* 5. 3: 275–99.

Goffman, E. (1956) *The Presentation of Self in Everyday Life*, Edinburgh: University of Edinburgh Social Sciences Research Centre.

Gonzalez, J. (1995) 'Envisioning Cyborg Bodies: Notes from current research', in C. H. Gray, H. J. Figueroa-Sarriera and S. Mentor (eds) *The Cyborg Handbook*, London: Routledge.

Goodwin, A. (1993) *Dancing in the Distraction Factory*, London: Routledge.

Gordon, M. (1983) *Lazzi: The comic routines of the* commedia dell'arte, New York: Performing Arts Journal Publications.

Gossett, S. (1988) '"Man-maid, begone!": Women in masques', *ELR* 18: 96–113.

Gosson, S. (?1590) *Playes Confuted in Five Actions*, London: Thomas Gosson.

Gray, C. H. (1995) 'An Interview with Manfred Clynes', in C. H. Gray, H. J. Figueroa-Sarriera and S. Mentor (eds) *The Cyborg Handbook*, London: Routledge.

Gray, C. H., Mentor, S. and Figueroa-Sarriera, H. J. (1995) 'Cyborgology: Constructing the knowledge of cybernetic organisms', in C. H. Gray, H. J. Figueroa-Sarriera, and S. Mentor (eds) *The Cyborg Handbook*, London: Routledge.

Greenblatt, S. (1988) *Shakespearean Negotiations: The circulation of social energy in Renaissance England*, Oxford: Clarendon Press.

—— (1997) 'Mutilation and Meaning', in D. Hillman and C. Mazzio (eds) *The Body in Parts: Fantasies of corporeality in early modern Europe*, New York and London: Routledge.

Greene, R. (1970) *The Historie of Orlando Furioso* (>1592), in *Plays and Poems*, ed. J. C. Collins, New York: Books for Libraries Press.

Grewar, A. (1993) 'Shakespeare and the Actors of the *Commedia dell'Arte*', in D. J. George and C. J. Gossip (eds) *Studies in the* Commedia dell'Arte, Cardiff: University of Wales Press.

—— (1996) 'The Old Man's Spectacles and Other Traces of the *Commedia dell'Arte* in Early Shakespearean Comedy', in C. Cairns (ed.) *Scenery, Set and Staging in the Italian Renaissance: Studies in the practice of theatre*, Lampeter: The Edwin Mellen Press.

Gropius, W. (ed.) (1961) *The Theater of the Bauhaus*, Middletown, Conn.: Wesleyan University Press.

Grosz, E. (1994) *Volatile Bodies: Toward a corporeal feminism*, Bloomington: Indiana University Press.

—— (1995) *Space, Time, and Perversion: Essays on the politics of bodies*, New York and London: Routledge.

Gumbrecht, H. U. (1994) 'Rhythm and Meaning', in H. U. Gumbrecht and K. L. Pfeiffer (eds) *Materialities of Communication*, trans. W. Whobrey, Stanford, Calif.: Stanford University Press.

Gurr, A. (1963) 'Who Strutted and Bellowed?', *Shakespeare Survey* 16: 95–102.

—— (1987) *Playgoing in Shakespeare's London*, Cambridge: Cambridge University Press.

Hadomi, L. (1988) 'Fantasy and Reality: Dramatic rhythm in *Death of a Salesman*', *Modern Drama* 31.2: 157–74.

Halliwell, S. (trans. and commentary) (1987) *The Poetics of Aristotle*, London: Duckworth.

Hammond, P. E. and Hammond, S. N. (1979) 'The Internal Logic of Dance: A Weberian perspective on the history of ballet', *Journal of Social History* 12: 591–608.

Haraway, D. (1991) *Simians, Cyborgs, and Women: The reinvention of nature*, London: Free Association Books.

Harvey, D. (1989) *The Condition of Postmodernity: An enquiry into the origins of cultural change*, Oxford: Basil Blackwell.

Hazlewood, C. (1972) *Lady Audley's Secret* (1863), in G. Rowell (ed.) *Nineteenth Century Plays*, Oxford: Oxford University Press.

Heinemann, M. (1980) *Puritanism and Theatre: Thomas Middleton and opposition drama under the early Stuarts*, Cambridge: Cambridge University Press.

Hess, D. J. (1995) 'On Low-tech Cyborgs', in C. H. Gray, H. J. Figueroa-Sarriera and S. Mentor (eds) *The Cyborg Handbook*, London: Routledge.

Hetherington, K. (1997) *The Badlands of Modernity: Heterotopia and social ordering*, London and New York: Routledge.

Heywood, T. (1941) *An Apology for Actors* (1612), ed. R. H. Perkinson, New York: Scholars' Facsimiles & Reprints.

Hodgdon, B. (1980) 'Shakespeare's Directorial Eye: A look at the early history plays', in S. Holman (ed.) *Shakespeare's More Than Words Can Witness: Essays on visual and nonverbal enactment in the plays*, London: Associated University Presses.

Hodge, A. (ed.) (2000) *Twentieth Century Actor Training*, London: Routledge.

Hogle, L. F. (1995) 'Tales for the Cryptic: Technology meets organism in the living cadaver', in C. H. Gray, H. J. Figueroa-Sarriera and S. Mentor (eds) *The Cyborg Handbook*, London: Routledge.

Holbrook, P. (1998) 'Jacobean Masques and the Jacobean Peace', in *The Politics of the Stuart Court Masque*, ed. D. Bevington and P. Holbrook, Cambridge: Cambridge University Press.

Holcroft, T. (1802) *A Tale of Mystery*, London: R. Phillips.

Holland, E. W. (1996) 'Schizoanalysis and Baudelaire: Some illustration of decoding at work', in P. Patton (ed.) *Deleuze: A Critical Reader*, Oxford: Blackwell Publishers.

Holland, P. (1979) *The Ornament of Action: Text and performance in Restoration comedy*, Cambridge: Cambridge University Press.

Holland, S. (1995) 'Descartes Goes to Hollywood: Mind, body and gender in contemporary cyborg cinema', in M. Featherstone and R. Burrows (eds) *Cyberspace/Cyberbodies/Cyberpunk*, London: Sage.

Holman, P. (1993) *Four and Twenty Fiddlers: The violin at the English court 1540–1690*, Oxford: Clarendon Press.

Howard, J. (1984) *Shakespeare's Art of Orchestration: Stage technique and audience response*, Urbana: University of Illinois Press.

Howard, S. (1998) *The Politics of Courtly Dancing in Early Modern England*, Amherst: University of Massachusetts Press.

Hughes, W. (1980) *The Maniac in the Cellar: Sensation novels of the 1860s*, Princeton: Princeton University Press.

Huizinga, J. (1949) *Homo Ludens: A study of the play-element in culture*, London: Routledge & Kegan Paul.

Ian, M. (1996) 'When is a Body not a Body? When it's a Building', in J. Sanders (ed.) *Stud: Architectures of masculinity*, New York: Princeton Architectural Press.

Ihde, D. (2002) *Bodies in Technology*, Electronic Mediations, vol. 5, Minneapolis: University of Minnesota Press.

James, M. (1983) 'Ritual, Drama and the Social Body in the Late Medieval Town', *Past & Present* 98: 3–29.

Jerrold, D. (1990) *Black-Ey'd Susan, or, 'All in the Downs'* (1829), in G. Rowell (ed.) *Nineteenth-Century Plays*, Oxford: Oxford University Press.

Johnson, M. (1987) *The Body in the Mind: The bodily basis of meaning, imagination, and reason*, Chicago and London: The University of Chicago Press.

Jones, A. (1998) *Body Art/Performing the Subject*, Minneapolis: University of Minnesota Press.

Jonson, B. (1941) *The Masque of Queens*, in *Ben Jonson*, vol. 7, ed. C. H. Herford, P. Simpson and E. Simpson, Oxford: Clarendon Press.

—— (1947) *Discoveries*, in *Ben Jonson*, vol. 8, ed. C. H. Herford, P. Simpson and E. Simpson, Oxford: Clarendon Press.

Joseph, B. L. (1964) *Elizabethan Acting*, revised edition, London: Oxford University Press.

Jousse, M. (1990) *The Oral Style* (1925), trans. E. Sienaert and R. Whitaker, New York: Garland.

Kalb, J. (1998) *The Theatre of Heiner Muller*, Cambridge: Cambridge University Press.

Kalikoff, B. (1986) *Murder and Moral Decay in Victorian Popular Literature*, Ann Arbor, Mich.: UMI Research Press.

Kaplan, J. H. and Stowell, S. (1994) *Theatre and Fashion: Oscar Wilde to the Suffragettes*, Cambridge: Cambridge University Press.

Kern, S. (2003) *The Culture of Time and Space 1880–1918*, Cambridge, Mass.: Harvard University Press.

Kernodle, G. R. (1944) *From Art to Theatre: Form and convention in the Renaissance*, Chicago: University of Chicago Press.

King, B. (1985) 'Articulating Stardom', *Screen* 26. 5: 27–50.

—— (1989) 'The Burden of Headroom', *Screen* 30. 1–2: 122–38.

Kirby, M. (1985) 'Happenings: An introduction', in M. R. Sandford (ed.) *Happenings and Other Acts*, London: Routledge.

Kleist, H. von (1989) 'On the Marionette Theater', in M. Feher, with R. Naddaff and N. Tazi (eds) *Fragments for a History of the Human Body: Part one*, New York: Zone.

Knight, W. G. (1997) *A Major London 'Minor': The Surrey Theatre 1805–1865*, London: The Society for Theatre Research.

Knopp, L. (1995) 'Sexuality and Urban Space: A framework for analysis', in D. Bell and G. Valentine (eds) *Mapping Desire: Geographies of sexuality*, London and New York: Routledge.

Kracauer, S. (1995) *The Mass Ornament*, trans. T. Y. Levin, Cambridge, Mass.: Harvard University Press.

Laban, R. (1960) *The Mastery of Movement*, revised L. Ullmann, London: Macdonald & Evans.

—— (1988) *Modern Educational Dance*, revised L. Ullmann, Plymouth: Northcote House.

Lakoff, G. and Johnson, M. (1999) *Philosophy in the Flesh: The embodied mind and its challenge to western thought*, New York: Basic Books.

——— (2003) *Metaphors We Live By*, Chicago and London: The University of Chicago Press.

Langer, S. (1953) *Feeling and Form: A theory of art developed from philosophy in a new key*, London: Routledge & Kegan Paul.

Latimer, J. (1978) *Maria Marten or the Murder in the Red Barn*, ed. M. Slater, London: Heinemann Educational Books.

Laughlin, C. D. Jr., McManus, J. and d'Aquili, E. D. (1990) *Brain, Symbol and Experience*, Boston, Mass. and Shaftesbury: New Science Library.

Lawrence, D. H. (1974a) *The Daughter-in-Law* (1912), in *Three Plays*, introd. R. Williams, Harmondsworth: Penguin Books.

—— (1974b) *The Widowing of Mrs Holroyd* (1914), in *Three Plays*, introd. R. Williams, Harmondsworth: Penguin Books.

Lea, K. M. (1934) *Italian Popular Comedy: A study in the* commedia dell'arte, *1560–1620 with special reference to the English stage*, Oxford: Clarendon Press.

Lecoq, J. (2000) *The Moving Body: Teaching creative theatre*, trans. D. Bradby, London: Methuen.

Lefebvre, H. (1998) *The Production of Space*, trans. D. Nicholson-Smith, Oxford: Blackwell Publishers.

Léger, F. (1973) 'The Spectacle: Light, color, moving image, object-spectacle', in *Functions of Painting*, trans. A. Anderson, ed. E. F. Fry, London: Thames & Hudson.

Lewalski, B. (1993) 'Anne of Denmark and the Subversion of Masquing', *Criticism* 35.

Lingis, A. (1983) *Excesses: Eros and culture*, Albany: State University of New York Press.

—— (1994) 'The Society of Dismembered Body Parts', in C. V. Boundas and D. Olkowski (eds) *Gilles Deleuze and the Theater of Philosophy*, New York and London: Routledge.

—— (1994) *Foreign Bodies*, London: Routledge.

Lorentzen, J. L. (1995) 'Reich Dreams: Ritual horror and armoured bodies', in C. Jenks (ed.), *Visual Culture*, London and New York: Routledge.

Lupton, D. (1995) 'The Embodied Computer/User', in M. Featherstone and R. Burrows (eds) *Cyberspace/Cyberbodies/Cyberpunk*, London: Sage.

Lury, C. (1998) *Prosthetic Culture: Photography, memory and identity*, London: Routledge.

Lynch, K. (1972) *What Time is this Place?*, Cambridge, Mass.: MIT Press.

McAuley, G. (2000) *Space in Performance: Making meaning in the theatre*, Ann Arbor: The University of Michigan Press.

McClary, S. (1998) 'Unruly Passions and Courtly Dances: Technologies of the body in Baroque music', in S. E. Melzer and K. Norberg (eds) *From the Royal to the Republican Body: Incorporating the political in seventeenth- and eighteenth-century France*, Berkeley: University of California Press.

Mackintosh, I. (1993) *Architecture, Actor and Audience*, London and New York: Routledge.

McMillin, S. and MacLean, S. B. (1998) *The Queen's Men and their Plays*, Cambridge: Cambridge University Press.

McNamara, K. R. (1987) 'Golden Worlds at Court: *The Tempest* and its masque', *Shakespeare Studies* 19: 183–202.

McNeill, W. H. (1995) *Keeping Together in Time: Dance and drill in human history*, Cambridge, Mass.: Harvard University Press.

Maier, C. S. (1987) 'The Politics of Time: Changing paradigms of collective time and private time in the modern era', in C. S. Maier (ed.) *Changing Boundaries of the Political: Essays on the evolving balance between the state and society, public and private in Europe*, Cambridge: Cambridge University Press.

Maisel, E. (ed.) (1974) *The Alexander Technique: The essential writings of F. Matthias Alexander*, London: Thames & Hudson.

Malbon, B. (1999) *Clubbing: Dancing, ecstasy and vitality*, London and New York: Routledge.

Mann, C. (1985) 'How to Produce Meerut (1933)', in R. Samuel, E. MacColl and S. Cosgrove (eds) *Theatres of the Left 1880–1935*, London: Routledge & Kegan Paul.

Manning, S. (1997) 'The Female Dancer and the Male Gaze', in J. Desmond (ed.) *Meaning in Motion: New cultural studies of dance*, Durham, N.C.: Duke University Press.

Maquerlot, J.-P. (1995) 'Time and Tragic Mode in *The Duchess of Malfi*', in J.-M. Maguin and M. Willems (eds), *French Essays on Shakespeare and his Contemporaries*, London: Associated University Presses.

Marker, L.-L. (1970) 'Nature and Decorum in the Theory of Elizabethan Acting', in D. Galloway (ed.) *The Elizabethan Theatre*, vol. 2, Waterloo, Ontario: Archon Books.

Marlowe, C. (1971) *Tamburlaine*, ed. J. W. Harper, London: Ernest Benn.

Marx, K. (1982) *Capital*, vol. 1, trans. B. Fowkes, intro. E. Mandel, Harmondsworth: Penguin.

Massinger P. (1976) *The Roman Actor* (1626), in *Plays and Poems*, vol. 3, ed. P. Edwards and C. Gibson, Oxford: Clarendon Press.

Massumi, B. (1999) *A User's Guide to Capitalism and Schizophrenia: Deviations from Deleuze and Guattari*, Cambridge, Mass. and London: MIT Press.

Maurer, M. (1989) 'Reading Ben Jonson's *Queens*', in S. Fisher and J. E. Halley (eds) *Seeking the Woman in Late Medieval and Renaissance Writings: Essays in feminist contextual criticism*, Knoxville: University of Tennessee Press.

Mauss, M. (1992) 'Techniques of the Body', in J. Crary and S. Kwinter (eds) *Incorporations*, New York: Zone.

Mayer, D. (1980) *Henry Irving and* The Bells: *Irving's personal script of the play*, Manchester: Manchester University Press.

Mazzio, C. (1997) 'Sins of the Tongue', in D. Hillman and C. Mazzio (eds) *The Body in Parts*, London: Routledge.

Meagher, J. C. (1962) 'The Dance and Masques of Ben Jonson', *Journal of the Warburg and Courtauld Institutes* 25: 258–77.

—— (1966) *Method and Meaning in Jonson's Masques*, Notre Dame, Ind.: University of Notre Dame Press.

Mehl, D. (1969) 'Emblems in English Renaissance Drama', *Renaissance Drama* n.s. 2: 39–57.

Mellamphy, N. (1980) 'Pantaloons and Zanies: Shakespeare's "apprenticeship" to Italian professional comedy troupes', in M. Charney (ed.) *Shakespearean Comedy*, New York: New York Literary Forum.

Melrose, S. (1994) *A Semiotics of the Dramatic Text*, Basingstoke: Macmillan.

Melzi, R. C. (1966) 'From Lelia to Viola', *Renaissance Drama* 9: 67–81.

Mennell, S. (1995) 'On the Civilizing of Appetite', in M. Featherstone, M. Hepworth and B. S. Turner (eds) *The Body: Social process and cultural theory*, London: Sage.

Merleau-Ponty, M. (1996) *Phenomenology of Perception*, trans. C. Smith, London and New York: Routledge.

Merrick, J. (1998) 'The Body Politics of French Absolutism', in S. E. Melzer and K. Norberg (eds) *From the Royal to the Republican Body: Incorporating the political in seventeenth- and eighteenth-century France*, Berkeley: University of California Press.

Middleton, T. (1975) *Women Beware Women*, ed. J. R. Mulryne, London: Methuen & Co.

Molière (1982) *The Miser*, trans. J. Wood, Harmondsworth: Penguin.

Montaigne, M. de (1908) *Essayes*, trans. J. Florio, introd. T. Seccombe, London: Grant Richards.

Moore, J. R. (1949) 'Pantaloon as Shylock', *Boston Public Library Quarterly* 1: 33–42.

Muchembled, R. (1993) 'The Order of Gestures: A social history of sensibilities under the ancien régime in France', in J. Bremner and H. Roodenburg (eds) *A Cultural History of Gesture: From antiquity to the present day*, Cambridge: Polity Press.

Mumford, L. (1934) *Technics and Civilization*, London: George Routledge & Sons.

Nashe, T. (1972) *Pierce Penilesse* (1592), in *The Unfortunate Traveller and Other Works*, ed. J. B. Steane, Harmondsworth: Penguin Books.

Neher, A. (1962) 'A Physiological Explanation of Unusual Behaviour in Ceremonies Involving Drums', *Human Biology: A record of research* 34: 51–60.

Nield, S. (2004) 'Popular Theatre, 1895–1940', in B. Kershaw (ed.), *The Cambridge History of British Theatre*, vol. 1 *Since 1895*, Cambridge: Cambridge University Press.

Orgel, S. (1975) *The Illusion of Power: Political theater in the English Renaissance*, Berkeley: University of California Press.

—— (1985) 'The Spectacles of State', in *Persons in Groups: Social behaviour as identity formation in Medieval and Renaissance Europe*, Binghamton, N.Y.: Medieval and Renaissance Texts & Studies.

—— (1987) 'Introduction', in W. Shakespeare, *The Tempest*, ed. S Orgel, Oxford: Oxford University Press.

—— (1990) 'Jonson and the Amazons', in E. Harvey and K. E. Maus (eds) *Soliciting Interpretation*, Chicago: University of Chicago Press.

Paster, G. K. (1993) *The Body Embarrassed: Drama and the disciplines of shame in early modern England*, Ithaca, N.Y.: Cornell University Press.

—— (1997) 'Nervous Tension: Networks of blood and spirit in the early modern body', in D. Hillman and C. Mazzio (eds) *The Body in Parts*, London: Routledge.

Pavis, P. (ed.) (1996) *The Intercultural Performance Reader*, London: Routledge.

Peacock, J. (1990) 'Inigo Jones as a Figurative Artist', in *Renaissance Bodies: The human figure in English culture c. 1540–1660*, ed. L. Gent and N. Llewellyn, London: Reaktion Books.

Penley, C. and Ross, A. (1991) 'Cyborgs at Large: Interview with Donna Haraway', *Social Text* 25/26.

Pfister, M. (1988) *The Theory and Analysis of Drama*, Cambridge: Cambridge University Press.

Pile, S. (1996) *The Body and the City*, London: Routledge.

Pinero, A. W. (1995) *Trelawny of the 'Wells' and Other Plays*, ed. J. S. Bratton, Oxford: Oxford University Press.

Pini, N. (1997) 'Cyborgs, Nomads and the Raving Feminine', in H. Thomas (ed.) *Dance in the City*, Basingstoke: Macmillan.

Pocock, I. (1974) *The Miller and his Men* (1813), in M. R. Booth (ed.) *The Magistrate and other Nineteenth-Century Plays*, Oxford: Oxford University Press.

Polanyi, M. (1967) *The Tacit Dimension*, London: Routledge & Kegan Paul.

Polhemus, T. (1998) 'Dance, Gender and Culture', in A. Carter (ed.) *The Routledge Dance Studies Reader*, London and New York: Routledge.

Poster, M. (1995) 'Postmodern Virtualities', in M. Featherstone and R. Burrows (eds) *Cyberspace/Cyberbodies/Cyberpunk*, London: Sage.

Pykett, L. (1994) *The Sensation Novel from* The Woman in White *to* The Moonstone, Plymouth: Northcote House.

Rabkin, G. (ed.) (1999) *Richard Foreman*, Baltimore, Md. and London: The Johns Hopkins University Press.

Ravelhofer, B. (1998) '"Virgin Wax" and "Hairy Men-Monsters": Unstable movement codes in the Stuart masque', in D. Bevington and P. Holbrook (eds) *The Politics of the Stuart Court Masque*, Cambridge: Cambridge University Press.

Reichardt, J. (1978) *Robots: Fact, fiction and prediction*, London: Thames & Hudson.

Reynolds, S. (1998) *Energy Flash: A journey through rave music and dance culture*, London: Picador.

Richards, K. (1989) 'Inigo Jones and the *Commedia dell'Arte*', in C. Cairns (ed.) *The Commedia dell'Arte from the Renaissance to Dario Fo*, Lewiston: The Edwin Mellen Press.

—— (1994) 'Elizabethan Perceptions of the *Commedia dell'Arte*', in G. Sorelius and M. Svigley (eds) *Cultural Exchange between European Nations during the Renaissance*, Uppsala: Acta Universitatis Upsaliensis.

Richards, K. and Richards, L. (1990) *The* Commedia dell'Arte: *A documentary history*, Oxford: Basil Blackwell.

Richardson, B. (1987) '"Time is out of Joint": Narrative models and the temporality of the drama', *Poetics Today* 8: 299–309.

Roach, J. (1993) *The Player's Passion: Studies in the science of acting*, Ann Arbor: The University of Michigan Press.

Roberts, P. (1976) *The Old Vic Story: A nation's theatre 1818–1976*, London: W. H. Allen.

Rose, M. B. (1984) 'Women in Men's Clothing: Apparel and social stability in *The Roaring Girl*', *ELR* 14. 3: 367–91.

Rosenberg, M. (1954) 'Elizabethan Actors: Men or marionettes?', *PMLA* 69: 915–27.

Rowell, G. (1993) *The Old Vic Theatre: A history*, Cambridge: Cambridge University Press.

Rudlin, J. (1994) Commedia dell'Arte: *An actor's handbook*, London: Routledge.

Sanders, J. (1996) 'Introduction', in J. Sanders (ed.), *Stud: Architectures of masculinity*, New York: Princeton Architectural Press.

Sawday, J. (1995) *The Body Emblazoned: Dissection and the human body in Renaissance culture*, London: Routledge.

Schafer, R. M. (1994) *The Soundscape: Our sonic environment and the tuning of the world*, Rochester, Vt.: Destiny Books.

Schechner, R. (2002) *Performance Studies: An introduction*, London; Routledge.

Schmitt, J.-C. (1989) 'The Ethics of Gesture', in M. Feher, with R. Naddaff and N. Tazi (eds) *Fragments for a History of the Human Body: Part two*, New York: Zone.

Schneider, R. (1997) *The Explicit Body in Performance*, London: Routledge.

Schwartz, H. (1992) 'Torque: The new kinaesthetic of the twentieth century', in J. Crary and S. Kwinter (eds) *Incorporations*, New York: Zone.

Segel, H. B. (1995) *Pinocchio's Progeny: Puppets, marionettes, automatons, and robots in modernist and avant-garde drama*, Baltimore, Md.: The Johns Hopkins University Press.

—— (1998) *Body Ascendant: Modernism and the physical imperative*, Baltimore, Md.: The Johns Hopkins University Press.

Shakespeare, W. (1968) *The Two Gentlemen of Verona*, ed. N. Sanders, Harmondsworth: Penguin.

—— (1982) *Hamlet*, ed. H. Jenkins, London and New York: Methuen.

—— (1987) *The Tempest*, ed. S Orgel, Oxford: Oxford University Press.

Shepherd, J. (1991) *Music as Social Text*, Cambridge: Polity Press.

Shepherd, S. (1994) 'Pauses of Mutual Agitation', in J. S. Bratton et al. (eds) *Melodrama: Stage picture screen*, London: British Film Institute.

Shepherd, S. and Wallis, M. (2004) *Drama/Theatre/Performance*, London and New York: Routledge.

Shepherd, S. and Womack, P. (1996) *English Drama: A cultural history*, Oxford: Blackwell Publishers.

Sidney, P. (1975) *A Defence of Poetry*, ed. J. A. Van Druten, Oxford: Oxford University Press.

Simmel, G. (1997) *Simmel on Culture: Selected writings*, ed. D. Frisby and M. Featherstone, London: Sage.

Singer, B. (2001) *Melodrama and Modernity: Early sensational cinema and its contexts*, New York: Columbia University Press.

Skey, M. A. (1979/80) 'Herod the Great in Medieval European Drama', *Comparative Drama* 13.4: 330–64.

Slater, A. P. (1982) *Shakespeare the Director*, Hassocks: Harvester Press.

Smith, B. R. (1999) *The Acoustic World of Early Modern England: Attending to the O-factor*, Chicago and London: University of Chicago Press.

Sobchack, V. (1994) 'New Age Mutant Ninja Hackers: Reading *Mondo 2000*', in M. Dery (ed.) *Flame Wars: The discourse of cyber culture*, Durham, N.J.: Duke University Press.

Sofer, A. (2003) *The Stage Life of Props*, Ann Arbor: The University of Michigan Press.

Spingler, M. (1991/2) 'The Actor and the Statue: Space, time, and court performance in Molière's *Don Juan*', *Comparative Drama* 25.4: 351–68.

Springer, C. (1991) 'The Pleasure of the Interface', *Screen* 32.3: 303–23.

—— (1994) 'Sex, Memories, and Angry Women', in M. Dery (ed.) *Flame Wars: The discourse of cyber culture*, Durham, N.J.: Duke University Press.

Staines, D. (1976) 'To Out-Herod Herod: The development of a dramatic character', *Comparative Drama* 10.1: 29–53.

Stallybrass, P. (1986) 'Patriarchal Territories: The body enclosed', in M. W. Ferguson, M. Quilligan and N. J. Vickers (eds) *Rewriting the Renaissance: The discourses of sexual difference in early modern England*, Chicago: University of Chicago Press.

—— (1987) 'Reading the Body: *The Revenger's Tragedy* and the Jacobean theater of consumption', *Renaissance Drama* 18: 121–48.

—— (1996) 'Worn Worlds: Clothes and identity on the Renaissance stage', in M. de Grazia, M. Quilligan and P. Stallybrass (eds) *Subject and Object in Renaissance Culture*, Cambridge: Cambridge University Press.

Stallybrass, P. and White, A. (1986) *The Politics and Poetics of Transgression*, London: Methuen.

States, B. O. (1985) *Great Reckonings in Little Rooms: On the phenomenology of theatre*, Berkeley: University of California Press.

—— (1992) 'The Phenomenological Attitude', in J. G. Reinelt and J. R. Roach (eds) *Critical Theory and Performance*, Ann Arbor: University of Michigan Press.

—— (1994) *The Pleasure of the Play*, Ithaca, N.Y. and London: Cornell University Press.

Steele, E. (1977) 'Shakespeare, Goldoni, and the Clowns', *Comparative Drama* 11.3: 209–26.

Stelarc (1998) 'From Psych-Body to Cyber-Systems: Images as post-human entities', in J. Broadhurst Dixon and E. J. Cassidy (eds) *Virtual Futures: Cyberotics, technology and post-human pragmatism*, London: Routledge.

—— (2000) 'Parasite Visions: Alternate, intimate and involuntary experiences', in M. Featherstone (ed.) *Body Modification*, London: Sage.

Stoppard, T. (1967) *Rosencrantz and Guildenstern Are Dead*, London: Faber & Faber.

Storr, A. (1992) *Music and the Mind*, New York: The Free Press.

Strong, R. (1984) *Art and Power: Renaissance festivals 1450–1650*, Woodbridge: The Boydell Press.

Stryker, S. (2000) 'Transsexuality: The postmodern body and/as technology', in D. Bell and B. M. Kennedy (eds) *The Cyberculture Reader*, London and New York: Routledge.

Sullivan, H. W. (1992) '*Mimesis Hysteresis*: What in the audience is moved when the audience is moved?' *Gestos* 7, 14: 45–57.

Suvin, D. (1984) 'Reflections on Happenings', in *To Brecht and Beyond*, Brighton: Harvester Press.

—— (1987) 'Approach to Topoanalysis and the Paradigmatics of Dramaturgic Space', *Poetics Today* 8: 311–34.

Suzuki, T. (1986) *The Way of Acting*, trans. J. T. Rimer, New York: Theatre Communications Group.

Tagg, P. (1984) 'Understanding Musical "Time Sense" – Concepts, sketches and consequences', in *Tvärspel: trettisen artikler om musik*, Göteborg: Musikvetenskapliga institutionen.

Tasker, Y. (1993) *Spectacular Bodies: Gender, genre and the action cinema*, London: Routledge.

Taussig, M. (1993) *Mimesis and Alterity: A particular history of the senses*, London: Routledge.

Tennenhouse, L. (1986) *Power on Display: The politics of Shakespearean genres*, London: Methuen.

Theweleit, K. (1992) 'Circles, Lines and Bits', in J. Crary and S. Kwinter (eds) *Incorporations*, New York: Zone.

Thompson, E. (2002) *The Soundscape of Modernity: Architectural acoustics and the culture of listening in America, 1900–1933*, Cambridge, Mass.: The MIT Press.

Thrift, N. (1983) 'On the Determination of Social Action in Space and Time', *Environment and Planning D. Society and Space* 1.1: 23–57.

Toffler, A. (1970) *Future Shock*, London: Bodley Head.

Tomas, D. (1995) 'Art, Psychasthenic Assimilation and the Cybernetic Automaton', in C. H. Gray, H. J. Figueroa-Sarriera and S. Mentor (eds) *The Cyborg Handbook*, London: Routledge.

Tuan, Y. (1977) *Space and Place: The perspective of experience*, Minneapolis: University of Minnesota Press.

Turner, B. S. (1982) 'The Government of the Body: Medical regimens and the rationalization of diet', *British Journal of Sociology* 33.2: 254–69.

—— (1996) *The Body & Society* (second edition), London: Sage.

van Leeuwen, T. (1999) *Speech, Music, Sound*, Basingstoke: Macmillan.

Vanden Heuvel, M. (1991) *Performing Drama / Dramatizing Performance: Alternative theater and the dramatic text*, Ann Arbor: University of Michigan Press.

Venet, G. (1995) 'Baroque Space and Time in Chapman's Tragedy: *The Conspiracy and Tragedy of Byron*', in J.-M. Maguin and M. Willems (eds) *French Essays on Shakespeare and his Contemporaries*, London: Associated University Presses.

Vigarello, G. (1989) 'The Upward Training of the Body from the Age of Chivalry to Courtly Civility', in M. Feher, with R. Naddaff and N. Tazi (eds) *Fragments for a History of the Human Body: Part two*, New York: Zone.

Virilio, P. (1991) *The Aesthetics of Disappearance*, trans. P. Beitchman, New York: Semiotext(e).

—— (1994) *The Vision Machine*, trans. J. Rose, London: British Film Institute.

Walker, J. (1992) 'Voiceless Bodies and Bodiless Voices: The drama of human perception in *Coriolanus*', *Shakespeare Quarterly* 43: 170–85.

Walker, J. A. (1999) 'It is Getting to the Point: A proposal for historicizing performance form', *Nineteenth Century Theatre* 27. 1: 5–40.

Wallis, M. (1994) '"To Be, or Not to Be" – What are the Questions?', in I. Clarke (ed.) *Hamlet. Essays*, Loughborough: Loughborough Drama Texts.

Wallis, M. and Shepherd, S. (1998) *Studying Plays*, London: Arnold.

Walser, R. (1993) *Running with the Devil: Power, gender, and madness in heavy metal music*, Hanover, N. H. and London: Wesleyan University Press.

Ward, J. (1988) 'Newly Devis'd Measures for Jacobean Masques', *Acta Musicologica* 60: 111–42.

Webber, M., Stephens, C. and Laughlin, C. D. Jr. (1983) 'Masks: A re-examination, or "Masks? You mean they affect the brain?"', in N. R. Crumrine and M. Halpin (eds) *The Power of Symbols: Masks and masquerade in the Americas*, Vancouver: University of British Columbia Press.

Weimann, R. (1999) 'Playing with a Difference: Revisiting "pen" and "voice" in Shakespeare's theater', *Shakespeare Quarterly* 50.4: 415–32.

—— (2000) *Author's Pen and Actor's Voice: Playing and writing in Shakespeare's theatre*, Cambridge: Cambridge University Press.

West, S. (1991) *The Image of the Actor: Verbal and visual representation in the age of Garrick and Kemble*, London: Pinter.

Whigham, F. (1984) *Ambition and Privilege: The social tropes of Elizabethan courtesy theory*, Berkeley: University of California Press.

White, M. (1998) *Renaissance Drama in Action: An introduction to aspects of theatre practice and performance*, London: Routledge.

Wickham, G. (1963) *Early English Stages, 1300–1660*, vol. 2 *1576–1660*, London: Routledge & Kegan Paul.

—— (ed.) (1985) *Mankind*, in *English Moral Interludes*, London: J. M. Dent & Sons.

Wigley, M. (1992) 'Untitled: The housing of gender', in B. Colomina (ed.) *Sexuality and Space*, New York: Princeton Architectural Press.

Wiles, D. (1987) *Shakespeare's Clown*, Cambridge: Cambridge University Press.

Williams, S. J. and Bendelow, G. (1998) *The Lived Body: Sociological themes, embodied issues*, London and New York: Routledge.

Wilshire, B. (1982) *Role Playing and Identity: The limits of theatre as metaphor*, Bloomington: Indiana University Press.

Wilson, M. S. (1990) 'Columbine's Picturesque Passage: The demise of dramatic action in the evolution of sublime spectacle on the London stage', *The Eighteenth Century: Theory and interpretation* 31.3: 191–210.

Wilson, R. (1993) *Will Power: Essays on Shakespearean authority*, New York and London: Harvester Wheatsheaf.

Wilson, R. R. (1995) 'Cyber(body)parts: Prosthetic consciousness', in M. Featherstone and R. Burrows (eds) *Cyberspace/Cyberbodies/Cyberpunk*, London: Sage.

Wiseman, S. J. (1990) '*'Tis Pity She's a Whore*: Representing the incestuous body', in L. Gent and N. Llewellyn (eds) *Renaissance Bodies: The human figure in English culture c.1540–1660*, London: Reaktion Books.

Wollen, P. (1993) *Raiding the Icebox: Reflections on twentieth-century culture*, Bloomington: Indiana University Press.

Wright, R. (1984) 'Prospero's Lime Tree and the Pursuit of "Vanitas"', *Shakespeare Survey* 37: 133–40.

Wycherley, W. (1949) *The Gentleman Dancing-Master*, in *William Wycherley*, ed. W. C. Ward, London: Ernest Benn.

—— (1973) *The Country Wife*, ed. J. D. Hunt, London: Ernest Benn.

Yates, F. A. (1936) *A Study of* Love's Labours Lost, Cambridge: Cambridge University Press.

Zerubavel, E. (1981) *Hidden Rhythms: Schedules and calendars in social life*, Chicago and London: University of Chicago Press.

Zumthor, P. (1994) 'Body and Performance', in H. U. Gumbrecht and K. L. Pfeiffer (eds) *Materialities of Communication*, trans. W. Whobrey. Stanford, Calif.: Stanford University Press.

Channel 4 (1999) *Frasier: An Affair to Forget*, repeat broadcast Channel 4, 8 October.

Look at Lolo written and produced by Peter Stuart: Planet Rapido for Channel 4.

http://www.stelarc.va.com.au (24.03.05)

Index